WITHDRAWN

Psychotherapy with High-Risk Clients:

Legal and Professional Standards

Psychotherapy with High-Risk Clients:
Legal and Professional Standards

Richard L. Bednar, Ph.D.
Brigham Young University

Steven C. Bednar, J.D.
Holme, Roberts, & Owen

Michael J. Lambert, Ph.D.
Brigham Young University

Dan Roland Waite, J.D.
Beckley, Singleton, DeLanoy, Jemison, & List

 Brooks/Cole Publishing Company
Pacific Grove, California

MURDOCK LEARNING RESOURCE CENTER
GEORGE FOX UNIVERSITY
NEWBERG, OR. 97132

Brooks/Cole Publishing Company
A Division of Wadsworth, Inc.

Printed in the United States of America

10 9 8 7 6 5 4 3 2 1

Library of Congress Cataloging-in-Publication Data
Psychotherapy with high-risk clients : legal and professional
  standards / Richard L. Bednar . . . [et al.].
    p. cm.
  Includes bibliographical references and index.
  ISBN 0-534-15408-5 (hardback)
  1. Psychotherapists—Legal status, laws, etc.—United States.
  2. Psychotherapists—Malpractice—United States. 3. Insanity—
  Jurisprudence—United States. 4. Insane—Commitment and detention—
  United States. 5. Insane, Criminal and dangerous—United States.
  6. Psychotherapist and patient—United States. I. Bednar, Richard L.
  [DNLM: 1. Commitment of Mentally Ill—United States. 2. Informed
  Consent. 3. Malpractice—United States—Legislation.
  4. Psychotherapy. 5. Suicide. 6. Violence. WM 33 AA1 P97]
  KF2910.P75P75 1991
  344.73 '041—dc20
  [347.30441]
  DNLM/DLC
  for Library of Congress   90-15159
                                                                 CIP

Sponsoring Editor: *Claire Verduin*
Editorial Associate: *Gay C. Bond*
Production Services Manager: *Joan Marsh*
Production Service: *Bookman Productions*
Manuscript Editor: *Eva Marie Strock*
Permissions Editor: *Carline Haga*
Interior Design: *Judith Levinson*
Cover Design: *Nani Hudson*
Typesetting: *Bookends Typesetting*
Cover Printing: *Phoenix Color Corporation*
Printing and Binding: *Arcata Graphics/Fairfield*

Preface

Mental health services in this country are rapidly becoming an integral part of our nation's health-delivery system. Psychologists, social workers, marriage and family therapists, and psychiatrists provide these services in a variety of public and private settings. With increasing frequency, we find that some of these services are being supported by tax dollars from various community sources and third parties. It should come as no surprise to find that the increase in social acceptance and public funding of mental health services has brought with it a corresponding concern for public accountability.

The recent rise in prominence of the mental health professions has been accompanied by other events that were entirely predictable. Fees for clinical services are higher, but so are liability insurance premiums. The exposure of the public to core questions and problems in mental health care on television has resulted in a more enlightened and sophisticated clinical clientele. Many clients seem to have a good grasp of their rights and the therapist's obligations in a therapeutic relationship. Clients and their lawyers respond more quickly and more aggressively to questionable clinical practices. Courses on the legal and ethical issues in the delivery of clinical services have always been required in the professions, but now they are being taught with more rigor and care than they were just several years ago.

This book speaks to the legal and professional standards that apply in high-risk, clinical, decision-making areas. It is intended for therapists and therapists-in-training (of all persuasions and settings) simply because clinical risk is usually determined by the facts of a clinical case far more than the orienting theory of the clinician. Both the professional and legal standards that apply to suicide, dangerousness, informed consent, and involuntary hospitalization are discussed in considerable depth and detail. Numerous examples are provided to illustrate basic legal and professional standards in applied cases.

Special thanks are extended to Melissa Peterson for her exceptional skill in typing, proofreading, and editing the manuscript of this book. However, her real contribution to the development of the book was less obvious and more profound. She took upon herself many clinic responsibilities that were clearly beyond her job description so that we would have more time to write. We truly appreciate her thoughtfulness and her skill.

Thanks are also extended to Dr. Virginia Allen, Idaho State University, Dr. Robert Chope, Florida State University, Dr. Wallace Kennedy, Seattle Pacific University, and Dr. Donald MacDonald, San Francisco University, for helpful comments and suggestions after reviewing our manuscript.

Richard L. Bednar   *Michael J. Lambert*
Steven C. Bednar   *Dan Roland Waite*

v

Contents

5
Suicidal Clients: Legal Duties   93

6
Suicidal Clients: Clinical Duties   104

7
Informed Consent: Legal Duties   133

8
Informed Consent: Clinical Duties   156

9

Involuntary Civil Commitment: Legal Duties   **188**

10

Involuntary Civil Commitment: Clinical Duties   **209**

Introduction

The relationship between psychology and the law is moving from that of an adversary to that of an ally but at an almost painfully sluggish pace. When intelligent and well-trained professionals from different disciplines are prevented from necessary and meaningful collaboration because of ambiguity in fundamental terms and concepts, the results are problematic at best and catastrophic at worst. The following conversation between a well-trained therapist seeking the advice of a well-trained attorney on a common clinical/legal problem illustrates the dilemma.

THERAPIST: I hate to say this to you again, but your question is almost meaningless in a clinical context!

ATTORNEY: Look, it may be a meaningless clinical question, but it's a fundamental legal question.

THERAPIST: OK, let me put it this way. There is no empirically demonstrated method or information that allows one to predict dangerousness with any degree of accuracy. The psychological and legal literature on this point is abundantly clear. So I have no idea what standard of care could possibly be violated! Given this, what on earth is the legal relevance of your question?

ATTORNEY: It is still of fundamental legal importance. The legal system will *impose* a standard of care on you in this situation, and your conduct will be measured against that standard.

THERAPIST: And where is this standard of care coming from? What is it based on, and why on earth is the legal system dictating what it is?

ATTORNEY: The standard may be arbitrary and may even be ill-founded, but the role of the legal system is to determine fault and negligence when innocent parties are harmed as a result of deviations from professional standards.

THERAPIST: Do you realize what you are saying to me? This is absolutely crazy! This is nothing more than semantic nonsense. I just told you there is no standard to deviate from. How can you disregard such fundamental conceptual realities and not call your legal analysis mythology?

ATTORNEY: In the final analysis, what the court deems prudent and reasonable is the standard.

THERAPIST: I object to the legal system imposing clinical standards they are not qualified to make or understand.

ATTORNEY: Objection overruled. I understand that you may not like the rules of the game, but your objections won't change any of the rules! You still need to know and to tell me what information a reasonable and prudent psychologist would have gathered in this situation and what conclusions would be suggested by these data.

The ability of professionals to speak cogently and coherently between disciplines may be every bit as important as their ability to speak cogently and coherently within their own disciplines. As we will illustrate, the cross-discipline gap between law and clinical practice can only be bridged when intelligent and well-trained professionals from each discipline come to a more complete understanding of the issues that divide them.

1

Paradoxes and Contradictions in Legal Standards

As psychologists, we know relatively little about law. Many of us read books like this one to help soothe our nerves about the explosion of malpractice litigation. We believe that the more we know about legal issues, the less likely we are to get sued. Undoubtedly there is some truth to this belief, and legal naiveté really can be dangerous. Paradoxically, however, an incisive understanding of the legal issues involved in mental health services literally teaches quite another lesson: The more one knows about the law and our legal system, the more clearly one understands the futility of trying to avoid lawsuits that involve angry clients and determined lawyers. The best protection from problems of malpractice is not legal expertise but *clinical* expertise. And the best way of minimizing (please note that we did not say completely avoiding) costly and unpleasant legal detours in the practice of psychotherapy is by being very good at psychotherapy.

LEGAL INVULNERABILITY: A MYTH AND AN ILLUSION

There are many reasons for malpractice litigation besides negligence. These include expressions of client pathology, opportunities for financial gain, and symptoms of unresolved problems between therapist and client. These are not matters of negligence or substandard care; they are personality issues that have found their way into the courtroom because a professional relationship failed. These problems are usually a matter of either the client's or the therapist's expectations not being met or being misunderstood. Assessing blame in these matters should not be a legal matter, particularly for judges and juries who know so little about client pathology and care. But unfortunately, the ultimate resolution of these issues involves more legal persuasion by lawyers and value judgments by judges than the dispassionate application of legal principles. Such problems make the very idea of legal invulnerability a myth and an illusion. Legal expertise is not a solution— even lawyers have to defend themselves from malpractice suits filed by other lawyers! Furthermore, the inherent risk of liability in the delivery of mental health services is infinitely higher than in the legal profession. Our clients are disturbed. They project, deny, distort, blame, get angry, and punish. Sometimes they transfer these feelings to us with extreme vigor. How well we therapeutically manage these unpredictable and volatile relationships often determines whether or not we get sued.

Additionally, our professional services are usually more of an art than a science, and some of our standards of care are vague and at times contradictory. Thus we can expect to regularly engage in clinical practices that simply do not work the way we plan, not because we do something wrong or malicious or we do not have the best of motives or intentions, but because our treatment plans and practices do not always work, and our clinically desperate clients become angry because they hope for so much but often receive so little. The real issue in these cases is our lack of public modesty about our fledgling discipline. As London (1964) noted in *The Modes and Morals of Psychotherapy*: "Its professors and practitioners, once contemptuously regarded as eccentrics mumbling arcane obscenities at the fringe of medicine, have advanced from relative obscurity to chairs of eminence and couches of opulence in the finest universities and neighborhoods in the Western World" (p. v). Seldom do practicing clinicians tell their clinical clientele that our advances in status and professional recognition have not been accompanied by parallel improvements in knowledge and treatment.

Finally, and most regrettably, a number of malpractice suits involve valid legal issues and genuine professional incompetence. For a variety of reasons, some clinicians engage in unwise and self-serving clinical practices and simply get caught. We should be grateful for such lawsuits because they help raise the lowest level of professional care that can still be considered acceptable and also protect an unsuspecting public and enforce our professional standards by imposing unpleasant sanctions.

While an incisive understanding of our legal system cannot protect us from litigation, it does offer us the greatest insight into the myth of legal invulnerability. Let us explain. Generally, it is fair to suggest that most clinicians would use their code of ethics and known legal guidelines to define proper conduct in high-risk clinical situations. We can also assume that a clinician's knowledge of these standards and statutes and adherence to them are the best protection from professional liability. This in fact is *not* necessarily true; for example, the therapist's duty to protect innocent third parties from harm by dangerous clients simply did not exist prior to this precedent-setting *Tarasoff v. Regents of University of California* (1976) case. But as a result of this case, the court imposed a duty on psychotherapists to protect potential victims of dangerous clients and found the therapist negligent because of his failure to protect the innocent victim. Ironically, this ruling actually contradicted an accepted ethical standard prior to this trial: to protect client confidentiality.

We hope our major point is clear. Some successful malpractice litigation will be the result of the court's interpretation of events in hindsight rather than a failure of the therapist's foresight. In *Tarasoff*, the courts defined professional negligence in terms of a legal standard that did not exist at the time the offense occurred!

We discuss this problem more in a later section. For now, we only wish to point out that laws frequently emerge from litigated cases, which means that lawsuits are the grist on which the legal mill grinds. Practicing clinicians in states that have not had a test case on the primacy of "confidentiality" or the "duty to warn" cannot be sure of what constitutes proper clinical conduct in this high-risk situation. They will know only after this issue has been litigated in their state, and that litigation probably will be instigated to clarify vague and poorly defined legal and ethical standards rather than to respond to flagrant violation of known standards. This is not professional negligence in the true meaning of the term; it is an evolutionary process by which standards of care are redefined with our society's changing views and values.

Practicing clinicians then can find themselves at legal risk for various reasons, some of which may have nothing to do with existent law, ethical violations, or substandard care. The more obvious reasons for legal complications include (1) actually being negligent or providing substandard care, (2) being caught in situations in which incompatible and contradictory standards could apply (duty to warn and client confidentiality), (3) having vague and poorly defined standards challenged and subsequently clarified, (4) ambiguity in the law allowing angry clients and determined lawyers to construe the law in ways that would enhance their personal interest, and (5) clients litigating as an expression of nothing more than deep-seated pathology. Considering all the forces that can be combined to form malpractice suits, practicing clinicians can easily be placed in uniquely disturbing situations (regardless of their exceptional skill or competence).

As mental health professionals, we know that the function of an illusion is to excuse one's self from facing unpleasant and unwanted realities. Legal liability is becoming a reality for more practicing clinicians each day, and it is becoming progressively more dangerous to deny this reality with the illusion that legal understanding creates legal invulnerability. Several actual clinical cases that expose the paradoxes and contradictions of our legal and ethical standards are discussed in the next section.

Double-Bind Dilemmas

The virtue and value of polished legal and ethical thinking are seldom evident in the daily diet of clinical activity. The most common dilemmas are covered rather nicely by professional codes of ethics and familiarity with a few important state statutes regarding commitment, dangerousness, and abuses. The more common violations include a breach of confidentiality, failure to inform authorities about child abuse (for a variety of reasons), involvement in a conflict of interest situation, and poor maintenance of client welfare in the fiduciary relationship. A therapist's transgressions at this level are usually the result of poor judgment, limited knowledge, or self-indulgence. A modicum of academic discipline and a fair amount of self-control are usually sufficient to prevent problems in these common and highly visible trouble spots.

The real benefits of high-level legal and ethical thinking are most obvious in the inevitable double-bind dilemmas every clinician eventually encounters: situations in which right and wrong are neither obvious nor defined by traditional standards. In some cases, contradictory standards may actually apply. It is a no-win situation for the clinician. Any course of action involves known risks, and clinicians must select the risks to which they are most willing to expose themselves. Of course these personal decisions must be balanced against other considerations, such as client welfare, possible harm to others, and the potential for malpractice litigation. These are the dilemmas clinicians dread and situations in which legal and ethical thinking are most appreciated. Let us illustrate this point with several clinical case studies that provide the basis for an in-depth analysis and review of the clinical and legal issues involved in the dangerous and suicidal cases discussed later.

Dangerous Clients.   It was about 8:00 in the evening. The therapist had just finished what he assumed was the last session of the evening. As he prepared to lock the reception area, the door opened, and a middle-aged man walked in, looked around, and then asked if a doctor was available. There was nothing particularly unusual about the man—he dressed neatly, did not appear overly distressed, and gave the impression of being coherent and deliberate. He certainly did not appear ready to commit a murder.

Even though the therapist was anxious to go home, he asked the stranger what he wanted. The man replied that he was on the verge of a very important decision and felt he should talk with somebody about it. He did not know where else to go, so he came to the clinic. The therapist assumed the man was maybe filing for divorce, possibly quitting his job, or even perhaps disappearing without a trace. The therapist decided to talk with him, thinking this might be an important conversation for the client. Usually the therapist would not accept walk-ins without an intake evaluation, but in this situation it seemed that an exception to the rule would be both proper and potentially profitable for the client.

Once seated in the consulting room, the therapist started the conversation by asking what the stranger, Brad, had on his mind. With only the slightest hint of nervousness, Brad cleared his throat and said he was thinking about killing Helen this evening. She was his supervisor at work, and he reported that she had been insulting him publicly for about 9 months. For whatever reason, it appeared that Helen had crossed the line this afternoon. The therapist asked how Brad was going to kill her. Brad pulled a razor-blade knife from his jacket pocket and said he was going to slice her face open and then pour acid on the wounds. He opened a small paper bag to show the therapist a small bottle of muriatic acid.

Two hours later, it was clear to the therapist that this client was not mentally ill in the legal sense of the term. Brad's comprehension of right and wrong was unimpaired, as was his understanding of the consequences of his behavior. His level of dangerousness was more difficult to assess. He reported no history of violent behavior in his past. He had also come to the clinic to talk instead of proceeding directly to Helen's home. Furthermore, he now thought it would be best if he had several sessions with the therapist before deciding what to do. However, the fact that Brad was carrying a knife and a bottle of acid deeply troubled the therapist. Even though Brad surrendered his weapons with little hesitation when asked to do so, the therapist knew they could easily be replaced at a dozen or more stores. The therapist suspected that the catharsis Brad experienced by openly expressing his anger toward Helen had substantially reduced his capacity for actual violence.

At this point, the therapist really did not know what to do. Involuntary hospitalization was not feasible; the client may have actually been dangerous, but he certainly was not mentally ill (both conditions were required for involuntary commitment in the state where this situation occurred). Additionally, the client showed a real interest in seeing the therapist in order to "talk" this problem out, and he had agreed to not see Helen before another session the next morning. On the other hand, the client's anger was based on a long history of perceived mistreatment and accumulated rage, and he had the means to inflict a heinous form of violent retribution. It was simply not possible to predict whether this relatively quiet man was about to explode or whether he would sink back into his relatively private world of psychic frustration. The therapist felt that any attempt to warn the potential victim at this point would seriously jeopardize the fragile therapeutic alliance that had been forming during the last 2 hours. Such action would destroy the best and perhaps only opportunity that this individual might have for learning how to cope without violence with his suppressed feelings of anger.

As the therapist pondered his alternatives carefully, the only thing clear to him was that he had a difficult situation on his hands. A breach of confidentiality could be involved if he warned unnecessarily. Additionally, his diagnosis of the client not being mentally ill had to be considered tentative in the absence of a more complete and objective psychological evaluation. And finally, if the client did go to Helen's home and inflict harm, the therapist certainly faced the prospects of a malpractice suit for failing to warn Helen, even though the client's behavior was fundamentally unpredictable at the time the therapist had to make this decision.

Keep this case in mind while reading about the legal principles described throughout the book. This is a good test case for applying many of the principles we will be discussing.

Increasing Suicide Potential by Hospitalization. Norma was in her mid-20s, extraordinarily intelligent, and severely disturbed. She had been diagnosed as a paranoid schizophrenic about 5 years earlier. She was currently receiving weekly injections of an antipsychotic medication (Haldol) because she could not be trusted to take oral medication regularly. She had never been hospitalized. Her medication was quite effective at controlling both her auditory and occasional visual hallucinations for 4 or 5 days; the last 2, and sometimes 3, days before her next injection were more problematic.

Norma was not a prototypical paranoid schizophrenic. She also had what appeared to be impulse-control problems that involved drugs, alcohol, and a variety of other behavioral manifestations. She was a splendid manipulator and a world-class liar. She was not amoral or without guilt, however. She suffered deep and desperate shame over past deeds she found inexcusable. One such deed involved an abortion. Much of Norma's drinking, lying, and manipulating was her way of trying to hide "personal truths" from herself and others. Her greatest and most profound fear was that others would find out about her mental illness, a totally intolerable thought to her. She would do anything, go to any length, to be sure no one found out. And her various disguises worked remarkably well; she was seen as eccentric, and occasionally irresponsible, but no one really suspected how emotionally disturbed she was. When Norma started hallucinating, whether at home, at work, or with friends, she had the presence of mind to quickly find a place of privacy until the episode was over. She had a remarkable ability to function rather well in spite of her psychological disturbance. As she put it, "I simply turn the voice down low so I can pay attention and respond—otherwise everyone will know."

Several weeks earlier, the frequency of Norma's auditory hallucinations started to increase, as did "the voices'" insistence that she destroy herself. Her suicide potential dramatically increased, not because of the insistence of the voices but because of the difficulty of "faking" normalcy with the voices talking so much. Her fear of getting caught escalated greatly. As a result, Norma gained access to a university lab, looked up the dose of arsenic lethal for her body weight, and started hiding quantities of the deadly poison at strategic locations in her environment. Her plan was to kill herself immediately if she was about to get caught being "crazy."

The dilemma is now clear. The therapist faces a situation with the following characteristics:

1. The client is an extremely high suicide risk. She has (a) a specific plan, (b) lethal means, (c) predetermined cues to activate the suicide attempt, (d) a prior suicide attempt under similar conditions, (e) auditory voices insisting on the suicide, and (f) no meaningful support group available.

2. The client is mentally ill and poses an imminent danger to herself. The conditions for immediate hospitalization appear optimal—anything less would usually constitute substandard care. But two points need serious consideration before any attempt to hospitalize is made. First, is there any chance the client would agree to a voluntary commitment. The answer is an emphatic "No"; everyone would then know her "horrible" secret. Second, if the client is committed involuntarily, can enough persuasive evidence be presented so she is retained long enough for the pathology underlying this entire dilemma (loss of face from public exposure) to be effectively resolved? It must be remembered that a premature release would virtually ensure a successful suicide attempt inasmuch as the most important elements to activate the client's suicide will have been satisfied: Everyone will know and she will have "lost face" completely. Furthermore, this client has a demonstrated capacity to fake "normalcy," even during periods of extreme stress associated with her hallucinations. Attempts at involuntary hospitalizations could actually increase the chances of a serious suicide attempt if a judge or other mental health professionals released her early and failed to crack or recognize her psychological disguise and her true level of dangerousness during their first evaluation of her.

3. The therapist now knows that little packages containing terribly lethal doses of arsenic have been strategically hidden throughout the client's environment. Innocent parties, particularly children, could find and ingest the poison. Yet any attempt to report this situation to authorities so they could systematically search the client's environment could prove fatal to the client.

Keep the facts of this case in mind reading through the book. This is another good test case for applying the legal principles we will be discussing. For now, note that the therapist, who is not yet guilty of any obvious act of negligence or substandard care, is suddenly emersed in a genuine double-bind dilemma. Issues of client welfare, potential substandard care, dangerousness to others, breach of confidentiality, and protection of self-interests are all in conflict with each other. It is a situation in which the preservation of one legal/ethical standard will probably violate another.

While this dilemma is a psychological nightmare for practitioners, it is a fertile opportunity for lawyers. Any move the therapist now makes will violate someone's best interests and the laws and/or ethical codes designed to protect them. Opportunities for malpractice litigation are both obvious and numerous, all based on the same premise: A known standard of professional care applies to these situations, and the violation of this standard is the basis for defining professional negligence.

In fact, no compass in the legal, ethical, or professional standards exists to guide practitioners in these dilemmas, nor should we suppose that double-bind circumstances similar to these are rare occurrences in clinical practice. They appear with a predictable regularity with high-risk clientele, and each occurrence leaves the practitioner unprotected from exposure to severe liability.

Moreover, once a suicide, homicide, or other harm has taken place, the legal system, with all the benefits of hindsight, has an undeniable urge to argue that the dangers of any situation were more obvious than they really were. And they are usually right because with the benefits of hindsight, the hints of danger in any situation are more obvious than they originally were. This fact alone makes it difficult for judges and juries to resist the natural temptation to believe that if the therapist had been slightly more astute, harm could have been prevented. And under these conditions, there is little benefit in trying to arouse in the minds of a judge or jury a dispassionate understanding of the factual difficulties of predicting or controlling outpatient behavior.

Ingredients in both these clinical dilemmas are two myths that are seldom made obvious in discussions of high-risk clinical situations. First, legal invulnerability really is a myth. Professional negligence and violations of law are not the only determinants of successful malpractice litigation. They may not even be the most important ones in some cases. Angry clients, ambiguous laws, vague standards of care, and persuasive lawyers can play an influential role in this equation. These are not legal factors or failures in professional judgment; they are social psychological factors. *Mastery of the law does little to enhance one's understanding of these social psychological events or how to combat them. These events are problems that may fade in the face of persuasion, the successful development of a therapeutic alliance, and strategic problem solving, but not legal debate.* Therapists must understand this concept before they can understand the basis for a major portion of malpractice litigation and how to prevent it.

Second, there is no "cookbook" approach to these problems. These dilemmas are seldom the result of either careless or obvious violations of ethical or legal standards, and their successful resolution is hardly ever the result of the rote application of existing legal or ethical codes. Much more imaginative solutions are required that recognize the contradictions in our legal and ethical codes and integrate these considerations into treatment plans that focus on a positive therapeutic relationship.

AMBIGUITY: LANGUAGE, LAW, AND PSYCHOTHERAPY

We must now face a paradox of major proportion. Simply stated, the more diligently we seek to understand the language of law and psychology, the more obvious it becomes that ambiguity is a staple element of both languages. Philosophers of science (Fiegel & Brodbeck, 1953) taught us long ago that semantic precision and conceptual clarity require that we use dissimilar words when referring to different events and similar words when referring to the same events. Generally, confusion is considered the result of limited knowledge, lack of understanding, or confusing and inconsistent language. The more we understand the language of law and psychology, the more obvious it becomes that many of the most crucial concepts involved are inherently ambiguous.

The problem is not that we use words with imprecise meaning; it is more that we use words with precise meaning when referring to ambiguous concepts and events. And under scrutiny, the illusion of clarity can be obliterated and the ambiguity of the concept fully exposed, usually at rather inopportune times. How judges, juries, and lawyers interpret this ambiguity on a case-by-case basis is one of the greatest sources of risk for legal liability among the mental health professions. Nowhere is the lack of semantic precision more obvious than at the juncture where psychology and law meet. This is the point where semantic elasticity is more the rule than the exception and the meaning of words is defined more by circumstance than by substance. Regrettably, this unfortunate state of affairs is seldom accepted for the problem it is. Let us explain and illustrate this statement.

Negligence: Substance and Sterility

The very heart of malpractice litigation is professional negligence. At first glance, the term *negligence* appears to have very precise legal and professional meaning. Upon careful examination, however, it becomes obvious that the very meaning of the term is often quite arbitrary, both legally and professionally. The term is truly defined more by circumstance than by enduring meaning, and each new circumstance in which this term is defined yields slightly different results. Because negligence plays a central role in malpractice litigation, we examine it in detail in Chapter 2.

Negligence As a Substantive Concept.   In professional malpractice, negligence is a term that refers to professional behavior judged as falling below the standards established by the profession to protect clients from the risk of unreasonable harm by unskilled clinicians (Slovenko, 1973). Four conditions are required to establish a cause of action for negligence: (1) establishment of a duty to the plaintiff, (2) breach of the duty, (3) damages, and (4) causation. These four components provide form and content to negligence doctrine; they are further reviewed in Chapter 2.

Negligence As a Sterile Concept.   The precision and clarity with which we can define standards of care and professional competence are of paramount importance in malpractice litigation. Ultimately, and certainly legally, negligence is an ill-advised and significant deviation from the profession's standard of care. However, before the concept of negligence can have any substantive or functional meaning, we simply must be able to recognize professional conduct that falls above or below this standard. This is the litmus test for establishing negligence and liability in malpractice cases. The validity of this test ultimately rests on the supposition that standards for professional care exist and that the adequacy of professional conduct can be measured against these standards. These are reasonable requirements for professions whose practices are more of a science than an art. The failure of a physician, for example, to check the cholesterol level of an overweight client past the age of 50 during a yearly physical exam would require compelling justification before it could be considered anything but negligent.

Because psychotherapy is more an art than a science, the consequences of different psychological practices are not very well understood. But more importantly, there really are few, if any, psychological practices that are consensually accepted as standards for professional care. Regrettably, but quite literally, our customary criteria for judging the adequacy of professional conduct are for the most part improvised and oblique.

This unhappy state of affairs is not the result of indifference by the professions. In fact, it is a matter of vital concern. Psychology, psychiatry, social work, and marriage and family therapy face rather difficult technical and conceptual problems that must be at least partially resolved before they can develop more robust standards of care. One of the best ways of understanding the depth of these dilemmas and the uncertainty they create in our standards of practice is to examine the origin and meaning of many of our professional standards.

Professional Standards:
Substance or Semantics?

Basically, professional standards derive from three primary and fundamentally different sources.

1. First are the standards developed by our professional organizations. As a result of debate, extensive reviews of literature, surveys of common practices, and expert opinion, the profession formalizes guides for acceptable professional conduct. These guides are usually applicable to the entire profession and are formalized in ethical codes and treatment practices.

2. Second, different geographical regions or specific agencies may adopt standards of practice uniquely applicable to their setting. The development of local standards is the mechanism that encourages a practitioner in a small, rural town 100 miles from the nearest hospital and a colleague to be held to a different standard of practice than someone working at a university-affiliated teaching hospital.

3. Finally, there are court-imposed standards, which are usually the result of litigated cases in which the court holds a profession to a higher standard than it normally practices as a means of increasing public protection. In spite of the benevolent motives that inspire these rulings, court-imposed standards are usually problematic, almost always based on the assumption that the judiciary knows enough about a profession's conceptual issues and technical capabilities to instruct it in its capabilities and preferred practices.

In spite of the obvious differences in the origin of these standards of practice in the mental health professions, they all share one common factor: They are all ultimately a reflection of "expert opinions." When professional practices are derived and modified by research evidence, the opinions of experts tend to converge toward similar conclusions, and it is these conclusions that seem to be the major ingredients of which standards are made. This statement is not meant to imply that controversy and disagreement evaporate when expert opinions are based on research data—clearly, that is not the case. In fact, most research evidence (that is, the cause and consequences of various disorders and their treatments) is the subject of substantial controversy, but it does provide a more objective and substantive foundation for the formation of expert opinions.

But quality research findings are not available to guide professional practice in many areas. The absence of research evidences helps create a conceptual vacuum that invites professional experience and values to play a more influential role in shaping expert opinion. These opinions can be expected to be more variable from one situation to another and from person to person than those anchored to research data and interpretation. *Regrettably, but undeniably, the subjective elements in expert opinion can compromise the very expertise that is assumed to be at the heart of expert opinion.* Any discussion of professional standards of care, then, must include a discussion of the diversity, objectivity, and reliability of its experts. As the reader will quickly see, our analysis of these topics in the mental health professions is not a reassuring one. This is the point where rather precise language (standards of care) is used when referring to rather vague and poorly defined events and concepts.

Expert Opinions: Diversity, Objectivity, and Reliability. The mental health professions are far from being exact sciences—some people may even question if they are sciences at all. Psychologists, psychiatrists, social workers, and family therapists disagree widely and frequently on (1) what constitutes mental illness, (2) the type of diagnosis that best fits different patterns of symptoms and behavior, and (3) the most important elements in psychological treatment.

An imminent psychiatrist, Sasz (1960), argued persuasively that mental illness is a myth and suggested that client confinement (hospitalization) is a moral issue, not a medical one. Most of his psychiatric colleagues, however, consider psychotic episodes an expression of biochemical irregularities that are best treated in a hospital where medications can be carefully regulated. It is important to note that either point of view can muster substantial expert support for its position, but neither can produce evidence that transcends the personal beliefs of its experts—beliefs which are, ultimately, a matter of social philosophy and differences in professional training.

Consequently, what is the standard of professional conduct expected when psychotic episodes start occurring in outpatient clientele? There really is not one! The outcome of a case being litigated on this count probably will not be determined by measuring the quality of client care against a known standard of professional conduct. Because of the ambiguity inherent in the language of law and the mental health professions, such cases probably will be determined by the persuasive power of the lawyers, the biases of the judge, and the sympathies of the jury. These are not matters of legal merit, nor is this dilemma confined to this one dimension of professional care. The dilemma is easily extended to such fundamental considerations as the (1) use of drugs in the treatment of a variety of disorders, (2) treatment of choice for different types of disorders, (3) means of assessing client improvement or deterioration, (4) duration and setting for treatment, (5) training and qualifications required of practitioners, and (6) predictability and controllability of disordered behavior. Obviously, when intelligent and well-trained professionals cannot agree on issues as fundamental to clinical practice as these, there can be little hope for agreement on less fundamental and more divergent practices.

We hope our major point is clear. The mental health professions are still in their infancy and are founded on diversity. A variety of professionals are developing highly divergent methods and models for understanding and treating emotional and behavioral problems. For example, Barr, Lang, Holt, Goldberger, and Klein (1972) suggested the unique benefits to be derived from psychotic experiences, Janov (1970) has a loyal following for his Primal Scream Therapy, and some of the more radical group treatment procedures have included nudity as a treatment factor. There is also substantial controversy over more traditional issues such as the role of support, paradoxical injunctions, aversive conditioning, and confrontation in treatment. The value and utility of all these views are arguable from someone's perspective, and virtually any clinical practice has a loyal following. In most cases, these practices will have the support of some experts from some field of psychology. With such a broad and diverse range of activities included in clinical practice, it is easy to understand why professional standards of care for mental health professionals cannot be extended beyond the most rudimentary consideration in clinical care.

And the legal profession has not failed to notice how the diversity of common clinical activities effects our inability to define standards of care. The *Tarasoff* (1974) trial brought the legal profession face-to-face with this problem. In this case, negligence was defined in terms of a therapist's failure to take steps to protect an innocent victim from a dangerous client. Naturally, the standard of care for predicting client dangerousness became a pivotal issue in this case. It became clear to the judiciary that the mental health professions do not have a standard practice for predicting dangerousness. Nevertheless, the ability of a therapist to predict client dangerousness was examined under the ordinary malpractice criterion of "conformity to standards of the profession." But now the courts had to face the problem of determining what standard of practice could be applied to the problem of predicting client dangerousness. Ultimately, of course, there are no standards for this problem, for all the reasons we have already discussed, which is probably what led Justice Mosk (1974, p. 34) to note that dependence on such standards (really their absence) "will take us from the world of reality into the wonderland of clairvoyance."

Similarly, the American Psychological Association (1987) made the same point in an amicus brief filed as a friend of the court. In this brief, they quoted extensively from the original *Tarasoff* (1974) ruling as follows:

> Many recent decisions, in this and other contexts, have recognized the difficulties inherent in therapists' efforts to predict dangerousness. For this reason, the courts have generally held—as did the District Court in this case—that therapists seeking to predict patient violence must stay "within the broad *range* of reasonable practices and treatment in which professional opinion and judgment may differ." The problem with this approach is that the existence of such a range of reasonable professional judgment is negated by empirical evidence. The consistent research finding is that mental health professionals fail to predict accurately future violence in two out of three cases, and that there is not consistent professional standards for predicting violence. In light of these findings, the "standards of the profession" or the "range of reasonable practice and treatment" is inherently unreliable, and ultimately unworkable, as a standard by which to judge the assessments of a particular therapist and to impose liability based on those judgments. (pp. 13–15)

This is precisely the type of situation that leaves us all in the uncomfortable position of wondering how we might go about applying standards of care that are premised on professional skills and knowledge that may not even exist. Because our attempts to identify standards of practice are based more on semantics than substance, the integrity and vitality of the legal concept of negligence are in serious doubt when applied to the mental health professions. The rigorous exactitude of legal jargon, regardless of intent, does little to alleviate the inexactitude of this "soft science." Furthermore, if our analysis is only partially valid, *we can only speculate about the real basis for malpractice rulings, and these speculations should be as frightening to the legal profession as they are enlightening to the mental health professions.*

Clinical Competence: Substance or Semantics?   Now we turn our attention away from the legal ambiguity of the concept of negligence and face a more sensitive problem: Can any of the mental health professions define competence in the practice of psychotherapy? This is an intriguing question, to say the least. And once again we find the same abuses of language and meaning that we encountered in our attempts to understand professional negligence—the use of language that lacks conceptual meaning or operational definitions. It is entirely possible that even the mental health professions cannot adequately define competence or the most essential ingredients of psychotherapy.

In a fascinating discussion of professional competence and licensing, Pottinger (1979) reminded us that a primary reason the American Psychological Association pursued licensing was to establish a psychologist's right to practice psychotherapy. Yet there is no agreement about what this single and important function entails. In fact, even proponents of licensure have rarely defined any dimensions of competence beyond entry-level educational requirements.

Similarly, Pottinger (1979) noted that:

> Psychology as a profession is unique in the following respect: we educate, train, certify, license, distribute, select, and evaluate mental health care workers (psychiatrists, psychologists, social workers, mental health paraprofessionals, allied mental health personnel) with few agreed upon guiding concepts and no uniform definitions of what our professions are or for what our professional titles stand for. (p. 2)

Historically, educational standards have been the regular mechanism for admission into the mental health professions. Recently, however, it has become less acceptable to consider education as a proxy for competence. It is now widely recognized that we tend to use education and experience as proxies only because we lack more rigorous definitions of competence or ways of assessing it. And as Pottinger (1979) already documented, there are good reasons for being uneasy about the relationship between education and professional competence. Consider the following:

1. The development of an organized sequence of study in higher education does not: (a) simultaneously define the outcomes or competencies that may result from that study or (b) automatically ensure the development of the competencies required for professional practice. Thus educational standards may have little to do with the competencies that are essential to mental health workers.

2. A substantial body of literature exists that fails to demonstrate a significant relationship between academic work and subsequent professional

performance (Bergin & Jasper, 1969; Bergin & Solomon, 1970; Holland & Richards, 1965; Kelly & Fiske, 1951; Kelly & Goldberg, 1959; Livingston, 1971; McClelland, 1973; Meehl, 1971; Price, Taylor, Richards, & Jacobsen, 1964; Taylor, Smith, & Ghiselin, 1963; Thorndike & Hagen, 1959). Even though educators may claim that students are better prepared for work because they are more knowledgeable, these reports fail to substantiate that claim, at least in areas related to mental health services.

3. A number of prominent professional experts have raised disturbing questions about the level of competence in the professional ranks (Meehl, 1971; Rogers, 1973; Strupp, 1972; Truax & Mitchell, 1971). Collectively, these reports suggest that the number of skilled practitioners is probably between 20 to 30%, with far more certified charlatans and exploiters than any of us would care to imagine.

All this leads to a rather disturbing conclusion. The concept of professional competence, just like standards of care, is a staple element in professional practice and malpractice litigation. But, as a profession, we do not appear to know a great deal about the conceptual or operational meaning of professional competence, and the consequences of our confusion may be starting to show. In the introduction to a book on therapy and ethics, Finkel (1980) articulately summarized our unhappy state of affairs as follows:

> . . . with increasing frequency, he [the mental health professional] has been called before the court of public opinion, not so much to defend the defendant, but to defend himself and his practices. The old adage, "Healer, heal thyself" is heard again.
> So he pauses, . . . and for good reason. The voices calling him into question come from within the profession as well as from without, and cut across varying ideologies and politics. He is hearing from more than "fringe elements" whose usual utterances can be taken apart and shrugged off. Now, it is eminent spokesmen in the fields of psychiatry, psychology, law, and ethics who are wondering aloud whether the patient needs protection from the healer—and their refrain is getting louder. The therapist is hearing from another voice too—this one from within: not hallucinations, mind you, but the voice of conscience. (p. 2)

Earlier, we noted that the mental health profession must at least partially resolve some fundamental conceptual and measurement problems before it can develop more robust standards of care. Our current use of ambiguous language is only the tip of the iceberg. The underlying problem is the ambiguity and complexity of some of our most basic concepts. The more obvious examples include terms such as *competence, therapeutic improvement, standards of care, client deterioration, eminent danger,* and *effective treatment*; all these terms are easier to define semantically than to understand operationally. Furthermore, we see little reason to be optimistic about future improvements until we stop using relatively clear language to refer to complex and poorly defined concepts and events.

Recently, many advocates of various psychotherapies have developed and tested treatment manuals (Lambert & Ogles, 1988). These manuals operationalize competence, and some have even developed rating scales that allow therapists' skill levels to be assessed. While these manuals have obvious training and evaluation advantages, they provide no ready-made solution to the problems already raised here. There is little agreement across practitioners about competence and skill; what the point of view of one theory may strictly forbid may be widely advocated by other theories.

MALPRACTICE: EXAGGERATED FEARS AND MISCONCEPTIONS

We have known for a long time that fear is a two-edged sword. Low to moderate levels of fear tend to enhance performance on a variety of performance tasks, but high levels can dramatically interfere with optimal performance (Morgan & King, 1971). The fears associated with a substantial lawsuit in high-risk clinical situations are seldom the catalysts that bring the best out of most practicing clinicians—just the opposite is more likely. When incisive clinical interventions are required to deal with a crisis effectively, it is not the time to be burdened with irrational fears while second-guessing the prospects of a malpractice suit. The only reasonable response to these fears is to obtain information in advance, the type of information that exposes irrational fears to be the frauds they really are and preserves the rational ones and the risks they represent. Rumors and myths can bc particularly problematic, and they are usually the companions of most irrational fears. Ironically, rumors can breed levels of fear and suspicion that create the very stress and anxiety our rational beliefs are intended to protect us from. It is these stereotypes we now discuss. But first a story—a factual illustration of a true malpractice case. We did not select a mental health case because our primary points here are more legal than psychological and more generic than specific.

A family retained a relatively well-known and respected surgeon to operate on their 4-year-old daughter, who had a congenital heart defect and whose death was imminent without corrective surgery. At the time this surgery occurred, the technical capability for open-heart surgery had existed for only several years. The surgery was not considered an experimental procedure, but neither was it a standard practice. Unfortunately, and quite unexpectedly, complications arose during the surgery and the little girl died. At first, nobody knew why, but an autopsy revealed a rare secondary heart defect, and this secondary defect had unknowingly and substantially increased the risk and complexity of the proposed surgery.

The family filed suit, claiming their daughter's death was a result of the surgeon's negligence. Their attorney argued that the surgeon had failed to meet the standard of care expected with open-heart surgery by (1) not knowing about the secondary heart defect prior to the surgery and (2) not taking appropriate precautions to guard against the surgical complications that were known to accompany the secondary heart defect.

Well before these charges were filed, the plaintiff's attorney engaged in a massive search for expert medical advice regarding the known effects of the secondary heart defect. And eventually he found what he was looking for. In a relatively obscure medical journal with a circulation of about 500, he found a report outlining the risks of open-heart surgery when this rare secondary heart defect existed.

The battle lines for the trial were now clearly drawn. The plaintiff's attorney found a variety of different ways to repeatedly ask the surgeon the same incisive question "Would the little girl be alive today if you had known about the secondary heart defect?" The answer was always the same: "Yes, she most likely would still be alive."

When it was time for the surgeon to take the stand in his own defense, his attorney skillfully guided him through a prolonged series of questions about the precise practices he followed to stay current in his professional knowledge. The lawyer wanted to know what journals the doctor read, how he selected them, if he kept notes on reports dealing with open-heart surgery, and the number of educational conferences he attended each year. The surgeon's attorney even had his client summarize the major findings of several current reports on open-heart surgery that were selected randomly while he was testifying on the stand.

As you might well imagine, a major issue in the trial was why the surgeon did not know about the published report that clearly identified the increased risk of open-heart surgery when the rare heart defect existed. When the surgeon was asked why he was not aware of this particular report, he responded by explaining that he made it a practice to deliberately avoid reports contained in secondary professional journals. Past experience had taught him that these reports were often less credible than those in the primary medical journals. He felt it was too risky to modify his treatment plans based on these preliminary reports.

Eventually, the legal debate ended. Naturally, it was a horrible ordeal for the surgeon. He often found himself taking long walks late at night. He was no longer sure that his personal decision to base his treatment practices on only the most credible information was very wise after all. He understood that a girl may have died needlessly.

The court found no negligence in the surgeon's professional conduct, and he was completely exonerated. While the court was deeply grieved about the death of the little girl, it was quick to add that the skill and knowledge of the surgeon seemed exemplary. In this case, there was no guilt because there was no negligence, and there was no negligence because the surgeon's skill and expertise were in harmony with the profession's standard of practice. The fact that the surgeon did not know everything is regrettable—few of us do, but far more important, it is simply not the meaning of professional negligence.

We presented this case to illustrate the following points about malpractice litigation:

1. *Although it may be difficult for many of us to believe, and there are numerous stories to the contrary, the courts are as committed to holding profes-*

sionals to reasonable standards of care as they are to protecting the public from unreasonable professional practices. This case represents a situation many professionals would fear because they believe that the courts have a continuing bias favoring casualties of professional care. Because of this bias, many professionals are believed to be financially victimized by the blind sympathies of the courts. We cannot say this never happens or that it does not happen less than it could. Human sympathy can be a powerful motive.

But more than any other social institution, the courts understand the necessity of balancing the welfare of the professions as well as the individual. If inflated and unreasonable standards of care are imposed on *new* professional practices, no one will develop new practices. And if inflated and unreasonable standards are imposed on *any* professional practice, no one will offer that service because of the inflated risk involved. These reasons are why the courts are as committed to holding professionals to reasonable standards as they are to protecting the public from unreasonable practices. This is the only way the courts can preserve the vital and valid benefits of professional services in a complex society without favoring individuals or professions.

In the final analysis, the long-term interests of professions, individuals, and society are best served by the courts' ruling doctrine being "reasonableness" for all parties. Many of our irrational fears about professionals being financially victimized by the courts are simply exaggerated because many of us do not believe or do not understand the underlying necessity of the courts continually trying to preserve their commitment to fairness for all parties, even in malpractice litigation.

2. *Many professionals do not understand the fundamental difference between mistakes, errors of judgment, unfavorable outcomes, and professional negligence.* In our case illustration, there was an unfavorable outcome (the client died), the surgeon made a mistake (he was unaware of the secondary defect), and his judgment was in error (he deliberately avoided educational material in secondary medical journals). Yet there was no negligence. It is important to remember why. Negligence is an ill-advised and significant deviation from the profession's standard of practice. It simply is not against the law to be wrong, to make mistakes, or have our clients suffer unexpected and unpleasant outcomes. *Why* these things happen is the essence of legal negligence, not *if* they happen.

Another case helps illustrate our primary point. Suppose you have a suicidal client. You formally assess the client's suicide potential and, in the process, ask all the standard questions. You judge the suicide potential to be moderate. In light of this information, you invite the client to schedule additional appointments any time it becomes necessary. You also extend telephone privileges that will allow contact with you 24 hours a day. Your client understands the risks and benefits of your plan and endorses it. Ten hours after the session, the client is found dead with a gunshot wound in the head.

Again, we have a bad outcome, clinical mistakes, and errors of judgment. But do we have negligence? Probably not. You would have fulfilled your duty by using a diagnostic procedure that was consistent with professional standards, and you took affirmative steps to protect the client's life because of the information revealed in the diagnostic interview.

As professionals, we are expected to be clairvoyant only on rare and unreasonable occasions. We are usually held accountable only for failures to exercise the ordinary skill and expertise that can be expected from similarly trained professionals. Any of our beliefs that imply that more can be expected of us, or that it is against the law to make mistakes or have unfavorable client outcomes, only enhance the fear that deters quality clinical care.

3. *The more ambiguous a profession's standard of care, the more likely its bad outcomes, mistakes, and errors of judgment are to be considered as professional negligence.* During the last 10 years or so, we have participated in a number of clinic board meetings for the purpose of discussing strategies to minimize malpractice suits. Most of these meetings seem to share a common element: a fear of being sued. This fear evokes two rather noticeable responses: (1) to hardly ever talk about actual problems of staff competence or limiting services to areas of demonstrated expertise, and (2) to almost always talk about the ways agency policies and standards can be written so as to minimize accountability in the event of a lawsuit. The rationale for this approach is obvious enough. An agency is almost automatically held liable if there is a noticeable discrepancy between what the agency says it will do and what it actually does in the delivery of mental health service. This being the case, why be clear about agency standards or policies? It only seems to enhance the chances of a successful malpractice suit. And this rationale is essentially accurate to a point. Professional conduct that significantly deviates from agency policies or standards is quite likely going to provide a basis for establishing negligence.

But this rationale overlooks one important point. It is virtually impossible to establish negligence when professional conduct is consistent with clear professional standards. In our case of open-heart surgery, it seems fairly obvious that the only reason the bad outcome and errors of judgment were not considered negligence was because the surgeon's conduct was measured against a known standard of professional conduct. We suggest that the more vague and ambiguous a profession's standard of care, the more likely it is that errors of judgment and unfavorable outcomes will be considered professional negligence.

4. *Many lawsuits are social psychological events that may have social psychological solutions.* A lack of medical expertise was probably not the most important cause of the lawsuit we described earlier; it was that an angry client had experienced an unhappy and unexpected treatment outcome. When the family first contacted a lawyer, they probably had no idea if medical negligence was even a factor in the death of their daughter. They were most likely angry and wanted to strike back because of their loss. This is an interesting possibility, one that Gutheil and Appelbaum (1982) skillfully discussed in their penetrating analysis of the psychological factors affecting malpractice litigation.

Gutheil and Appelbaum suggested that two factors create the optimal conditions for a lawsuit: (1) the client has high and unreasonable expectations for receiving help; (2) the client experiences an unpleasant and unexpected outcome. Please notice that neither condition is a legal or professional consideration; both conditions are client responses to stress and anger.

The best antidote for these dangerous conditions involves two steps. Step 1 is to realign clients' high expectations to more reasonable and realistic levels. Step 2 is to ensure that the client shares and understands the risks involved in the treatment process. This can be done by having the client endorse or participate in treatment decisions—an issue that we extensively discuss later. The ultimate goal of these steps is of course to take the professional out of the role of the all-knowing magician and form a more mature relationship that is a working alliance between the professional and the clients.

When we apply these considerations to our medical illustration, we obtain interesting results. First, the busy professional did not take the time necessary to discuss the surgery with his client in any detail. He did have them sign the standard informed consent forms, but clearly he did not discuss the risks of the surgery or the unexpected complications that could possibly arise. It is not that he did not know that unexpected events regularly occur during surgery; it is more likely that he did not want to worry the parents with needless speculation because he was that sort of person. When the little girl died, he had a hard time expressing his personal grief over the loss because of his grief for what had happened. Again, it was not that he did not care, it was that he cared too much. But the parents did not know that, and, finally, his professional style did not lend itself to the development of a working alliance with his clients. He really was a high-caliber expert. He was also a little shy, and it was difficult for him to discuss risks and decisions with clients who were easily upset and knew so little. And so a lawsuit ensued.

But the role of unmet expectations, frustration, and anger in human relationships is the area of expertise for most therapists. And just because these emotions can be turned on us in the form of potential malpractice suits does not mean that we have to stop responding to our clients' feelings therapeutically. This may be precisely the time we should pay the most attention to what our clients are telling us instead of frantically seeking the advice of an attorney. More than with any other profession, we should be able to understand that many lawsuits are social psychological events that may have social psychological resolutions.

So Why This Book: A Strategic Response to Ambiguity!

Any attempt to discuss the more important clinical considerations involved with dangerous clients must acknowledge a major paradox. How can we *precisely* and *carefully* discuss basic issues when the underlying professional and legal concepts are saturated with ambiguity? Remember, our analysis of the law and the mental health disciplines revealed some unsettling observations. Such fundamental concepts as negligence, standards of care, and clinical competence have limited substantive meaning, yet they are the most crucial considerations in malpractice law and clinical practice. One can only wonder how any significant enlightenment might emerge from such profound ambiguities.

Our answer to this vital question is deceptively simple. Even though the level of conceptual development in clinical/legal malpractice cases is clearly less than any of us might hope for, therapists still see dangerous clients and judges presiding over malpractice cases. And it is the nuts and bolts of these daily clinical activities we now address. We want to set aside questions about the adequacy and relevance of professional standards and legal concepts, instead focusing our attention on the "what" and "how" of clinical work in high-risk situations. Our guiding assumption is the same in all cases: Familiarity with the most current issues and knowledge relevant to high-risk situations, no matter how limited or controversial, is the best guide for clinical practice and legal defense. The practicing clinicians simply must be fully aware of the current issues and information in the major high-risk areas of clinical practice because this information is what defines and differentiates what every clinician *can* or *should* know and what *nobody* knows. In any malpractice case, the clinician will be held accountable to some standard of care, even if that standard is based on vague or ambiguous concepts. Accordingly, the astute clinician will be the most conversant with the issues and controversies that attend the topics we seem to know the least about. The value of any information is at a premium when it is most needed and least available. Paradoxically, then, high-risk clinical situations that are defined by ambiguous legal/professional concepts are the areas in which content mastery of *all* available professional literature is as important as it is scarce. In subsequent chapters we review the most current information, issues, and controversies relevant to clinical practice in high-risk areas.

SUMMARY AND CONCLUSIONS

Any attempt to understand the dynamics of malpractice litigation is doomed if a variety of nonlegal considerations is not taken into account. Because of unresolved conceptual and measurement problems in the mental health professions, it is difficult to define many of the most fundamental concepts and practices. Some of the more obvious examples include such basic considerations as competence, client improvement, eminent danger, client deterioration, effective treatment, and appropriate training.

When considered from a legal point of view, these problems escalate to nearly unimaginable proportions. Because of the ambiguity and diversity inherent in the mental health professions, expert opinion can be found to support almost any doctrine or practice. This fact alone almost completely negates the validity and vitality of the concept of professional standards, and by implication, the essence of the legal concept of negligence. Surrounded by this unhappy state of affairs, one cannot, and certainly should not, help but wonder out loud about the real basis for liability rulings when the legal foundations for these rulings appear so impoverished and oblique.

In the mental health professions, the concept of negligence and liability may be applied only to "procedural" violations such as breaches of confidentiality or conflicts of interests. These elementary but important points of professional practice may be the only areas in which we can currently agree on standards of practice. And as important as these considerations are, they should not be confused with the more essential elements involved in competent clinical care.

We suggested that many malpractice suits are more easily and accurately understood as social psychological events rather than legal violations. Because of this assumption, legal expertise is not always the most important consideration in preventing or resolving problems that initially appear as legal disputes. Unrealistic expectations for help combined with an unexpected or unfavorable treatment outcome may provide the optimal conditions for a malpractice suit. Interestingly, neither considerations are legal matters, and both are most amenable to social psychological sources of influence.

Finally, we discussed a number of fear-inducing myths about malpractice litigation. In our opinion, the most important one was our suggestion that the more obscure a profession's standards, the more likely it is that unfavorable client outcomes or errors of clinical judgment can be construed as, and confused with, legal negligence, a sobering and frightening thought for both the legal and mental health professions.

REFERENCES

American Psychological Association. (1987). *Brief amicus curiae.* Friedman, P. R., & Bersoff, D. N. (authors). Arlington, VA: Author.

Barr, H. L., Lang, R. J., Holt, R. R., Goldberger, L., & Klein, G. S. (1972). *LSD: Personality and experience.* New York: Wiley.

Bergin, A. E., & Jasper, L. G. (1969). Correlated of empathy in psychotherapy: A replication. *Journal of Abnormal Psychology, 74,* 477–481.

Bergin, A. E., & Solomon, S. (1970). Personality and performance correlates of empathic understanding in psychotherapy. In J. T. Hart & T. M. Tomlinson (Eds.), *New directions in client-centered therapy.* Boston: Houghton Mifflin.

Fiegel, H., & Brodbeck, M. (1953). *Readings in the philosophy of science.* New York: Appleton-Century-Crofts.

Finkel, N. J. (1980). *Therapy and ethics: The courtship of law and psychology.* New York: Grune & Stratton.

Gutheil, T. G., & Appelbaum, P. S. (1982). *Clinical handbook of psychiatry and the law.* New York: McGraw-Hill.

Holland, J. L., & Richards, J. M. (1965). Academic and nonacademic accomplishment: Correlated or uncorrelated. *Journal of Educational Psychology, 56,* 165–174.

Janov, A. (1970). *The primal scream.* New York: Putnam.

Kelly, E. L., & Fiske, D. W. (1951). *The prediction of performance in clinical psychology.* Ann Arbor: University of Michigan Press.

Kelly, E. L., & Goldberg, L. R. (1959). Correlates of later performance and specialization in psychology. *Psychological Monographs, 73.*

Lambert, M. J., & Ogles, B. (1988). Psychotherapy treatment manuals: Problems and promise. *Journal of Integrative and Eclectic Psychotherapy, 7,* 187–204.

Livingston, J. S. (1971). Myth of the well-educated manager. *Harvard Business Review, 49,* 79–89.

London, P. (1964). *The modes and morals of psychotherapy.* Washington, D.C.: Hemisphere Publishing Co.

McClelland, D. C. (1973). Testing for competence rather than intelligence. *American Psychologist, 28,* 1–14.

Meehl, P. E. (1971). A scientific, scholarly, nonresearch doctorate for clinical practitioners: Arguments pro and con. In R. R. Holt (Ed.), *New horizon for psychotherapy: Autonomy as a profession.* New York: International Universities Press.

Morgan, C. T., & King, R. A. (1971). *Introduction to psychology* (4th ed.). New York: McGraw-Hill.

Pottinger, P. S. (1979). *Defining competence in the mental health professions.* Paper presented at the annual meeting of the American Psychological Association, New York.

Price, P. B., Taylor, C. W., Richards, J. M., Jr., & Jacobsen, T. C. (1964). Measurement of physician performance. *Journal of Medical Education, 39,* 203–211.

Rogers, C. R. (1973). Some new challenges. *American Psychologist, 28,* 379–387.

Slovenko, R. (1973). *Psychiatry and law.* Boston: Little, Brown.

Strupp, H. H. (1972). *Changing frontiers in the science of psychotherapy.* Chicago: Aldine-Atherton.

Szasz, T. S. (1960). The myth of mental illness. *American Psychologist, 15,* 113–118.

Tarasoff v. Regents of University of California. 529 P.2d 533, 118 Cal. Rptr 129 (1974).

Taylor, C. W., Smith, W. R., & Ghiselin, B. (1963). The creative and other contributions of one sample of research scientists. In C. W. Taylor & F. Barron (Eds.). *Scientific creativity: Its recognition and development.* New York: Wiley.

Thorndike, R. C., & Hagen, E. (1959). *Ten thousand careers.* New York: Wiley.

Truax, C. B., & Mitchell, K. M. (1971). Research on certain therapist interpersonal skills in relation to process & outcome. In A. E. Bergin & S. L. Garfield (Eds.). *Handbook of Psychotherapy and Behavior Change.* New York: Wiley.

2

Legal Liability and Social Responsibility: An Introduction to Legal Reasoning

Psychotherapists, of course, believe that their role is to help others and do not perceive that anyone in society should need to be protected from them. From this perspective, the possibility of civil law suits in the course of psychotherapeutic practice seems difficult to fathom, if not outright unfair. From the perspective of the legal system and disgruntled consumers, however, therapists, like any other identifiable group, sometimes behave badly and should be held accountable.[1]

A malpractice lawsuit can have devastating effects on the practice of an unfortunate professional. Even suits filed with absolutely no merit can catastrophically impact the psychotherapist's professional reputation, personal life, and financial stability. Frivolous lawsuits must be seriously defended, which usually requires hiring an attorney to draft dismissal documents and argue them before the court, no small investment. Practicing therapists are therefore understandably concerned with why they may be subject to suit, what they can be sued for, and how they can reasonably prevent liability.

This chapter will briefly explain (1) the principles and policies underlying the branch of law governing malpractice suits (tort law) and (2) the malpractice cause of action itself and what must be proved to establish a case of psychiatric malpractice.

Malpractice is negligence law applied to professionals. To illustrate the elements of malpractice law and its application, we introduce the facts of an actual medical malpractice case, selected because it most clearly illustrates the underlying principles of malpractice law. Note that medical malpractice examples are used sparingly throughout the text. In fact, we have included all relevant legal decisions involving psychotherapy. We restricted medical examples to situations in which such an example is the only means of illustrating a principle of case law.

[1]R. Meyer, E. Landis, & J. Hays, Law for the Psychotherapist 11 (1988) [hereinafter Law for the Psychotherapist].

CASE FACTS AND INTRODUCTION

Anna Salinetro suffered injuries to her back in an automobile accident. Several days after the accident, she obtained a medical examination in order to recover insurance benefits. The physician, Dr. Nystrom, took X rays of Anna's lower back and abdomen. Anna had visited her gynecologist 6 days prior to the X rays because she suspected she was pregnant. Anna's gynecologist told her the test results were negative—she was not pregnant. Prior to taking the X rays, Dr. Nystrom, his receptionist, and the X-ray technician all failed to ask Anna whether she was pregnant. Two days after the examination and X rays, it was determined that Anna was 4 to 6 weeks pregnant. Approximately 1 month later, Anna's gynecologist found out that X rays had been taken and advised that the pregnancy be terminated because of suspected damage to the fetus. Anna underwent a therapeutic abortion. A pathology report conclusively determined that the fetus was dead at the time of the abortion. Anna sued Dr. Nystrom for malpractice.[2]

Considerations in this case might include:

1. Was Dr. Nystrom negligent in failing to inquire if Anna was pregnant before ordering X rays?

2. Was Anna negligent in failing to inform Dr. Nystrom of the possibility that she might be pregnant?

3. If both Dr. Nystrom and Anna are partially responsible for the death of the fetus, how is legal responsibility determined?

4. If both parties are partially at fault, whose negligence can be said to have caused the damages?

5. May the law infer that the fetus would not have died "but for" the X rays?

With the facts and issues of this case in mind, we now examine the role of tort law and the underlying policies it is designed to serve. We then examine malpractice as a specific component of tort law and analyze the elements of proof required for a successful malpractice action. At the chapter's close, we return to the case presented to illustrate how malpractice law is applied in a real case.

TORT LAW IN PERSPECTIVE

We all have a multitude of interests that we want and expect the law to protect. Beyond our basic needs, we want the freedom to work and interact with others. We want to be protected from interferences into our private lives, our family relations, our honor, and our reputation. We are concerned with freedom of thought and movement. In short, the catalog of our interests is "as long as the list of legitimate human desires; and not the least of them is the desire to do what [we]

---

[2]Case illustration drawn from *Salinetro v. Nystrom*, 341 So. 2d 1059 (Fla. Ct. App. 1977).

please, without restraint and without undue consideration for the interests and claims of others."[3]

Inevitably, however, the interests of one individual conflict with the interests of another, and losses or injuries result. Primitive cultures remedied these conflicts with fists, clubs, or swords. In other words, "might made right." In civilized communities, however, "it is the law which is called upon to act as arbiter."[4]

Some conflicts, however—such as acts of ingratitude or name-calling—cause insults or injuries that are so trivial that they are simply accepted as part of life's routine. The aggrieved party's only remedy for such injury is to develop a tough hide.

Other injuries are less trivial but still regarded as a private matter and best dealt with privately. While the law may provide a cause of action, the corresponding social and financial costs practically prohibit prosecution of an action for these relatively minor injuries. Accordingly, the injured party can usually best be protected from these types of harm through private insurance.[5]

Some misfortunes are sufficiently important to justify state intervention in demanding that the injurer compensate the injured. Such occurrences are called torts and accordingly are governed by tort law.

A *tort* is a civil wrong for which the courts will provide a remedy in the form of an action for monetary damages.[6] To demonstrate the function of the law of torts, let us compare tort law with other, more familiar areas of the law.

Contract law protects a single, individual interest: requiring that the promises of others be performed. In reality, contract law frequently allows a breaching party to escape performance but, accordingly, requires that party to compensate the nonbreaching party. The amount of required compensation is usually equal to the level of profits the nonbreacher would have realized had the contract been honored.

Criminal law, on the other hand, protects interests that are common to the public at large. For example, society as a whole has an interest in deterring antisocial behavior, rehabilitating those who engage in such behavior, and seeking retribution against those deemed beyond rehabilitation. In this way, the law theoretically can preclude the moral and social decay of its people. Therefore, criminal law focuses on when and how the wrongdoer should be punished, not on when and how the injured person should be compensated—this latter unfulfilled purpose is the function of tort law.

In short, tort law "is a body of legal principles [that serves] to control or regulate harmful behavior; to assign responsibility for injuries that arise in social interaction; and to provide recompense for victims with meritorious claims."[7] Figure 2-1 shows how the law of torts is related to contract and criminal law.

[3]Prosser & Keeton, The Law of Torts 16 (5th ed. 1984).
[4]*Id.*
[5]*See* P. Atiyah, Accidents, Compensation and the Law 9 (3d ed. 1980).
[6]Prosser & Keeton, *supra* note 3, at 2.
[7]P. Keeton, R. Keeton, L Sargentich, & H. Steiner, Cases and Materials on Tort and Accident Law 1 (1983).

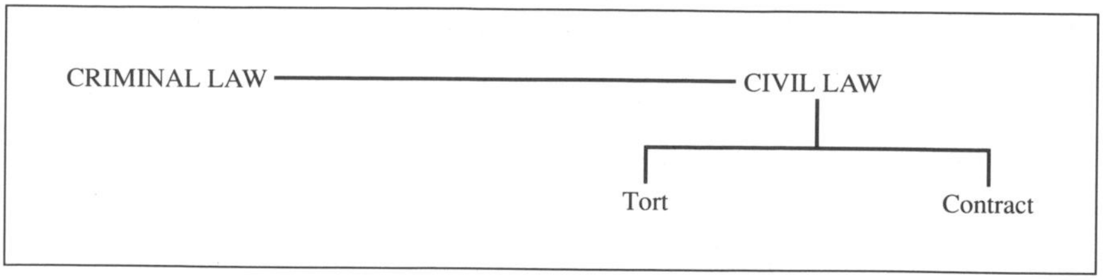

Figure 2-1   Relation of tort law to criminal and contract law.

PRINCIPLES OF TORT LAW

The central theme of tort law is that liability must be based on conduct which is socially unreasonable. That is, when a wrongdoer (*tortfeasor*) unreasonably interferes with the protected interests of others, the tortfeasor will be required to pay compensation for such interferences.[8]

Unreasonableness, however, is "in the eye of the beholder." What is completely acceptable to one person may be viewed as clearly unreasonable to another.[9] Much of tort law, however, is not concerned with the tortfeasor's subjective state of mind, nor is tort law generally concerned with what the injured party considers unreasonable (most people consider any injury to their self unreasonable). Rather, tort law seeks to measure by an objective, disinterested standard the acts and the harm the tortfeasor causes. "It may consider that the actor's behavior, *although entirely reasonable in itself from the point of view of anyone in the actor's position,* has created a risk or has resulted in harm to neighbors which is so far unreasonable that the actor should nevertheless pay for harm done."[10]

If tort law is concerned with basing liability on unreasonable conduct, why would it impose liability on a person whose conduct is considered reasonable by others similarly situated? The short answer is that as between any two parties—even two relatively innocent parties, neither of whose conduct is considered unreasonable—one must still bear the loss. The law makes the difficult decision of which party's conduct most invites the harm and assigns the loss accordingly.

For example, consider the following two hypothetical situations:

Conjecture A: Seller advertises used car for sale in the want-ad section of the local newspaper. Buyer 1 responds to the ad, inspects the car, and purchases it, tendering a check for $1000. Seller accordingly signs title over to Buyer 1 and gives Buyer 1 the car. Later that same day, Buyer 1 resells the car to Buyer 2 for $900 cash.

---

[8]Prosser & Keeton, *supra* note 3, at 6.

[9]This point is demonstrated in the divided and often heated lines drawn by the abortion issue. Both sides of the issue are flanked by vast numbers of supporters who strongly feel that the act of abortion is or is not socially reasonable conduct.

[10]Prosser & Keeton, *supra* note 3, at 6.

One week later, Seller learns from the bank that: (1) Buyer 1's check has been dishonored, and (2) Buyer 2 has the car (bank lent Buyer 2 the $900). Buyer 1 is nowhere to be found, and Buyer 2 refuses to return the car. Seller therefore sues Buyer 2 for return of the car.

Conjecture B: Thief steals Owner's car, forges a title document, and sells the car to Buyer for $900. Owner learns the car is in Buyer's possession and asks that it be returned. Thief has seemingly vanished from the face of the earth. When Buyer refuses, Owner sues Buyer for return of the car.

In each hypothetical situation, the real culprit, Buyer 1 or Thief, are long gone and accordingly the lawsuit is between two relatively innocent parties. How does the court decide who should win? More correctly, how should the court decide who should bear the loss? In Conjecture A, should the loss remain with Seller or be shifted to Buyer 2? Interestingly, the universal result in Conjecture A is that the loss remain with Seller—that is, Buyer 2 keeps the car—while the loss is shifted to Buyer in Conjecture B—that is, Buyer must return the car to owner.

The underlying reason for the different result is that while Seller in Conjecture A was relatively innocent, Seller could have avoided the problem by calling the bank and verifying the check before transferring possession and title to Buyer 1. In contrast, Owner had no contact with Thief in Conjecture B and is therefore completely blameless.

Many psychiatric malpractice actions involve two relatively innocent parties. A therapist may act innocently but nevertheless accidentally injure a client. Who should bear the loss? What are the relevant policy considerations affecting the liability decision?[11] Tort law implements the following considerations.

Need to Compensate Injury

Certainly, the law cannot attempt to compensate all losses. Along the spectrum of possible injuries, beginning with mere insults and ending with death, every legal system must determine where to draw the line between compensable and noncompensable injuries. Although no real continuum exists wherein we can say "here is where the line has been drawn," the liability decision values certain losses more than others. For example, an individual's first need, after life itself, is an income. Therefore, an injury that causes a permanent or temporary loss of income is the type of injury which ranks high for compensation.[12]

In the psychiatric malpractice context, other losses resulting from an injury are also compensable; that is, not only may an injured client recover for lost

[11]For additional material on this issue, see Prosser & Keeton, *supra* note 3, at 20; D. Harris, M. Maclean, H. Genn, S. Lloyd-Bostock, P. Fenn, P. Corfield, Y. Brittan, Compensation and Support for Illness and Injury 17 (1984) [hereinafter Compensation and Support]; J. Fleming, An Introduction to the Law of Torts 179 (1985).

[12]Atiyah, *supra* note 5, at 12.

income and of course medical bills, the client may also be able to recover compensation for physical pain and suffering and emotional distress. Further, most states recognize an action whereby the spouse of the injured client may recover for the loss of the injured spouse's domestic and sexual "services."[13]

In short, the mere fact that a client suffers a demonstrated loss tends to influence the liability decision toward assessing liability against the therapist. This tendency exists even though the therapist acted on pure therapeutic motives and therefore lacked any intent to cause injury.

Loss Spreading

Another major consideration in the calculus of deciding which party should bear the loss, especially when two parties are relatively innocent, is which party is in the better position to initially absorb and ultimately spread the loss.[14] This is not so much a matter of respective wealth as it is a question of who is better able to avoid the loss, absorb the loss, or distribute it in smaller portions among a larger group.[15]

In the malpractice context, the plaintiff is almost always an injured client or a relative of the client, while the defendant is either a hospital or therapist. Courts generally view the hospital or therapist as being in a much better position to absorb and spread the loss for two reasons. First, the mental health professions sell a variety of services and can therefore raise the price of these services to provide a surplus from which to pay tort judgments. Second, providers can obtain insurance to indemnify themselves against any judgments. The price of insurance is viewed as a standard cost of doing business, a cost that is both definite and known in advance. Therefore, while the individual client may be ruined if forced to bear the loss of a debilitating injury, the therapist or hospital can disseminate the loss in small portions among a large section of the community in the form of higher fees.[16] This factor also cuts in favor of assessing liability against the hospital or therapist.

Deterrence

A third objective of tort law is to deter people from acting in a careless manner. The whole idea of carelessness, however, implies fault, and therefore the liability decision often necessarily focuses on each party's blameworthiness. Many medical malpractice cases involve clear examples of careless behavior because fairly standardized procedures have been established for many applications. The mental health field, however, is generally devoid of standardized treatment procedures, so carelessness loses much of its meaning because it is a relative concept that has meaning only when measured against some standard. However, even in

[13]This action is one for loss of consortium.
[14]"There is a strong and growing tendency, where there is no blame on either side, to ask in view of the exigencies of social justice; who can best bear the loss." R. Pound, The Spirit of the Common Law 189 (1921).
[15]Prosser & Keeton, *supra* note 3, at 24.
[16]J. Fleming, *supra* note 11, at 6–7.

the mental health field, some treatment decisions are considered riskier than others. The law seeks to discourage therapists from practicing "on the fringe."

Fault

The type of carelessness detailed so far compares the carelessness of the therapist to professional standards. Another comparison, however, is relevant to the liability decision: comparing carelessness between the parties themselves. A declining number of jurisdictions deny all compensation to an injured plaintiff who is even minimally blameworthy for his or her own injuries (doctrine of contributory negligence). Most jurisdictions, however, simply allow a defendant to reduce an adverse judgment by an amount proportionate to the percentage of fault attributed to the plaintiff (doctrine of comparative negligence). For example, if a jury awards an injured client $100,000 but apportions 60% of the fault to the therapist and 40% to the client, the therapist will be allowed to reduce the judgment by $40,000. Furthermore, many jurisdictions have modified their comparative fault statutes so as to completely bar recovery when the plaintiff's fault exceeds 50%. In other words, those jurisdictions using a so-called modified comparative negligence statute, as compared to the "pure" form, do not allow plaintiffs to recover when the level of their carelessness exceeds that of the defendant. Therefore, in some professional malpractice actions—for example, client suicide cases—the therapist will argue that she or he should not be found liable because the client was more responsible than the therapist for the injury.

Other Factors

The factors detailed above are just a few of the many that affect the tort liability decision. Other factors include convenience of administration, retribution, and minimalization of transaction costs.[17] Keep in mind, however, that no one factor is of such importance as to be the determining one in any given case. While the specific facts of a case may justify giving more emphasis to some factors and less emphasis to others, all these factors combine to make up the calculation that is the liability decision.

PROFESSIONAL MALPRACTICE

Malpractice Generally

The most basic division within tort law is between acts that are intentional and those that are unintentional, or accidental.[18] Intentional torts arise when one voluntarily acts to invade another's rights and causes injury to that person's body,

---

[17]*See* Compensation and Support, *supra* note 11, at 21; Prosser & Keeton, *supra* note 3, at 23–26; Fleming, *supra* note 11, at 182.

[18]*See, e.g.,* Law for the Psychotherapist, *supra* note 1, at 13 (1988); Cohen, *The Professional Liability of Behavioral Scientists: An Overview,* in Psychotherapy and the Law 253 (1986).

emotional state, reputation, or property. Unintentional torts arise when one voluntarily acts out of a reckless or careless disregard for another's rights and consequently causes injury.

For all practical purposes, unintentional torts fall within the legal category called *negligence.* Every person in society is duty bound to take reasonable care not to injure others. Negligence will be found when this duty is breached and the breach causes injury to another.

Malpractice is a special species of negligence—that is, malpractice is "a convenient term that describes the legal [liability] of professionals in the conduct of their special relationships with their patients."[19] Malpractice, then, refers to the negligent execution of professional duties, as distinguished from the negligent performance of personal or business/manufacturing duties. Figure 2-2 displays the place of malpractice within the law.[20]

An understanding of what malpractice is can be enhanced by a brief study of what it is not. A therapist failing to exercise an extraordinary amount of skill, knowledge, or judgment in treating clients is *not* guilty of malpractice; the therapist is not charged by the law to be brilliant. Further, it technically is not malpractice

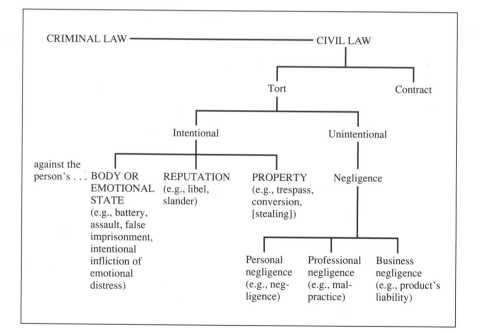

Figure 2-2   The place of malpractice within the law.

[19]Mariano & Wolman, *Boundaries Between the Law and Behavioral Therapies,* Psychotherapy and the Law 267 (1986).
[20]Throughout this book, the terms *malpractice, professional negligence,* and *negligence* are used synonymously.

if the professional intends to cause the harm that results because malpractice is, by definition, an unintentional tort.[21]

Malpractice Litigation and the Burden of Proof

The plaintiff bears the initial *burden of proof* and the ultimate *burden of persuasion.* In practical terms, this statement means that the plaintiff presents his evidence first in each trial, and that in doing so, he must make a *prima facie* showing. Thus the plaintiff must prove each and every element of the cause of action. If the plaintiff fails to establish one or more elements, the case is dismissed even without evidence from the defendant because the plaintiff has failed to satisfy his initial burden of proof. If, however, the plaintiff presents a *prima facie* case, the burden of proof shifts to the defendant to present evidence that either tends to rebut the plaintiff's allegations or demonstrates the existence of a defense. Rebutting the plaintiff's evidence is denying the negligent conduct alleged; stating a defense is admitting the conduct but providing a legal justification. If the defendant states a defense or presents evidence contrary to that presented by the plaintiff, the case goes to the judge or jury for a decision. However, the ultimate burden of persuasion remains with the plaintiff—all the evidence will be weighed and the case decided in favor of the defendant unless the plaintiff proves his case by a "preponderance of the evidence," which is the standard of proof required in civil cases.[22] Evidence preponderates when it is more convincing, by any measure, to the judge or jury than the opposing evidence.[23] If, however, the judge or jury feels that the evidence is equally weighted and equally believable, the plaintiff will lose because he bears the ultimate burden of persuasion.

Malpractice: The Prima Facie Case

What must a plaintiff prove to satisfy the initial burden of proof? The professional malpractice action consists of four elements that must be proved before liability can be found: (1) the therapist owed the client a duty, (2) the duty was breached, (3) the client suffered injury, and (4) the injury was caused by the therapist's breach. These elements are discussed in detail throughout the book in

[21]Cohen, *supra* note 18, at 252–253. Note, however, that the therapist can be subject to suits for intentional torts (for example, a false imprisonment action is a real possibility when a patient has been wrongfully hospitalized) and even breach of contract.

[22]*See* Law for the Psychotherapist, *supra* note 1, at 14.

[23]Note that the "preponderance of the evidence" standard required in civil actions differs from the "beyond a reasonable doubt" burden required of the prosecutor in criminal actions. Whereas the civil standard merely requires the plaintiff to have a slightly stronger case than the defendant, the criminal standard requires that the prosecutor prove the case beyond any reasonable doubt. Therefore, even if the criminal prosecutor presents more credible evidence than the defendant presents, the defendant must still be found not guilty unless the prosecutor's evidence goes so far as to establish guilt beyond a reasonable doubt.

connection with various and specific high-risk clinical situations. Here's an overview of these elements, to facilitate their application in specific settings.

Duty. While everyone in society has a duty to act as a reasonable and ordinary person, the professional has an additional duty to act as a reasonable professional. This duty of professional reasonableness has been described as follows:

> In the absence of a special contract, a [professional] is not required to exercise extraordinary skill and care or the highest degree of skill and care possible; but as a general rule he is only required to possess and exercise the degree of skill and learning ordinarily possessed and exercised under similar circumstances, by the members of his profession in good standing, and to use ordinary and reasonable care and diligence, and his best judgment, in the application of his skill to the case.[24]

In short, the duty is determined by the level of knowledge, skill, judgment, and expertise others in the profession use.[25] While this statement defines the duty, liability for psychiatric malpractice does not attach unless the therapist owed the duty to the specific plaintiff of the case, usually a matter of showing that a professional relationship existed between the therapist and the plaintiff.[26] Proving the existence of a professional relationship is very fact-dependent but relatively easy to satisfy—for example, it may be found to exist as a result of a single 1-hour examination[27] or even as a result of a telephone conversation between the professional and the client.[28]

Breach of Duty. Once the plaintiff has proved the existence of a special relationship between the therapist and himself, the plaintiff must demonstrate that the duty was breached. That is, the defendant must be found to have departed from the conduct of a reasonable and prudent therapist.

The breach of the professional's duty may involve affirmative actions, such as involuntarily committing a client who is neither dangerous nor gravely disabled, or may arise from omissions, such as failing to prevent a client's foreseeable suicide. In any event, the court will look to the actual practices of other therapists or to the codes of professional conduct to determine whether the defendant therapist breached a duty to the plaintiff client.[29]

It is important to distinguish between choosing a wrong course of treatment and negligently choosing a wrong course of treatment—simple incorrect decisions do not constitute a breach of duty. The law recognizes that people make mistakes and that even highly qualified professionals can err, an especially applicable point in the mental health field, which lacks certain accepted standards.

---

[24]70 C.J.S. *Physicians and Surgeons* Sec. 41 (1987).
[25]Law for the Psychotherapist, *supra* note 1, at 13.
[26]*Id.* at 15.
[27]*See Farrow v. Health Services Corp.*, 604 P.2d 474 (Utah 1979).
[28]*See O'Neill v. Montefiore Hosp.*, 11 App. Div. 2d 132, 202 N.Y.S.2d 436 (1960).
[29]*See* Law for the Psychotherapist, *supra* note 1, at 15.

Therefore therapists are not required to exercise extraordinary skill or be omniscient; they must simply possess and use the skills, knowledge, and judgment common to the average therapist.[30]

Injury.   Even if a therapist employs clearly substandard techniques, liability will not be found unless the client is injured in some manner. Further, it is not enough to show that the chosen course of treatment could have resulted in injury; the plaintiff must be injured in fact.

The plaintiff who complains of exclusively mental injuries, however, may have a difficult time satisfying this injury element for two reasons. First, allegations of mental injuries are somewhat speculative because of the state of knowledge regarding mental illnesses. Second, even if the plaintiff has in fact been injured, mental injuries are intangible and therefore difficult to demonstrate to the judge or jury.[31]

Causation.   Finally, a malpractice plaintiff must demonstrate that the therapist's breach of duty caused the injury. Because every event may be linked to multiple causes, the causation inquiry is the most conceptual negligence element. Causation is analyzed at both a factual and legal level.

Factual Causation.   Factual causation is determined by the "but for" test, which can be stated as follows: The defendant's breach of duty is a cause of injury only if the injury would not have been sustained "but for" the breach of duty. It is thus a question of fact whether or not the injury would have occurred absent the breach of duty. Curiously, however, this factual inquiry requires the "factfinder" (usually the jury) to compare what did occur with what might have occurred if hypothetical conditions had existed.

To illustrate, a therapist may recommend assertiveness training for a client complaining of excessive passivity. Assume the training succeeds but that the client's spouse has difficulty accepting the new, assertive personality and so the marriage ends in divorce. A finding that marital difficulties would not have occurred "but for" the assertiveness training requires the exclusion of countless, unrelated causes that may have occurred independent of the assertiveness training.

Any event resulting in injury may have countless causes, and for many causes it may be said that injury would not have occurred "but for" its influence. But legal liability does not attach to every minor contributing cause of each injury; if it did, the scope of social responsibility would be boundless. Thus satisfaction of the "but for" test is at most a rule that precludes liability if not met. To impose liability, considerations of legal (proximate) causation must also be satisfied.

Legal (Proximate) Cause.   When the "but for" test is satisfied, liability will attach only when the cause is so significant a contributing factor to the injury

---

[30]*See id.*
[31]Cohen, *supra* note 18, at 259.

that legal responsibility is justified. Legal causation does not seek to determine if an event caused injury in the factual sense, only whether it is reasonable and fair to hold the actor accountable for the consequences. Legal or proximate cause is thus a matter of policy, not causation. Legal responsibility is limited to those causes so closely connected with the result that the law is justified in imposing liability. Legal causation thus has a limiting purpose intended to set the boundaries of liability for the consequences of an act.

To illustrate, we return to the client whose assertiveness training introduced marital conflict. Clearly other causes may have contributed to the marital difficulty—for example, the husband's intolerance, financial stress, or simple failure to care for the relationship. The "but for" test may be satisfied; yet, how significantly must the assertiveness training contribute to the marital difficulty before it is considered a legal cause of the marital difficulty? At some point, a causal chain becomes so diluted that liability may not be fairly imposed, notwithstanding satisfaction of the "but for" test.

APPLICATION OF NEGLIGENCE ELEMENTS AND CONCLUSION

Having examined the principles of tort law generally, and the elements of malpractice law specifically, we return to the case facts presented at the chapter's beginning. This case illustrates application of these principles in an actual occurrence. Resolution of the malpractice case turns on the orderly application of each element of malpractice law. The logic the court uses in working through these elements is outlined as follows:

1. *Presence of a duty.* Professionals of every kind have a duty to their clients' welfare because clients concede increased control of their welfare to the professional based on the professional's expertise and knowledge. This duty requires the professional to exercise the knowledge, skill, judgment, and expertise others in the profession use. As a physician, Dr. Nystrom clearly owed Anna a duty to practice his profession at a level of skill and competence consistent with the standards of care of his profession.

2. *Breach of duty.* A duty is breached when professional conduct falls below the accepted standards of the profession. The inherent risk of X rays is common knowledge in the medical profession, and physicians are expected to protect their clients from these risks. Dr. Nystrom's failure to inquire about pregnancy before ordering X rays is clearly substandard medical care. This failure constitutes a breach of Dr. Nystrom's duty to Anna.

Commentary

The presence of a duty coupled with a breach of that duty constitute negligence. In this case, Dr. Nystrom's negligence has now been clearly established and is not the least bit controversial. Legal reasoning, however, does not stop at a finding of negligence; questions of damages and causation must be resolved to establish liability. Legal liability always requires a (1) demonstration of actual damages and (2) showing that the breach of duty is the cause of the damages sustained.

3. *Injury and/or damages.* Mere negligence will not provide a basis for liability; actual loss or damage must be sustained. Damages in this case are obvious—the fetus was terminally injured by the X rays.

4. *Causation.*

(a) *Factual causation.* A causal link must be established between the breach of duty and the injury sustained. Conceptually, this is a "but for" test—that is, "but for" the breach of duty, no injury would have occurred. Even though negligence and damages have already been established, no liability exists without satisfying the "but for" test. In this particular case, this test is not satisfied. Dr. Nystrom's failure to inquire about Anna's pregnancy was the breach of duty (negligence). But even if Dr. Nystrom had inquired and thereby satisfied his duty, Anna would have reported that she was not pregnant and the X rays would have been taken. Thus there is not a causal link between the breach of Dr. Nystrom's duty to inquire about Anna's pregnancy and the injuries sustained.

(b) *Legal (proximate) causation.* Because the factual causation, "but for" test, is not satisfied, the policy considerations of legal causation are not implicated.

5. *Verdict.* Negligent, but no liability.

Commentary and Summary

The principles illustrated in our medical malpractice case directly apply to all malpractice actions. In the mental health professions, negligence requires (1) existence of a professional duty and (2) a breach of that duty. Recovery for negligence further requires that (1) actual injury be sustained and (2) causation be established. These elements of malpractice are not unique to doctors and mental health professionals; they apply to every professional field.

GLOSSARY OF LEGAL TERMS

The following Glossary of Legal Terms, for the reader's convenience, contains definitions of all legal terms of art that appear throughout the book or are of general interest to the reader. Definitions are based on *Black's Law Dictionary*, abridged fifth edition.

Battery The consummation of an unlawful assault. The actual offer to use force to injure another person is assault, and the use of it is battery, which always includes an assault; hence the two terms are commonly combined in the term "assault and battery."

Burden of Persuasion   The onus on the party with the burden of proof to convince the trier of fact of all elements of the case.

Burden of Proof   In the law of evidence, the necessity or duty of affirmatively proving a fact(s) in dispute on an issue raised between the parties in a cause. The obligation of a party to establish by evidence a requisite degree of belief concerning a fact in the mind of the trier of fact or the court.

"But for" test   Test used in determining tort liability by applying the causative criterion as to whether the plaintiff would not have suffered the wrong "but for" the defendant's action.

Circuit Court of Appeals   Former name for federal intermediate appellate courts, changed in 1948 to the present designation of United States Courts of Appeals.

Common Law   As distinguished from law created by the enactment of legislatures, the common law comprises the body of those principles and rules of action, relating to the government and security of persons and property, that derive their authority solely from usages and customs of immemorial antiquity or from the judgments and decrees of the courts recognizing, affirming, and enforcing such usages and customs.

Comparative Negligence   Under comparative negligence statutes or doctrines, negligence is measured in terms of percentage, and any damages allowed shall be diminished in proportion to the amount of negligence attributable to the person for whose injury, damage, or death recovery is sought.

Compelling State Interest   Term used to uphold state action in the face of attack, grounded on Equal Protection or First Amendment rights because of serious need for such state action. Also used to justify state action under police power of state.

District Court   Each state is comprised of one or more federal judicial districts, and each district has a district court. The United States district courts are the trial courts with general federal jurisdiction.

Due Process Clause   Two such clauses are in the U.S. Constitution, one in the Fifth Amendment, pertaining to the federal government, the other in the Fourteenth Amendment, which protects persons from state actions. There are two aspects: procedural, whereby a person is guaranteed fair procedures, and substantive, which protects a person's property from unfair governmental interference or taking. Similar clauses are in most state constitutions.

False Imprisonment   The tort of "false imprisonment" is the nonconsensual, intentional confinement of a person, without lawful privilege, for an appreciable length of time, however short.

Judgment on Pleadings   After the pleadings are closed but within such time as not to delay the trial, any party may move for judgment on the pleadings.

Malice   The intentional doing of a wrongful act without just cause or excuse, with an intent to inflict an injury or under circumstances that the law will imply an evil intent. Malice in law is not necessarily personal hate or ill will, but it is that state of mind which is reckless of law and of the citizen's legal rights.

Malicious Prosecution   Prosecution begun in malice without probable cause to believe that the charges can be sustained. An action for damages brought by a person, against whom civil suit or criminal prosecution has been instituted maliciously and without probable cause, after termination of prosecution of such suit in favor of the person claiming damages.

Malpractice   Failure of one rendering professional services to exercise that degree of skill and learning commonly applied under all the circumstances in the community by the average prudent reputable member of the profession with the result of injury, loss or damage to the recipient of those services or to those entitled to rely on them.

Negligence   Conduct that falls below the standard established by law for the protection of others against unreasonable risk of harm; it is a departure from the conduct expected of a reasonably prudent person under like circumstances.

Parens Patriae   Parent of the country. The term refers traditionally to the role of the state as sovereign and guardian of persons under legal disability. It is a concept of standing used to protect those quasi-sovereign interests such as health, comfort, and welfare of the people.

Police Power   An authority conferred by the American constitutional system in the Tenth Amendment, U.S. Constitution, on the individual states, and, in turn, delegated to local governments, through which they are enabled to establish a special department of police; adopt such laws and regulations as tend to prevent the commission of fraud and crime; and secure generally the comfort, safety, morals, health, and prosperity of its citizens by preserving the public order.

Preponderance of Evidence   Evidence that is of greater weight or more convincing than the evidence offered in opposition to it—that is, evidence which as a whole shows that the fact sought to be proved is more probable than not. With respect to burden of proof in civil actions, the term means greater weight of evidence, or evidence that is more credible and convincing to the mind.

Prima Facie Case   Such as will prevail until contradicted and overcome by other evidence. A case that has proceeded on sufficient proof to that stage where it will support finding if evidence to contrary is disregarded. A *prima facie* case consists of sufficient evidence in the type of case to get the plaintiff past a motion for directed verdict in a jury case or motion to dismiss in a nonjury case; it is the evidence necessary to require defendant to proceed with the case.

Proximate Cause   The proximate cause of an injury is the primary or moving cause or that which, in a natural and continuous sequence, unbroken by any efficient intervening cause, produces the injury and without which the accident could not have happened, if the injury is one that might be reasonably anticipated or foreseen as a natural consequence of the wrongful act.

Rehearing   Second consideration of cause for the purpose of calling to the court's or administrative board's attention any error, omission, or oversight in the first consideration.

Remand   The sending by the appellate court of the cause back to the same court it came out of, for the purpose of having some further action taken on it there.

Res ipsa loquitur   The thing speaks for itself. Rebuttable presumption or inference that defendant was negligent, which arises from proof that instrumentality causing injury was in the defendant's exclusive control and that the accident was one which ordinarily does not happen in the absence of negligence.

Statute of Limitations   A statute prescribing limitations to the right of action on certain described causes of action; that is, declaring that no suit shall be maintained on such causes of action, nor any criminal charge be made, unless brought within a specified period of time after the right accrued.

Summary Judgment   Rule of Civil Procedure 56 permits any party to a civil action to move for a summary judgment on a claim when the party believes that there is no genuine issue of material fact and that the party is entitled to prevail as a matter of law.

Tort   A private or civil wrong or injury, other than breach of contract, for which the court will provide a remedy in the form of an action for damages.

Tortfeasor   A wrongdoer; one who commits or is guilty of a tort.

3

*Clinical Dangerousness: Legal Duties**

Violations of the client's right to therapeutic privacy generally have been considered a sacrilege, and for good reason. The therapeutic consulting room is the place where clients are expected to probe and explore the origin and meaning of their most private thoughts and feelings. Even though tact, politeness, and social conventions may be the governing determinants of human behavior in many settings, they are unwelcome distractions in the consulting room. This is the place for candor, the kind that is ultimately intended to bring clients face-to-face with their most intimate feelings and impulses. Needless to say, this can be a frightening experience. We all have our secrets—not just from others, but from ourselves as well. And candidly facing our less desirable human attributes and conflicts almost always precedes overcoming them. So client communications in the consulting room are considered confidential and protected by law. This client right is necessary and fundamental to a productive healing relationship and distinguishes psychotherapy from social relationships.

In recent years, however, the therapist's singular concern for the client's privacy and well-being has been diluted. As a result of the landmark *Tarasoff v. Regents of University of California* (1974) decision from the California Supreme Court, psychotherapists in many jurisdictions now have a legal duty to society as well as to their clients. In the opinion of the *Tarasoff* court, when a therapist is working with a dangerous client, that client's right to privacy ends where the public peril begins.[1] Although to many this ruling may be controversial and arguable, its legal implications are clear: Psychotherapists now have a legal duty to protect innocent victims from their dangerous clients. As readers will quickly see, this ruling raises many complex and unanswerable questions. We start our discussion of this fascinating topic by reviewing the evolution of the guiding legal principles that should influence the psychotherapist's work with dangerous clients.

TARASOFF: INFANCY TO ADOLESCENCE

In 1974, the door of legal liability opened wide to receive psychotherapists. The California Supreme Court announced in *Tarasoff v. Regents of University of*

*Portions of this chapter first appeared in the 1989 Brigham Young University Law Review and are reprinted with permission from the author and publisher.
[1] *Tarasoff v. Regents of University of California,* 17 Cal. 3d 425, 442, 551 P.2d 334, 347, 131 Cal. Rptr 14, 27 (1976).

California[2] its unequivocal, yet loosely defined, decision that psychotherapists' legal obligations include a duty to warn the intended victims of their clients.[3] After 15 years of legal maturation, the complexion of the *Tarasoff* doctrine and reasoning have changed significantly. In the most recent decision grounded in *Tarasoff* precepts,[4] the Wisconsin Supreme Court did more than any other jurisdiction to provide a larger stature and more potent personality to the now adolescent *Tarasoff* doctrine.

We use the Wisconsin Supreme Court decision of *Schuster v. Altenberg*[5] as a basis for identifying and discussing the remarkable changes from what the original *Tarasoff* duty was to what it is becoming. Because *Altenberg* represents the current apex of a maturing legal trend, other major decisions are also considered to provide a full review and analysis of *Tarasoff*'s development path.[6]

Tarasoff in Legal Infancy

Tarasoff I. The 1974 ruling in *Tarasoff I* stemmed from the murder of Tatiana Tarasoff by Prosenjit Poddar, a voluntary outpatient at the Cowell Memorial Hospital at the University of California at Berkeley. Two months prior to the homicide, Poddar confided his intention to kill Tatiana to Dr. Lawrence Moore, the treating psychologist. Dr. Moore contacted the campus police and requested that Poddar be detained. Poddar was apprehended but released by campus police because he appeared rational and because the police secured a promise from him to stay away from Tatiana. Dr. Moore's supervisor directed that no further action be taken to detain Poddar. Neither Tatiana nor any of her family members were warned of the threat. Two months after these events, Poddar went to Tatiana's home and killed her.[7]

These facts led to the California Supreme Court's ruling in *Tarasoff I*. As first announced, *Tarasoff* stood for the proposition that a psychotherapist has "a duty to use reasonable care to give threatened persons such *warnings* as are essential to avert foreseeable danger arising from his client's condition or treatment."[8] The court premised this duty on the special relationship between the psychotherapist and client, which was judged to satisfy the "special relationship" requirement in the RESTATEMENT (SECOND) OF TORTS Section 315 that creates a right to the third person for protection from the actor.[9] The *Tarasoff I* decision is the conceptual genesis for all psychotherapists' duties to third parties.

---

[2]529 P.2d 553, 118 Cal. Rptr 129 (1974) [hereinafter "*Tarasoff I*"] *reargued,* 17 Cal. 3d 425, 551 P.2d 334, 131 Cal. Rptr 14 (1976) [hereinafter "*Tarasoff II*"].

[3]*Tarasoff I,* 529 P.2d at 559, 118 Cal. Rptr at 135.

[4]*Schuster v. Altenberg,* 144 Wis. 2d 223, 424 N.W.2d 159 (1988).

[5]*Id.*

[6]*Tarasoff* is not binding as precedence in jurisdictions other than California. Nevertheless, *Tarasoff*-type actions are becoming more commonly recognized, and other states are using *Tarasoff* as a mold of legal reasoning to be applied in their own jurisdictions.

[7]*Tarasoff II,* 17 Cal. 3d at 430–432, 551 P.2d at 339–340, 131 Cal. Rptr at 19–20.

[8]*Tarasoff I,* 529 P.2d at 559, 118 Cal. Rptr at 135 (emphasis added).

[9]*See* RESTATEMENT (SECOND) OF TORTS Sec. 315–320 (1965). Although initially controversial, the finding of this "special relationship" has now become widely accepted and therefore is not evaluated at length herein.

Tarasoff II. Immediately after the California Supreme Court's announcement of the psychotherapist's new duty, the defendants in *Tarasoff I,* and the American Psychiatric Association, vigorously petitioned the court for a rehearing.[10] This effort was largely fueled by the American Psychiatric Association's fear of the impact the decision would have on the mental health care profession. The court's unusual step of granting reargument indicated its sensitivity to the weighty policy and legal arguments involved in the decision.

Pleased by the opportunity for reargument, the psychotherapeutic community was greatly distressed by the product of its efforts. *Tarasoff II*[11] resulted in a broader and more robust announcement of the California Supreme Court's earlier decision. Specifically, the court held:

> When a therapist determines, or pursuant to the standards of his profession should determine, that his patient presents a serious danger of violence to another, he incurs an obligation to use reasonable care to protect the intended victim against such danger. The discharge of his duty may require the therapist to take one or more of various steps, depending upon the nature of the case. Thus, it may call for him to warn the intended victim or others likely to apprise the victim of the danger, to notify the police, or to take whatever other steps are reasonably necessary under the circumstances.[12]

The court's restructuring of its opinion is significant in three important respects. First, and most importantly, the court held that the psychotherapist's duty was to "protect" the intended victim rather than to warn. Although phrased as a "duty to protect," many in the psychotherapeutic community fail to understand that their new duty is to *protect,* not merely to warn. In fact, a survey conducted almost 10 years after *Tarasoff* revealed that 92% of California psychiatrists believed their duty under *Tarasoff* was discharged merely by warning.[13]

Second, the court invoked the traditional "standards of the profession" criterion for use in determining when the psychotherapist should determine serious threats of danger. Although concurring in the judgment, Justice Mosk dissented vigorously because of the court's adoption of the standards of the profession as a measuring stick of liability. Justice Mosk stated:

> I would restructure the rule designed by the majority to eliminate all reference to conformity to standards of the profession in predicting violence. If a psychiatrist does in fact predict violence, then a duty to warn arises. The majority's expansion of that rule will take us from the world of reality into the wonderland of clairvoyance.[14]

---

[10]Disturbed by the court's holding, the American Psychiatric Association joined in the vigorous effort for reargument. *See* Mills, *The So-Called Duty to Warn: The Psychotherapeutic Duty to Protect Third Parties From Patients' Violent Acts,* 2 BEHAVIORAL SCIENCES & THE LAW 237 (1984) [hereinafter "Mills"].

[11]*Tarasoff II,* 17 Cal. 3d 425, 551 P.2d 334, 131 Cal. Rptr 14 (1976).

[12]*Id.* at 431, 551 P.2d at 340, 131 Cal. Rptr at 20.

[13]Givelber, Bowers & Blitch, *Tarasoff, Myth and Reality: An Empirical Study of Private Law in Action,* 1984 WIS. L. REV. 443, 467 (1984).

[14]*Tarasoff II,* 17 Cal. 3d at 452, 551 P.2d at 354, 131 Cal. Rptr at 34. (Mosk, J., concurring and dissenting).

Third, the court was unacceptably vague in explaining how the newly prescribed duty should be discharged. The court suggested that the duty could be discharged by warning the victim or calling the police but left open the possibility of clinical interventions psychotherapists conventionally use when confronting potentially violent clients.[15] In addition, the court failed to delineate to which mental health practitioners the duty applied. *Tarasoff* involved a staff psychologist at the University Hospital at Berkeley. The court did not make clear if the duty to protect applied to other mental health practitioners such as counselors, marriage and family therapists, and social workers.

Recognizing the inherent difficulty of the psychotherapist's new obligation, the court conceded to psychotherapists a broad buffer zone of reasonable professional standards as insulation from liability:

> We recognize the difficulty that a therapist encounters in attempting to forecast whether a patient presents a serious danger of violence. Obviously, we do not require that the therapist, in making that determination, render a perfect performance; the therapist need only exercise "that reasonable degree of skill, knowledge, and care ordinarily possessed and exercised by members of [that professional specialty] under similar circumstances." (*Bardesono v. Michels* (1970) 3 Cal.3d 780, 788, 91 Cal.Rptr 760, 764, 478 P.2d 480, 484) [other citations omitted]. *Within the broad range of reasonable practice and treatment in which professional opinion and judgment may differ, the therapist is free to exercise his or her own best judgment without liability;* proof aided by hindsight, that he or she judged wrongly is insufficient to establish negligence.[16]

Initially then, *Tarasoff* stood for the proposition that psychotherapists incurred a duty to use reasonable care to protect their clients' intended victims from serious threats of violence. The duty applied if the therapist either subjectively knew or, pursuant to the standards of the therapist's profession, should have known of the serious danger. Discharge of the duty required *whatever steps* were reasonably determined necessary[17] under the circumstances. In all these determinations, the judiciary conceded to the psychotherapists a buffer zone consisting of a "broad range of reasonable practice" in which professionals were free to exercise their own best judgment without liability.

Early Clarifications of the Infant Doctrine.   Two distinctive and well-defined features were quickly added to the *Tarasoff* doctrine. First, it was determined that the doctrine did not require that parents of suicidal clients be warned

---

[15]*Id.* at 431, 551 P.2d at 340, 131 Cal. Rptr at 20; *see also,* Mills, *supra* note 10.

[16]*Id.* at 438, 551 P.2d at 345, 131 Cal. Rptr at 25 (emphasis added).

[17]As to exercising "whatever other steps are reasonably necessary under the circumstances," 17 Cal. 3d at 431, 551 P.2d at 340, 131 Cal. Rptr at 20, the court failed to indicate whether the standards of the profession would be used to determine what other steps would be reasonably necessary. Yet, determining what steps are reasonably necessary under the circumstances hinges on a professional determination of the most effective method of deterring violence for each patient. What appears reasonable to practicing therapists as a method of deterring patient violence may not appear reasonable to the person of ordinary prudence.

of their child's suicidal inclination.[18] Second, and most importantly, in *Thompson v. County of Alameda*[19], the duty to warn became strictly limited to situations involving a prior threat to a specific, identifiable victim.[20]

Thompson involved the murder of a young boy by a juvenile delinquent released from the county's custody. The delinquent was known to have dangerous and violent propensities toward young children, and the county knew that violent sexual assaults were a likely result of releasing the juvenile into the community. The county also knew that the juvenile had indicated he would, if released, take the life of a young child residing in the neighborhood. The juvenile was released to his mother's temporary custody, however, and the county made no effort to warn her, or anyone in the neighborhood, of his dangerousness. Within 24 hours after his release, the delinquent murdered a young boy in the garage of his mother's home.

The *Thompson* court found that only in situations where a specific threat of harm is posed "to a named or readily identifiable victim or group of victims"[21] was there sufficient policy justification to impose a duty to warn. The *Thompson* court also found that warning large amorphous groups of public targets would involve the expenditure of time and limited resources that parole and probation agencies could not spare and would be of questionable value.[22] Such vague and generalized warnings were recognized as being of little value in relieving the anxiety and fear a general warning would raise among the populace.

The combination of *Tarasoff* and *Thompson* represents the *Tarasoff* doctrine at its first and most distinguishable stage. Subsequent decisions, although grounded in the *Tarasoff* reasoning, have produced a "duty to protect" doctrine that is in stark contrast to the image of its progenitor, as we now discuss.

Tarasoff in Adolescence: The *Altenberg* Case

Judicially developed law (known as common law) is the most frequent source of substantive law; the second greatest source is statutes, passed by legislatures. Because rules emerge from the courts on a case-by-case basis, the law is necessarily in a continuous state of flux. Each new case gives the judiciary an opportunity to refine the contours and features of existing law. The *Tarasoff* doctrine has been no exception. We now discuss the contrast between what the "duty to protect" doctrine first implied and what it now entails, using the most recent case based on *Tarasoff* precepts, *Schuster v. Altenberg*,[23] to illustrate these changes. *Altenberg* is the current apex of the doctrine's seeming maturation; other cases are used to illustrate the path *Tarasoff* has followed in developing its new and more robust personality and the key points of its development.

---

[18]*Bellah v. Greenson,* 81 Cal. App. 3d 614, 146 Cal. Rptr 535 (1978).
[19]27 Cal. 3d 741, 614 P.2d 728, 167 Cal. Rptr 70 (1980).
[20]*Id.* at 758, 614 P.2d at 738, 167 Cal. Rptr at 80.
[21]*Id.*
[22]*Id.* at 755–756, 614 P.2d at 737, 167 Cal. Rptr at 78.
[23]144 Wis. 2d 223, 424 N.W.2d 159 (1988).

Factual Background and Legal Claims.   Edith Schuster was a psychiatric client of Dr. Barry Altenberg from April 30, 1983, until her death on June 29, 1983.[24] Edith was killed in an accident in the automobile she was driving. Gwendolyn Schuster, Edith's daughter, was a passenger in the car and suffered severe injuries that caused her paralysis. Edith's husband and the injured daughter brought suit against Dr. Altenberg to recover for the daughter's pain and suffering, disability, medical expenses, and loss of earning capacity. Edith's husband claimed damages resulting from his obligation to pay his daughter's significant medical expenses while she was a minor.[25] The plaintiffs' complaint contained no allegation that Edith was homicidal, suicidal, or had any inclination to harm anyone.[26]

The plaintiffs alleged that Dr. Altenberg was negligent in his management and care of Edith Schuster in failing to recognize or manage her manic-depressive state, including failure to seek her commitment, to modify her medication, and to alert and warn the client or her family of her condition and its dangerous implications.[27] The court categorized the allegations as follows: (1) negligent diagnosis and treatment, (2) failure to warn the client's family of her condition and its dangerous implications, and (3) failure to seek commitment of the client.[28]

The trial court granted Dr. Altenberg judgment prior to trial based solely on the pleadings because plaintiffs did not allege that Gwendolyn Schuster was an identifiable victim of the alleged negligence. Plaintiffs appealed. Because Wisconsin had not yet adopted a position on psychotherapists' liability to third parties and because of the important legal and policy considerations involved, the case bypassed the court of appeals and was certified directly to the Wisconsin Supreme Court for adjudication.

Brief Summary of Legal Holding.   Because judgment was initially granted to Dr. Altenberg on the pleadings, the Wisconsin Supreme Court could not review the ultimate liability of Dr. Altenberg. Rather, the court had to determine if liability could possibly be established based on the facts in the pleadings. The court first found that judgment on the pleadings was improper because expert testimony could have revealed negligence in diagnosis and treatment, which, if established, could have constituted cause-in-fact harm to the client and third parties.[29] The court then went on to consider the claim of negligence for failing to confine Edith Schuster or to warn Edith and her family of her condition and

---

[24]*Id.* at 223, 424 N.W.2d at 160. Because judgment was entered on the pleadings in this case, the factual background is sparse.

[25]*Id.*

[26]Brief of Defendant-Respondents at 4, *Schuster v. Altenberg,* 144 Wis. 2d 223, 424 N.W.2d 159 (1988) (No. 87–0115) [hereinafter "Brief of defendant"].

[27]*Altenberg,* 144 Wis. 2d at 223, 424 N.W.2d at 160.

[28]*Id.*

[29]*Id.* at 230, 424 N.W.2d at 162.

its dangerous implications.[30] The court recognized a cause of action for failure to seek commitment of the client. The court further held that "the duty to warn or to institute commitment proceedings is not limited by a requirement that threats made be directed to an identifiable target."[31] With these rulings, the Wisconsin Supreme Court determined that the facts as contained in the pleadings did not preclude liability. The case was, therefore, remanded for a plenary trial.

Implications of the Court's Decision.   The *Altenberg* decision involves much more than is superficially apparent from the court's announced ruling. The facts of the case and the court's decision are marked departures from previous *Tarasoff*-type analysis.[32] In every area of *Tarasoff* controversy, the *Altenberg* decision radically departs from the original Tarasoff formulation, including such fundamental considerations as (1) the requirement of a specific victim, (2) the imminence of dangerousness required for liability, (3) the role of civil commitment, and (4) standards for predicting dangerousness.

EMERGING TRENDS IN *TARASOFF* DOCTRINE

The Specific Victim Requirement

Thompson v. County of Alameda[33] set forth the requirement that victims be specifically identifiable in order to invoke a duty to protect. Even though *Thompson* arose as a result of a custody release claim, the ruling requiring a specific victim became applicable to claims against psychotherapists. This action was a predictable clarification, not a departure from the original *Tarasoff* formulation. *Tarasoff* stated that the psychotherapist's duty was to protect the clients' *intended* victims from violence,[34] implying that the client must have a specific victim in mind in order to invoke the psychotherapist's duty. *Thompson* merely crystallized the requirement. This specific, identifiable victim requirement was initially well accepted and even received added emphasis in some jurisdictions. *Brady v. Hopper* best illustrated the requirement for a specific, identifiable victim and also clearly established that the specific victim requirement applied to psychotherapists.

---

[30]Once determining that a cause of action could be stated for negligent diagnosis, the court would normally not proceed to pass on the validity of other alleged theories. The court departed from this principle because the trial court had ruled against the validity of the negligent failure to warn and negligent failure to commit claim. Therefore the plaintiffs would have no opportunity to prove their case as to these claims on remand if the negligent diagnosis claim did not permit recovery. *Id.* at 223, 424 N.W.2d at 163.

[31]*Id.* at 234, 424 N.W.2d at 165.

[32]*Tarasoff*, of course, had no binding impact on Wisconsin's decision. Wisconsin's decision is uniquely significant, however, because the breadth of its departure from *Tarasoff* represents an increased pace in the trend toward broadening liability for psychotherapists.

[33]*See supra*, notes 18–22 and accompanying text.

[34]*Tarasoff II*, 17 Cal. 3d at 431, 551 P.2d at 340, 131 Cal. Rptr at 20.

Initial Fortification of the Specific Victim Requirement. *Brady* involved a suit to recover damages from the former psychiatrist of John W. Hinckley, Jr., at the time of the attempted assassination of President Ronald Reagan. Plaintiffs were all shot at and seriously injured in the incident. The court ruled as a matter of law that even if the treating psychiatrist was negligent in diagnosis and treatment of Hinckley, liability could not be imposed because of the absence of a specific threat and identifiable target. The court stated:

> Unless a patient makes specific threats, the possibility that he may inflict injury on another is vague, speculative, and a matter of conjecture. However, once the patient verbalizes his intentions and directs his threats to identifiable victims, then the possibility of harm to third persons becomes foreseeable, and the therapist has a duty to protect those third persons from the threatened harm.[35]

Initial Assaults on the Specific Victim Requirement. *Bardoni v. Kim*[36] first qualified *Thompson* by removing any doubt as to whether a psychotherapist's subjective knowledge of an identifiable victim was required to trigger the duty to protect. The court determined that the duty to protect did not arise when a therapist acquired actual knowledge, but rather when the therapist "should have known of the existence and identity of his client's violence."[37] In *Bardoni,* the Michigan court stated:

> Since our Court, as well as other jurisdictions, has extended a duty to protect or warn to situations where the psychiatrist knows or should have known of the danger posed by his client, we must also extend the duty to specific persons whom the psychiatrist knows or should have known were endangered.[38]

Attenuation of the *Thompson* reasoning began in 1983 with the California Supreme Court's decision in *Hedlund v. Superior Court.*[39] *Hedlund* involved an assault on LaNita Wilson, who received psychotherapy counseling from Bonnie Hedlund. LaNita's attacker, also a client of Hedlund, communicated to the therapist his specific intentions to commit serious bodily harm to LaNita. LaNita received no warnings from the therapist. When Hedlund's client shot LaNita, her son was seated next to her. LaNita covered her son with her own body to protect him. The son suffered severe emotional distress from the incident. It is important to note that no threats were made toward the woman's son, nor did the son claim a duty of warning was owed him. Instead, the son claimed that the duty owed to his mother extended to and was enforceable by him.[40]

In *Hedlund,* the court ruled that the minor son of LaNita had a cause of action against the therapist for failure to warn of the possible attack.[41] LaNita had

---

[35]*Brady v. Hopper,* 570 F. Supp. 1333, 1338 (D. Colo. 1983), *aff'd,* 751 F.2d 329 (10th Cir. 1984).
[36]151 Mich. App. 169, 390 N.W.2d 218 (1986).
[37]*Id.* at 176, 390 N.W. 2d at 224.
[38]*Id.* at n.7.
[39]34 Cal. 3d 695, 669 P.2d 41, 194 Cal. Rptr 805 (1983).
[40]*Hedlund,* 34 Cal. 3d at 705, 669 P.2d at 46, 194 Cal. Rptr at 810.
[41]*Id.* at 704–708, 669 P.2d at 46–48, 194 Cal. Rptr at 810–811; *See also,* Kelleher, *Psychotherapists and the Duty to Warn: An Attempt at Clarification,* 19 NEW. ENG. 597 (1983) [hereinafter "Kelleher"].

been the object of the client's verbal expressions, making her an identifiable victim. The court then found that the foreseeability of the minor son's proximity to his mother at the time of attack also rendered him an identifiable victim.[42]

Rejection of the Specific Victim Requirement. In *Altenberg,* the Wisconsin Supreme Court flatly rejected the *Thompson* identifiable victim requirement because it was deemed inconsistent with fundamental principles of Wisconsin tort law.[43] The court reaffirmed its commitment to the minority position articulated in *Palsgraff v. Long Island R.R.*:[44]

> A defendant's duty is established when it can be said that it was foreseeable that his act or omission to act may cause harm to someone. A party is negligent when he commits an act when some harm to someone is foreseeable. Once negligence is established, the defendant is liable for *unforeseeable consequences* as well as foreseeable ones. In addition, he is liable to *unforeseeable plaintiffs.*[45]

Under a strict reading of this approach, the potential scope of psychotherapists' liability to third parties is unusually broad. Generally, the scope of liability is determined by the foreseeability of the harm caused; it is the failure to take into account the foreseeability of the harm that constitutes the breach of duty and thus results in a finding of negligence. However, the Wisconsin approach suggests that once there is a finding of any negligence, by failing to act reasonably in view of *some specific* foreseeable harm, the psychotherapist is liable for *any harm* consequentially ensuing—whether or not it was foreseeable harm or to a foreseeable person.

While other jurisdictions have loosened or removed the *Thompson* identifiable victim requirement,[46] none have couched the decision on such a fundamental basis as Wisconsin or resulted in such a far-reaching and absolute impact.

[42]*Hedlund,* 34 Cal. 3d at 706, 669 P.2d at 46, 194 Cal. Rptr at 810. The court based its decision on *Dillon v. Legg,* 68 Cal. 2d 728, 441 P.2d 912, 69 Cal. Rptr 72 (1968). *Dillon* allowed a cause of action for emotional distress to a mother who witnessed the killing of her child by a negligent driver.

[43]*Altenberg,* 144 Wis. 2d at 234, 424 N.W.2d at 164. The court reviewed its previous decision involving duty and foreseeability in which the court refused to narrow the scope of liability to exclude third parties. *See A. E. Investment v. Link Builders Inc.,* 62 Wis. 2d 479, 214 N.W.2d 764 (1974) (narrow concept of duty rejected as applied to architects); *Schilling v. Stockel,* 26 Wis. 2d 525, 133 N.W.2d 335 (1965) (once it is determined that a negligent act has been committed, a finding of nonliability can be made only in terms of public policy); *Auric v. Continental Gas. Co.,* 111 Wis. 2d 507, 331 N.W.2d 325 (1983) (attorney may be held liable in negligence to a beneficiary of a will who was not in privity with the attorney).

[44]248 N.Y. 339, 162 N.E. 99 (1928).

[45]*Altenberg,* 144 Wis. 2d at 235, 424 N.W.2d at 164 (emphasis added); (citing *A. E. Investment v. Link Builders Inc.,* 62 Wis. 2d 483, 484–485, 214 N.W.2d 764 (1974). In a concurring opinion, Justice Steinmetz disagreed with the majority's characterization of Wisconsin's adherence to the *Palsgraff* minority. Instead, Justice Steinmetz determined that Wisconsin has followed its own distinct approach and limited liability through policy considerations after elements of duty and causation have been established. *Altenberg,* 144 Wis. 2d at 266, 424 N.W.2d at 176 (Steinmetz J., concurring).

[46]*See, e.g., Williams v. United States,* 450 F. Supp. 1040 (D.S.D. 1978); *Lipari v. Sears, Roebuck & Co.,* 497 F. Supp. 185 (D. Neb. 1980); *Chrite v. United States,* 564 F. Supp. 341 (E.D. Mich. 1983); *Durflinger v. Artiles,* 234 Kan. 484, 673 P.2d 86 (1983); *Naidu v. Laird,* 539 A.2d 1064 (Del. 1988).

Moreover, and most importantly, other cases rejecting the *Thompson* requirement differ from *Altenberg* on two important grounds: (1) control of the client through inpatient status and (2) the imminence of the danger.

Specific Victims: Inpatients vs. Outpatients.   *Tarasoff* and all its progeny have premised psychotherapist liability to third parties on the presence of a special relationship between the therapist and client. The special relationship is important because it supposedly grants the therapist a right or ability to control the conduct of the person inflicting the harm.[47] This right or ability to control is the cornerstone of the imposition of liability.

The broadest expansion of psychotherapist liability, based on a removal of the identifiable victim requirement, has arisen in a context distinguishable from the forum of this chapter: the negligent release of inpatients.[48] The distinction between outpatients and inpatients is important because of the psychotherapist's degree of control over an inpatient vis-à-vis an outpatient. Psychotherapists' ability to control the actions of inpatients far exceeds their ability to control casual outpatients. Indeed, in the inpatient setting, it is frequently the psychotherapist's permissive release that gives the client the requisite liberty to inflict the harm caused. Outpatients, on the other hand, are at liberty and frequently remain at liberty because they are not subject to involuntary confinement.[49]

Based on this important distinction, negligent release cases, which broaden liability by removing the *Thompson* identifiable victim requirement, are better viewed as a subset of *Tarasoff* cases. The increased liability in negligent release cases is distinguishable from outpatient situations and justified because of the increased control the psychotherapist has had over the client.[50]

Altenberg, however, expands psychotherapists' liability to third parties by removing the *Thompson* requirement in the outpatient setting. This result suggests that the important distinguishing feature in virtually all other liability expanding cases was either unnoticed or deemed irrelevant in *Altenberg.*

Specific Victims: Imminence of Danger.   The case most frequently cited for the proposition that an identifiable victim is not required is *Lipari v. Sears, Roebuck & Co.*[51] However, *Altenberg* has little in common with the *Lipari* decision because of important differences in the type and likelihood of harm. *Lipari* involved a mental client, Ulysses Cribbs, who purchased a shotgun at Sears and later fired the gun into a crowded night club, killing Mr. Lipari and seriously injuring his wife. Cribbs, the assailant, had been receiving psychiatric care from

---

[47]*See* RESTATEMENT (SECOND) OF TORTS Sec. 315–320 (1965).

[48]*See Peterson v. State,* 100 Wash. 2d 421, 671 P.2d 230 (1983); *Naidu v. Laird,* 539 A.2d 1064 (Del. 1988).

[49]*See e.g.,* WIS. STAT. Sec. 51.20(1)(a)1 1987). Standard for involuntary commitment requires a showing of both mental illness and a substantial probability of danger to others or himself.

[50]It is noteworthy that *Thompson,* the first clear statement of the identifiable victim requirement, occurred in a negligent release context.

[51]*Lipari v. Sears, Roebuck & Co.,* 497 F. Supp 185 (D. Neb. 1980).

the Veterans Administration Hospital immediately prior to the shooting. The district court, applying Nebraska law, refused to grant a motion for summary judgment in favor of the VA hospital that had been treating Cribbs. The court ruled that the victims were not, as a matter of law, unforeseeable and that plaintiffs could prevail on a showing that the VA hospital could have foreseen an unreasonable risk of harm to the Liparis or a class of persons of which the Liparis were members.[52]

The Fourth Circuit Court of Appeals has recognized *Lipari* as a lonesome and wayward decision.[53] Moreover, *Lipari* is distinguishable from *Altenberg* because of the imminence and type of harm foreseeable. Cribbs, the attacker in *Lipari,* had been committed to a mental institution prior to purchasing his shotgun and had received psychiatric treatment at the VA hospital after purchasing his gun. Cribbs then removed himself from treatment against the advice of his doctors shortly before the shooting incident. Compare this to Mrs. Schuster, whose treatment was strictly as an outpatient, who displayed no expressions or symptoms of violence, and whose daughter suffered injuries that were the result of an accident rather than an intentional act. Despite these differences, *Lipari* remains the closest company to *Altenberg*'s blanket rejection of the *Thompson* identifiable victim requirement.

Imminence of Danger Required for Liability

Prior to *Altenberg,* imposition of liability in an outpatient context had always been accompanied by either specific threats of violence or a demonstrated propensity for violence.[54] This well-defined trend has become less certain after *Altenberg. Altenberg* recognizes a cause of action for failure to warn a third-party victim, absent of any threats or suggestions of violence, which is in sharp contrast to other courts' requirements that specific threats be voiced. *Brady v. Hopper*[55] stated the requirement as follows: "Unless a patient makes specific threats, the possibility that he may inflict injury on another is vague, speculative, and a matter of conjecture. However, once the patient verbalizes his intentions . . . the possibility of harm to third persons *becomes* foreseeable. . . ."[56]

---

[52]*Lipari*, 497 F. Supp at 195.

[53]*See Currie v. United States,* 836 F.2d 209, 213 (4th Cir. 1987).

[54]*See, e.g., McIntosh v. Milano,* 168 N.J. 466, 403 A.2d 500 (Law Div. 1979) (specific threat to victim and past history of violence); *Leedy v. Hartnett,* 510 F. Supp 1125 (M.D. Pa. 1981), *aff'd,* 676 F.2d 686 (3d. Cir. 1982) (no liability absent a specific threat); *Doyle v. United States,* 530 F. Supp 1278 (C.D. Cal. 1982) (no liability absent specific threat or identifiable victim); *Hasenei v. United States,* 541 F. Supp 999 (D. Md. 1982) (no specific threat); *Furr v. Grove State Hosp.,* 53 Md. App. 474, 454 A.2d 414 (Ct. Spec. App. 1983) (no specific threats or victim); *Brady v. Hopper,* 570 F. Supp 1333 (D. Colo. 1983), *aff'd,* 751 F.2d 329 (10th Cir. 1984) (no specific threat); *Schrempf v. State,* 66 N.Y.2d 973, 487 N.E.2d 883, 496 N.Y.S.2d 973 (1985) (no liability based on propensity for violence because release was within standards of the profession); *Bardoni v. Kim,* 151 Mich. App 169, 390 N.W.2d 218 (1986); (victim should have been specifically identified).

[55]570 F. Supp 1333 (D. Colo. 1983).

[56]*Id.* at 1338 (emphasis added).

In *Altenberg*, plaintiffs made no allegation that the client either voiced threats or subjectively intended to harm anyone.[57] Yet the court left open the possibility that the harm caused was foreseeable. In *Altenberg*, then, harm may be deemed to have become foreseeable even before any intent to harm is verbalized or otherwise suggested by the defendant's behavior,[58] indicating that the Wisconsin Court deems foreseeability to arise from bare possibilities of harm rather than probabilities of harm.[59] Although foreseeability of harm must be proven, *Altenberg* places new and far-reaching demands on the powers of foreseeability exercised by psychotherapists.

Significantly, because the element of intent to harm is not present in *Altenberg*, the court implies that the psychotherapist is not only liable for failure to foresee and protect third parties from the client's *intentional* violent acts[60] but also from the client's foreseeable *negligent* acts. This action virtually dissolves the previous threshold of imminence at which liability for dangerousness is triggered.

Civil Commitment of Clients

The original *Tarasoff* formulation required the psychotherapist to protect the client's intended victim by warning or "whatever other steps are reasonably necessary under the circumstances,"[61] which left open the question of whether the therapist had a legal obligation to commit potentially dangerous clients. The *Tarasoff* court stated, however: "Within the broad range of reasonable practice and treatment in which professional opinion and judgment may differ, the therapist

---

[57]Brief of Defendant, *supra* note 27, at 14.

[58]For cases imposing liability absent specific threats in a negligent release context, see *Peterson v. State*, 100 Wash. 2d at 421, 671 P.2d at 230 (1983); *Naidu v. Laird*, 539 A.2d 1064 (Del. 1988). For cases imposing liability absent specific threats but with patients having demonstrated violent propensities, see *Jablonski v. United States*, 712 F.2d 391 (9th Cir. 1983).

[59]See 57 AM. JUR. 2D *Negligence*, Sec. 54 (1971). The Wisconsin Supreme Court's position in *Altenberg* contradicts earlier Wisconsin statements suggesting that duty to use due care arises from probabilities and not bare possibilities. "The duty to use due care arises from probabilities, rather than from bare possibilities of injury. Failure to guard against the bare possibility of injury is not actionable negligence." Brief of Defendant, *supra* note 26, at 14 (citing *Grube v. Moths*, 56 Wis. 2d 424, 202 N.W.2d 261 (1972)).

[60]If a psychotherapist fails to foresee the violence of his patient because of negligent diagnosis, a cause of action will stand on independent grounds. *Altenberg* demonstrates that a cause of action exists for negligent diagnosis if it can be shown that proper diagnosis and treatment would have avoided the harm caused to the third person. *Altenberg*, 144 Wis. 2d at 230, 424 N.W.2d at 162. This is congruent with the California Supreme Court's determination in *Hedlund*: "A negligent failure to diagnose dangerousness in a *Tarasoff* action is as much a basis of liability as is negligent failure to warn a known victim once such diagnosis has been made." *Hedlund*, 34 Cal. 3d at 704, 669 P.2d at 45, 194 Cal. Rptr at 809.

[61]*Tarasoff II*, 17 Cal. 3d at 431, 551 P.2d at 340, 131 Cal. Rptr at 20. Although praised as a duty to protect or "to take whatever steps are reasonably necessary under the circumstances." *Id.* Much of the psychotherapeutic community failed to understand that their new duty was to protect and not merely to warn. A study by Daniel Givelber demonstrated that more than 92% of California psychiatrists thought their duty under *Tarasoff* was discharged merely by warning. Givelber, Bowers, & Blitch, *Supra*, note 13, at 467. Only 30% of the same class believed *Tarasoff* required them to exercise reasonable care to protect the victim.

is free to exercise his or her own best judgment without liability."[62] With this state-ment, the judiciary conceded to psychotherapists the freedom to choose among the broad range of clinical alternatives available to deter violence without exposure to liability.[63] It is reasonable to assume that civil commitment was one example within this broad range of clinical alternatives which could be exercised by choice—not by duty, which is wholly appropriate given that lawyers and judges tend to think legally and therefore tend to underconsider the kinds of clinical alter-natives psychotherapists may use to reduce a client's violence.[64] Mounting evidence suggests, however, that the judiciary is coming to regard civil commitment as a legal duty, not a clinical alternative.

Civil Commitment: Clinical Choice or Legal Duty.   Recently, however, *Tarasoff*-type plaintiffs have alleged claims of therapists failing to exercise a *duty* to commit the client along with failing to exercise a duty to warn the victim.[65] *Currie v. United States*[66] is the most comprehensive treatment of the subject to date.

In *Currie,* Leonard Avery, a Vietnam veteran and ex-employee of IBM, had articulated to his therapist specific threats to blow up an IBM plant in Durham, North Carolina. Each time Avery's case was discussed, the participating team of psychotherapists concluded that Avery could not be committed because he was lucid and in touch with reality. His danger was determined to be a product of anger, not mental illness. The North Carolina statute required mental illness and danger-ousness in order to commit involuntarily.[67] To fulfill their duty under *Tarasoff,* the psychiatrists then explicitly warned the United States attorney general, the Veterans Administration district counsel, the Federal Bureau of Investigation, the Durham County Police Department, and IBM of Avery's threats. Despite the warnings, Avery was able to enter the IBM facility, where he shot and killed an IBM employee.

The claim for relief in *Currie* centered entirely on the psychiatrists' alleged affirmative duty to seek involuntary commitment. The Fourth Circuit Court of Appeals, ruling under North Carolina law, refused to recognize such a duty.[68] Apparently, persuaded by arguments by the American Psychological Association in its amicus brief, the court found that the policy considerations involved in find-ing a duty to warn were distinct from the policy considerations in finding a duty to

---

[62]*Tarasoff II,* 17 Cal. 3d at 438, 551 P.2d at 345, 131 Cal. Rptr at 24.
[63]Mills, *supra* note 10, at 246. Clinical remedies available include reassessment, consultation, changes in medication, or civil commitment.
[64]*Id.*
[65]836 F.2d 209 (4th Cir. 1987); *See also, Lipari,* 497 F. Supp at 185. At the time of *Currie, Lipari* was the only case clearly authorizing a claim for a duty to commit patients.
[66]*Id.*
[67]*Id.* at 211.
[68]*Id.* at 210. This conclusion overruled the Federal District Court's ruling that an affirmative duty to seek involuntary commitment should be recognized. The district court found *Lipari* persuasive in finding that "it would be improper to rule that psychotherapists would never have a duty to institute commitment proceedings against a patient." *Currie,* 644 F. Supp 1074, 1081 (M.D.N.C. 1986). The court believed that to rule otherwise would allow psychotherapists to act in careless disregard of members of the public known to be endangered by their patients.

commit.[69] The court found that involuntary commitment involved considerations of the client's constitutionally protected liberty interest[70] and that involuntary commitment would have a great likelihood of destroying the psychiatrist's potential for constructive influence over the client.[71]

The *Altenberg* court, unpersuaded by *Currie,* found failure to commit as a companion cause of action to failure to warn.[72] Contrary to *Currie,* the *Altenberg* court satisfied itself that warnings to third parties were more disruptive to the therapist/client relationship than commitment proceedings.[73] Based on this determination, the *Altenberg* court found it puzzling that the court in *Currie* would recognize a cause of action for failure to warn but not failure to commit.[74] Moreover, the *Altenberg* court believed that warnings alone were frequently ineffective in satisfying the duty to protect the potential victim.[75] A cause of action for failure to commit was limited, however, to situations where it could be established that the client was a proper subject of involuntary commitment under statutory standards.[76]

Legally Required Commitment: Risk Factors for the Therapist.   Wisconsin's willingness to recognize a cause of action for failure to commit is a serious dilemma for psychotherapists. The *Altenberg* court failed to balance the duty psychotherapists owed their clients with the duty owed potential victims. Psychotherapists stand in a fiduciary relationship with their clients, but not with the clients' potential victim(s). The clients' well-being is the psychotherapists' foremost consideration. The problem practitioners face, then, is that closing the walls of legal liability outside the fiduciary relationship renders the likelihood of legal liability from within the fiduciary relationship more threatening.[77] This dilemma is not reflected in any balancing considerations by the courts.

The recognition of an affirmative duty to commit indicates that the initial buffer zone of a "broad range of reasonable practice," which psychotherapists could use to avoid liability in *Tarasoff,* is becoming less real. It seems, at least in Wisconsin, that the courts are losing touch with what was initially recognized in *Tarasoff*: that judges are not qualified to be instructing psychotherapists on how to discharge their duty to protect.

[69]*Currie,* 836 F.2d at 213.
[70]*See* Kelleher, *supra* note 41, at 601; (citing National Institute of Mental Health, Civil Commitment and Social Policy: An Evaluation of the Massachusetts Mental Health Reform Act of 1970 at 47 (1981).
[71]*Currie,* 836 F.2d at 213.
[72]*Altenberg,* 144 Wis. 2d at 234, 424 N.W.2d at 165.
[73]*Id.* at 257–258, 424 N.W.2d at 173; *see also,* Stone, *The Tarasoff Decision: Suing Psychotherapists to Safeguard Society,* 90 HARV. L. REV. 358, 377 (1976).
[74]*Altenberg,* 144 Wis. 2d at 258, 424 N.W.2d at 173.
[75]*Id.*
[76]*Id.* at 248, 424 N.W.2d at 169.
[77]The energy and consideration a practitioner is now required to focus on outside the fiduciary relationship to avoid legal liability from third parties often comes at the expense of the patient. The psychotherapist will find it more difficult to put the patient's well-being first when the therapist's attention is consistently drawn outside that relationship.

In addition, recognition of a cause of action for failure to commit is especially burdensome to psychotherapists because of the increasing difficulty in successfully committing clients involuntarily. Commentators have noted that the infiltration of law into the mental health profession, with its focus on individual rights, has made it increasingly difficult to commit a person involuntarily.[78] The current trend toward recognizing and establishing the rights of mental health clients has led to the following potential complications with regard to commitment: (1) it is increasingly difficult to commit an individual involuntarily; (2) more and more people are being released from hospitals and treated on an outpatient basis; and (3) clients are more aware of their rights and are exercising them, particularly the right to refuse treatment.[79]

The Wisconsin statute for involuntary commitment is a prime example of the new and more stringent requirements for involuntary commitment. A client must not only exhibit a "substantial probability" of dangerousness but must also be mentally ill.[80] Needless to say, not all clients who have the potential for violence are mentally ill. Yet mere anger, or even a strong propensity for violence, are not grounds for commitment absent a mental illness.[81] Dangerous propensities, coupled with the fact that the person happens to be seeing a psychotherapist, does not provide a finding of mental illness. Furthermore, psychotherapists frequently disagree among themselves as to what constitutes mental illness. In commenting on this disagreement, the United States Supreme Court stated: "Psychiatry is not . . . an exact science, and psychiatrists disagree widely and frequently on what constitutes mental illness, on the appropriate diagnosis to be attached to given behavior and symptoms, on cure and treatment, and on the likelihood of future dangerousness."[82]

Notwithstanding this statement by the judiciary's highest court, the original buffer zone announced in *Tarasoff* has proven itself subject to attack via the increasing specificity of duties imposed on psychotherapists. Mental health professionals can only hope that the evaporating buffer zone of *Tarasoff* will not be replaced by dogmatic lawyers and judges assuming too quickly their own competence in a discipline subject to significant controversy and ambiguity.

---

[78]*See* Kelleher, *supra* note 41, at 601; (citing National Institute of Mental Health, Civil Commitment and Social Policy: An Evaluation of the Massachusetts Mental Health Reform Act of 1970 at 47 (1981)).

[79]Kelleher, *supra* note 41, at 602.

[80]WIS. STAT. Sec. 51.20 (1987) provides in relevant part as follows: "Involuntary commitment for treatment. (1) Petition for examination. (a) Except as provided in pars. (ab), (am) and (ar), every written petition for examination shall allege that the subject individual to be examined: 1. Is mentally ill, drug dependent, or developmentally disabled and is a proper subject for treatment; and 2. Is dangerous because the individual: . . . b. Evidences a substantial probability of physical harm to other individuals as manifest by evidence of recent homicidal or other violent behavior, or by evidence that others are placed in reasonable fear of violent behavior and serious physical harm to them, as evidenced by a recent overt act, attempt or threat to do serious physical harm. . . ."

[81]*Id.*

[82]*Ake v. Oklahoma*, 470 U.S. 68, 81 (1985).

Legally Required Commitment: Deprivation of Liberty and Least Restrictive Treatment. A fear commentators and the American Psychological Association share is that recognition of a duty to commit potentially dangerous clients will significantly and unnecessarily deprive mental clients of their liberty.[83] They contend that a duty to commit will increase the number of commitment proceedings based on therapists' fear of client violence.[84] Because therapists are unable to accurately predict violence, the unnecessary detention of numerous clients is a substantial reality.

This point is best illustrated by a hypothetical statistical analysis. Assume that 1 client out of 1000 will carry out a dangerous threat. Further assume that all psychotherapists could predict with 95% accuracy which one out of the 1000 is dangerous. If 100,000 clients are examined for dangerousness, 95 of the 100 dangerous clients would be isolated. Disappointingly, however, even a margin of error of only 5% means that of the 99,900 clients who are harmless, almost 5000 would be unnecessarily deprived of their liberty.[85] The point the American Psychological Association raised is that because therapists will fear liability where a duty to commit is imposed, more clients falling within the margin of error, which in fact greatly exceeds 5%, will be involuntarily committed.

A general guideline most states impose is that psychotherapists pursue the least restrictive treatment for their clients. If the American Psychological Association is right in its belief that imposition of a duty to commit will increase the number of commitment proceedings, then the policy of least restrictive treatment has encountered a hostile enemy. American criminal principles suggest that it is better that 10 guilty people go free than 1 innocent person be deprived of her or his liberty. How then can we explain a legal policy which suggests that in the area of civil commitment it is better that dozens of harmless people be committed, lest a single dangerous person be free?[86]

Predicting Dangerousness

The *Tarasoff* court's axiomatic statement "[t]he protective privilege ends where the public peril begins"[87] is not contested. The well-recognized problem for courts and psychotherapists, in fact, is determining where the public peril begins. Prior to *Altenberg,* the recognized difficulty of psychotherapists' ability to predict dangerousness was the fundamental justification for granting a buffer zone of conduct within a broad professional range of reasonably accepted practice. Although

---

[83]*See* Amicus Curiae Brief of the American Psychological Association at 28, *Currie v. United States* 826 F.2d 209 (4th Cir. 1987) (No. 86–2643) [hereinafter A.P.A. Brief].

[84]*Id.*

[85]Stone, *supra* note 73, at 363–364 n.23 (citing, Livermore, Malmquist & Meehl, *On the Justifications for Civil Commitment,* 117 U. PA. L. REV. 75, 84 (1968).

[86]Comment, *Tarasoff and Psychotherapists' Duty to Warn,* 12 SAN DIEGO L. REV. 932, 942–943, n.75 (1975). It is further significant that these numbers are based on an assumed accuracy of 95% in predicting violence. Actual precision is in fact much lower.

[87]17 Cal. 3d at 442, 551 P.2d at 347, 131 Cal. Rptr at 27.

the *Altenberg* court continues to pay lip service to this established buffer zone,[88] its justification appears to be attenuating. The *Altenberg* court stated: "Of further significance is the fact that a *survey* of psychotherapists suggests that practitioners are quite confident of their ability to assess dangerousness: '[T]he task of assessing dangerousness is not viewed as being beyond the competence of individual therapists or as a matter upon which therapists cannot agree.' "[89]

This statement is based largely on the results of a survey in which psychotherapists were asked to rate themselves as to their ability to predict dangerousness.[90] More than 75% of the therapists surveyed believed they could predict client violence within a range of "probable" to "certain".[91] In addition, 70% of the responding therapists believed that 90 to 100% of their colleagues would agree with their conclusion as to whether or not the client was dangerous.[92]

It is disquieting that the Wisconsin Supreme Court places stock in the results of this study in light of the overwhelming academic and empirical evidence to the contrary. Most every jurisdiction dealing with the predictability of violence has cited persuasive studies consistently showing that psychotherapists are not able to successfully predict violence.[93] Consistent research findings, in fact, show that mental health professionals fail to accurately predict future violence in two out of three cases[94] and that there is no consistent professional standard for predicting violence.[95] In addition, mental health has been proven to be the most important *non*correlate of violence.[96]

That mental health professionals' undocumented self-appraisals show practitioners as confident of their ability to predict violence does nothing to discredit the overwhelming empirical evidence to the contrary.[97] It does show, however, that psychotherapists' confidence in themselves, although undeniably flattering, is sorely misplaced. For psychotherapists, the importance of all these matters lies

---

[88]The court's literal wording of the established standard is reminiscent of the "broad range" standard established in *Tarasoff*: "[W]e emphasize that in determining whether harm was foreseeable, the psychotherapist is not held to a standard of omniscience, but merely that degree of care and skill which is exercised by the average practitioner in the class to which he belongs, acting in the same or similar circumstances." *Altenberg*, 144 Wis. 2d at 238, 424 N.W.2d at 165.

[89]*Id.* at 248, 424 N.W.2d at 169 (emphasis added) (quoting Givelber, Bowers, & Blitch, *supra* note 13).

[90]Givelber, Bowers, & Blitch, *supra* note 13. The study involved a survey sample of 2875 psychiatrists, psychologists, and social workers located in major cities across the United States.

[91]*Id.* at 463.

[92]*Id.* at 464.

[93]*See, e.g.*, J. Monahan, *The Clinical Prediction of Violent Behavior* (1981) [hereinafter "Monahan"]; Ennis & Litwack, *Psychiatry and the Presumption of Expertise: Flipping Coins in the Courtroom*, 62 CAL. L. REV. 693, 713 (1974). (cited in A.P.A. Brief, *supra* at note 83).

[94]*Id.*

[95]*See* Steadman, *The Right Not to Be a False Positive: Problems in the Application of the Dangerousness Standard*, 52 PSYCHIATRIC QUARTERLY 84, 96 (1980) ("Nowhere in the research literature is there any documentation that clinicians can predict dangerous behavior beyond the level of chance") (cited in A.P.A. Brief *supra* note 83.)

[96]J. Monahan, *The Clinical Prediction of Violent Behavior* (1981). (quoted in Amicus Curiae Brief of the American Psychological Association at 18, 19, *Currie v. United States* 836 F.2d 209 (4th Cir. 1987).

[97]*See supra* notes 93-96, and accompanying text.

in the expertise and knowledge the judiciary stands poised to impute to them. If psychotherapists are seen as expert predictors of violence, then courts are likely to find therapists negligent in more instances for failing to foresee their clients' violent acts. This trend threatens to destroy the "broad range of reasonable practice" buffer zone that *Tarasoff* first conceded to psychotherapists.

Legislative Responses.   The volatile nature of legal trends in *Tarasoff* case law has made legislative responses both desirable and necessary. As *Tarasoff*-related issues become more controversial, we can expect state statutes to rapidly increase. These statutes will likely differ significantly as to how therapists' duties are defined and discharged. Moreover, statutes will vary as to the scope of therapists' liability when dangerous clients carry out their threats. Because California has led the way in *Tarasoff* developments, we examine the California statute enacted in 1985. We can expect similar statutes to emerge in other jurisdictions as well.

The substance of the California statute draws from mainstream case law prior to the *Altenberg* decision. The statute provides, however, greater clarity than case law in defining when the therapist's duty to protect potential victims is triggered and how that duty is discharged:

> Section 43.92 [Psychotherapist's duty to warn of patient's violent behavior; Immunity from liability]
> (a) There shall be no monetary liability on the part of, and no cause of action shall arise against any person who is a psychotherapist . . . in failing to warn of, and protect from, a patient's threatened violent behavior except where the patient has communicated to the psychotherapist a serious threat of physical violence against a reasonably identifiable victim. (b) If there is a duty to warn and protect under the limited circumstances specified above, the duty shall be discharged by the psychotherapist making reasonable efforts to communicate the threat to the victim or victims and to a law enforcement agency.[98]

The California statute aids the psychotherapist by limiting the situations in which the duty to protect is triggered. The statute is also helpful because it clearly defines how the duty to protect may be discharged. However, the inconsistent nature of case law among jurisdictions offers great potential for commensurate diversity among legislative enactments. Psychotherapists should anticipate statutes in their jurisdictions and become familiar with them as they emerge.

SUMMARY AND IMPLICATIONS

Tarasoff was the first case to extend psychotherapists' obligations beyond the confines of the therapists' fiduciary relationship with their clients. Therapists first incurred a duty to warn targeted victims of clients' violence. This duty was

---

[98]CAL. CIV. CODE Sec. 43.92 (Deering 1971 & 1990 Supp.).

subsequently recouched in terms of a duty to protect. Compliance with this duty is measured by conformity to the standards of the profession, but because psychotherapeutic standards are difficult to define, the judiciary initially conceded a "broad range" of reasonable practice as a buffer zone from liability.

But emerging trends have displayed a pattern of expanding liability, as evidenced by the following:

1. The requirement of a specific and identifiable victim is losing strength.

2. The imminence of danger required to trigger the duty to protect appears to be lessening.

3. The initially broad buffer zone of reasonable practice is beginning to erode as clinical choices, such as civil commitment, become legal duties.

4. The judiciary appears to be generating more confidence in a psychotherapist's ability to predict dangerousness.

It remains to be seen if *Altenberg* is a prototype of an emerging legal logic, a mere aberration, or the arrival at a brief pinnacle in a reactionary trend of expanding liability.

The degree of *Altenberg*'s deviation from previous *Tarasoff*-type actions is largely attributable to the fact that Wisconsin purports to follow the minority position in *Palsgraff*. This, coupled with Wisconsin's refusal to limit its impact on policy grounds, has produced a new personality in the *Tarasoff* doctrine. What can be counted on is that the forces representing the policy interests on both sides of the controversy will become increasingly organized. The shape and personality of *Tarasoff* in adulthood will be largely determined by societal and judicial reaction to the new and more vigorous personality now emerging in the doctrine's adolescence.

What psychotherapists need to understand is that their profession is now subject to the scrutiny and absolute pronouncement of courts whose view of them is far from realistic or empirically founded. Although ambiguity in the principles and practices of the mental health discipline may prevent the courts from being able to understand major therapeutic issues, psychotherapists can understand what the judiciary is seeing through their veil of misunderstanding. This observation provides little comfort, but it can instruct psychotherapists on how to instruct the judiciary on relevant matters, which may be the therapist's most important defense against unwarranted liability.

In light of the fanciful and elaborate analytical gymnastics all the courts in the decisions reviewed used, it should be clearer than ever that the rules governing legal liability with dangerous clients are vague and evolving. Psychotherapists really do not yet know what legal ruling to expect from different legal jurisdictions. Until this dilemma is resolved, therapists' best protection from legal liability is their own clinical competence. And generally, competence is not subject to predetermined and carefully defined sets of thoughts and behaviors; it cannot be memorized, and it cannot be found in a manual of instructions. Rather, it is found in deliberate and collected reasoning and in a thoughtful balancing of risks that remain unknown until confronted situation by situation. Psychotherapists must remember that the law is structured and refined one fact pattern at a time. Only when a problem falls squarely and absolutely within clearly established precedent is there significant guidance and safety. A manual of instructions on how to avoid legal liability has little value relative to the thoughtful, perceptive, and deliberate behavior of an astute clinician after consulting with colleagues.

4

Clinical Dangerousness: Clinical Duties*

As we mentioned earlier, our discussion of clinical considerations with dangerous clients will focus on the "what" and "how" of clinical work. We integrate legal issues and professional knowledge into clinical practices that can survive courtroom scrutiny without compromising client care. Our analysis of the legal literature suggests that therapists need to be particularly mindful of the following legal/professional duties:

1. To exercise the ordinary skill and care of a reasonable professional in *identifying* those clients who may pose a significant risk of physical harm to third parties.

2. To exercise the ordinary skill and care of a reasonable professional in *protecting* third parties from those clients judged potentially dangerous.

3. To exercise the ordinary skill and care of a reasonable professional in *treating* those clients judged dangerous.

4. To take reasonable precautions in *record keeping* and collegial *consultations* that will most dramatically reduce the chances of successful malpractice suits.

To this end, we discuss the principles, practices, and issues associated with (1) assessment of dangerousness, (2) case management, and (3) fundamental precautionary considerations.

ASSESSING CLIENT DANGEROUSNESS

We have no wish to argue with research that suggests mental health professionals cannot predict client dangerousness with any degree of accuracy. We believe that a rigorous critique and an analysis of such research reveal a variety of conceptual and methodological issues not usually considered when these findings are discussed (for example, see Litwack, 1985, for critics of this literature). This type of analysis, when done by established experts under optimal conditions, could increase the perceived value and validity of predictions of dangerousness.

*Thanks are extended to Ben Ogles for his fine work in assisting with the development of this chapter. He was recently awarded his doctorate from the Clinical Psychology Training Program at Brigham Young University and is currently employed as an assistant professor of psychology at Ohio University in Athens.

One probable reason the courts have come to believe that mental health professionals can predict dangerousness is that so many of us kept telling them that we could (Givelber, Bowers, & Blitch, 1984). A higher level of professional modesty now seems more appropriate.

Nevertheless, a formal assessment of client dangerousness is absolutely essential to sound clinical practice and to a solid legal defense—should one become necessary (Sonkin, 1986; Gutheil, Bursztajn, & Brodsky, 1986). The formal assessment should be based on the most current knowledge in our profession—in spite of unresolved questions about predictive validity. Sound clinical procedures as well as legal considerations require us to know what questions are the best diagnostic guides in spite of their fallibility. Making a diagnostic error is not a violation of either legal or professional standards, but not asking the right questions before making a diagnosis may be a violation of both.

Prior to *Tarasoff*, the assessment of dangerousness was based largely on clinical lore. Since then, however, we have learned a bit more about this intriguing problem. Before reviewing this material, we need to clarify two points. The first point is the precise type of behavior we are trying to predict or assess—is it the capacity to murder, physically assault, physically abuse, or simply frighten others? Second, is the assessment going to provide a basis for a long- or short-term prediction? Obviously, long-term predictions are subject to many more sources of error and much more difficult to formulate with any degree of accuracy. The answer to both questions will determine the type of information needed to enhance the validity of the assessment.

The classic *Tarasoff* case easily illustrates the importance of these two considerations. Remember that Poddar first expressed his intention to kill Tatiana 2 months prior to the actual homicide. At the time of the threat, Tatiana was actually out of the country and not expected to return home for some time. The prospects of imminent harm or danger were low. A proper clinical assessment and response to this threat would have been radically different if Tatiana had been at her home and Poddar had expressed an intent to kill her that day with a gun he had just acquired!

Three areas of inquiry are particularly important in any attempt to assess dangerousness: (1) individual characteristics associated with violent behavior, (2) situational and environmental characteristics associated with violent behavior, and (3) combined or interactive influences of individual and environmental characteristics associated with violent behavior. We now discuss each area of inquiry.

Individual Characteristics

Individual characteristics that are related to potential violence include demographic variables, prior socialization experiences, prior violent acts, and other contributing factors.

Demographics.   A number of demographic factors are associated with violent behavior—for example, 90% of all crimes are committed by men. Younger people (15 to 30 years) commit the majority of crimes, and underprivileged groups (for example, lower socioeconomic classes, minorities, and the unemployed) commit a disproportionate percentage of crimes. Also, violent criminals are likely to have lower-than-average intelligence (Meloy, 1987; Mulvey & Lidz, 1984). Finally, individuals who frequently change jobs or residency tend to be over-represented in the population of violent offenders (Monahan, 1981).

Collectively, all these variables paint a picture of the most common violent offender as a younger male with a marginal social adjustment. While membership in any or all of these subgroups cannot be considered predictive of actual violent behavior, the astute clinician should recognize the increased risk associated with each demographic factor. And as the number of demographic factors that fit a client increase, the sense of urgency about the importance and adequacy of the remainder of the risk assessment should correspondingly increase.

Socialization.   A history of violence in the family may be one of the primary origins of violent behavior. Not only does family violence give children a model of intense anger, it is also the context in which most violent behavior takes place. Skodol and Karasu (1977) found that 77% of all emergency commitment cases in which the client was considered violent involved other family members as victims. A thorough exploration of early socialization experiences can reveal basic descriptive information about the social milieu in which a client was raised and the frequency and intensity of various responses to anger. A client's preferred mode of responding to intense anger is most likely a natural extension of a more basic socialization process, which is why childhood deprivation, violent parents, acceptance of violence in peer groups, and violence on the job are all considered factors that increase the risks of violent behavior (Meloy, 1987; Mulvey & Lidz, 1984; Skodol, 1984). These factors are the agents of social learning, and understanding the curriculum can tell us a great deal about the form, frequency, and substance of future violent acts.

History of Violence.   The psychological literature (Mulvey & Lidz, 1984) has repeatedly suggested that future violence is not predictable in the absence of a history of violent behavior. This revealing and compelling observation has a fair amount of empirical support. Generally, past violence is typically the best single predictor of future violence (Monahan, 1981). Any attempt to assess dangerousness must include a detailed history of prior violent acts. The more basic considerations include (1) juvenile arrests, (2) military experience, and (3) adult assaultive behavior. Additionally, childhood enuresis, fire-setting, and animal cruelty have been labeled the "violent triad" because of their ability to predict adult violence in at least one study (Hellman & Blackman, 1966). Hyman (1984) suggested five questions that will help reveal and clarify the frequency and severity of past violence:

1. Under what circumstances has past violence occurred?

2. What are the most common expressions of violence?

3. What is the most violent act ever committed (do not be shy about asking)?

4. What is the client's history of arrests as a juvenile and an adult?

5. What is the client's history of automobile misuse (for example, fights while driving, moving violations, outbursts, and so on)?

While past violence is not as predictive of future violence as we might hope, it is certainly the most revealing information we can obtain in a risk assessment. Conversely, a history of no violence is the best indicator of a future that is equally nonviolent.

Other Factors.   "Other" factors considered important to the assessment of dangerousness include (1) specific components of mental illness and (2) certain personality attributes. While mental illness by itself simply cannot be considered predictive of dangerous behavior, certain components of it can. Kutzer and Lion (1984) suggested four general categories that are important.

First, any type of disorder that seriously impairs reality functions, such as those involving delusion, hallucination, and thought disorders, including schizophrenia or toxic psychosis, can increase risk. Under these aberrant conditions, clients may not be legally or morally responsible for what they do.

Second, disorders that involve extreme mood shifts, such as mania or delusional depression, may lead to violence. Under these conditions, clients in a state of agitated excitement may actually do things they normally would not even consider a short time later.

Third, persons with certain personality disorders (antisocial and explosive personalities) are more likely than others to be violent. The more frequent indicators of these traits include resentment of authority, self-centeredness, problems of impulse control, superficial or ambivalent relationships, and repeated disputes with others (DeLeon, 1961; Kozol, Boucher, & Gawfalo, 1972; Soreff, 1984). These attributes are logical extensions of the underlying personality disorder and may be accompanied by other predictors of dangerousness.

Fourth, any number of organic problems, including tumors, dementia, and delirium, may lead to violence (Kutzer & Lion, 1984). Most of us still remember the "Texas Tower Massacre" at the University of Texas by a student being seen at the University Counseling Center. The ultimate cause of this tragedy may have been an undiagnosed brain tumor.

Finally, and for a variety of different reasons, substance abuse is intimately associated with violent behavior. As a group, substance abusers are overrepresented in the population of violent offenders (Monahan, 1981), for several reasons. First, substance abuse is more common in the personality types more prone to violence. Second, the disinhibiting affect of drugs can lead to greater impulsiveness, emotional lability, and loss of control. Third, prior to violent acts, offenders frequently consume both alcohol and drugs. A detailed inquiry about past and present substance abuse is essential in any risk-assessment procedure. Additionally, medications such as steroids, testosterone, L-dopa, and phenaciamide all have side effects that have been linked to violent behavior (Soreff, 1984).

Situational and Environmental Factors

Situational and environmental factors are undeniably important determinants of violence, but we know far less about them. Nevertheless, a thorough risk assessment should address the following areas of concern.

First, the influence of the family goes well beyond the initial socialization process. According to Mulvey and Lidz (1984), family interactions are a strong contextual influence on the expression of violence. Congested homes, overcrowded conditions, and lack of family support have been linked to increased hostility, violence, or rehospitalization (Mulvey & Lidz, 1984). Similarly, the most likely victims of violent behavior are other family members; this finding is particularly true for psychiatric clients (Steadman, 1982). A stressful family environment seems to increase the chances of a violent family environment.

Second, under some circumstances peer influences and job environment can be related to violence. The inhibition or disinhibition of violence by peer groups, particularly during adolescence, is well documented (Meloy, 1987). In fact, peer pressure and cultural norms can actually require violent retaliation as a continuing condition for group membership.

Employability and employment satisfaction appear negatively related to violent behavior, a difficult finding to interpret. It could be that the unemployed spend more time at home, which provides more opportunities for violence. It is equally likely that regularly employed people spend more time away from home, which reduces the opportunities for violence. We suggest that the personality attributes associated with violence also contribute to unsatisfying employment.

Finally, the availability of victims, weapons, and alcohol has been linked to the frequency of violent crimes (Monahan, 1981). The availability of weapons increases both the frequency of violent behavior and the severity and lethality of violent acts. Meloy (1987) suggested that there is a curvilinear relationship between alcohol consumption and violence. Low levels of alcohol consumption lower inhibitions and increase the chances of violence, but high levels of consumption reduce muscular control and the capacity for violent acts.

Thus situational and environmental factors can contribute to violent behavior by (1) causing stress and frustration (family environment) that either erode a person's tolerance for frustration or actually become the stimulus for violence, (2) providing social norms and expectations that encourage and reward violent behavior (peer pressure), or (3) providing the means (alcohol and weapons) that potentiate violent impulses. Each consideration should be noted in any risk assessment.

Individual/Situational Interactions

This stage of the assessment process is probably the most important but the least reliable. All the information that has been collected must now be combined, carefully considered, and placed to support one of two simple alternatives.

The first alternative is "Yes, this client is dangerous," and the second one is "No, this client is not dangerous." No clear rules or research findings direct the process for making this decision; it is clinical judgment in its purest form, and predictive accuracy is the test of validity. No explanations or discussions are allowed. All that really matters is will they or won't they? And the ultimate validity of this task is almost entirely dependent on therapists' ability to (1) accurately identify the client's uniquely germane features and the client's environment and (2) combine this complex information into a simple judgment without the assistance of many rules or principles regarding the significance of any single factor or pattern of findings.

Formulating Predictions

Monahan (1981) suggested several guidelines to help clinicians formulate predictions of violent behavior. We now illustrate these principles with the help of a clinical situation.

A slightly paranoid client believes that his wife has been cheating on him every time she comes home late from work. His typical response to her absence is to drink more than usual and angrily confront her when she comes home. The wife has become angry about these allegations, and the couple has exchanged vicious words over the problem. In the heat of an argument, the husband threatened to kill the wife if she came home late again. Neither spouse has a past history of assaultive violence, but they have slapped each other. Both start drinking when family stress increases. There is a gun in the upstairs closet.

Will they or won't they? To help make this decision, Monahan (1981) suggested the following three questions to help determine how the individual and environmental factors may interact to produce violent behavior:

1. Are the environmental or situational factors associated with the potential violence likely to reappear in the future?

2. Who is the potential victim, and how available will the victim be in the future?

3. In the client's environment, are means for committing violence available?

In our example, the answer to each question is "Yes." A lethal weapon is available, the potential victim is readily available, and the environmental circumstances that trigger violence are certain to reappear in the future. All these factors indicate a moderate to high risk of actual violence.

Before accepting all these observations and the conclusion they suggest, we should review the four most common mistakes clinicians make when trying to formulate predictions of dangerousness (Monahan, 1981):

1. *Ignoring base rates.* This error is usually of two distinct forms. The first is simply not understanding the role of base rates in clinical predictions or overlooking the extremely low frequency of violence that is typical of most base-rate tables. The second is assuming that the presence of one

or more of the risk factors we discussed dramatically increases the frequency of violence when the influence of the factor(s) is really rather minor.

2. *Not using environmental information.* Generally, clinicians are overly inclined to base their predictive efforts on individual risk factors; environmental factors, in spite of their obvious importance, tend to receive far less consideration. One of the best uses of environmental factors is determining the environmental circumstances in which violence has occurred in the past and then determining the likelihood that the client will be in similar circumstances in the future.

3. *Relying on erroneous predictor variables.* This error needs hardly any elaboration: The clinicians consider factors that are not associated with violent behavior.

4. *Having vague or unclear conceptions of what is being predicted.* As simple as this point appears, its importance cannot be overemphasized. Accurate predictions require a clear conceptual and operational understanding of the behavior one is trying to predict. Dangerous behavior can take many different forms, such as (a) physical assault, (b) destruction of property, (c) use of weapons, and (c) malicious forms of deceit designed to create trauma. Specifying the type of behavior one is trying to predict is an essential part of formulating meaningful predictions.

With all these considerations in mind, obviously our case illustration is one in which the risk of actual violence is at least moderate, and perhaps even high. But we must remember that *most* situations such as this will *not* result in actual violence. Even though we are not very good at predicting violence on an individual basis, we need not lose sight of other important clinical benefits that can be derived from our assessment data. We suggest that clinical precautions of some sort are clearly in order in this case because of the higher-than-average risk that our assessment process has established. Let us explain our reasoning.

Meehl (1954) taught us several decades ago that predictions about individuals are either right or wrong. This is a stringent test of utility. And in the assessment of dangerousness, our predictions about individuals have not been very accurate (Monahan, 1981). This finding is not surprising to those familiar with the historical literature that discusses the issues and results of individual clinical predictions (Meehl, 1954). But assessment data can also be used to classify individuals into subgroups that are defined by the presence of our best predictors of violence. And the frequency of violent acts by members of this subgroup can be expected to be higher than in the general population (in some cases it may be substantially higher).

For example, we might say that 4 individuals out of every 10 who are characterized by our best predictors of violence will actually engage in violent behavior. We cannot know in advance the actual acts specific individuals will commit, but we can know that, on the average, 4 out of 10 individuals from that subgroup will behave violently. Our point is simple. Absolute predictive accuracy for individuals is not a necessary precondition for substantially improving our knowledge about the potential for violence. Simply knowing that individuals belong to subgroups that are at higher-than-average risk of violence may be sufficient cause for taking precautions.

Applying these considerations to our example does not paint a happy prognostic picture. This couple definitely belongs to a subgroup of individuals at risk for violent behavior. We do not know if violence will actually occur, but we can be sure it will occur with people who share their characteristics more frequently than it does in the general population. Taking precautions when clients share attributes that define high-risk groups is a viable alternative to individual predictions. The only condition that could increase the risk factors for this couple would be either spouse having a family history of violence.

Individual Competence and Dangerousness

Up to this point, we have described the assessment of individual, environmental, and interactional variables that are associated with imminent clinical dangerousness. The assessment process has been mostly one dimensional—that is, how dangerous is the client. Gutheil et al. (1986) suggested a second dimension that requires careful evaluation in any attempt to accurately predict or manage dangerous clients: individual competence. Gutheil et al. (1986) suggested that clients are typically portrayed as children "in the hands of parentally responsible clinicians" (p. 124). Courts therefore expect clinicians to make responsible decisions on behalf of their irresponsible clients. However, there are few compelling reasons to believe that most clients with violent impulses cannot manage these feelings quite responsibly, at least under some conditions. Neither is it in the best interest of most clients to clinically approach them as passive victims of their own violent impulses.

To counteract the assumption of client incompetence, Gutheil et al. (1986) suggested the wisdom of assessing the client's capacity to participate in the therapeutic process in an informed and responsible manner. When properly documented, this assessment would constitute evidence of a client's capacity to understand choices, implement decisions, and act responsibly. In legal terms, it would be a clear demonstration of a client's capacity to be responsible for his or her own actions, thereby shifting the burden of accountability for the client's behavior from the therapist back to the client, where it belongs.

On the other hand, when clients are unwilling or unable to participate in the therapeutic processes in an informed and responsible manner, therapists must then be prepared to accept more responsibility for directing the affairs of their clients' lives. To illustrate this point, let us return to our previous example.

Suppose the husband has been attending outpatient individual therapy for the past 6 months. The therapist, on learning of the husband's threats to harm his wife, is alarmed and believes the level of imminent dangerousness to be moderate or high. During the session, the therapist and client discuss a number of issues concerning the best means for preventing actual violence. The therapist asks the client to consider removing the firearm, limiting alcohol consumption, including the wife in therapy for a few sessions, and increasing the frequency of therapy contacts. The client decides to participate in all these activities to reduce the threat of actual violence. Additionally, the clients believe they can control their violent impulses under these conditions, and they fully understand the consequences of their failure to do so.

This clearly demonstrates psychological competence which, when properly documented, suggests that it is not in the clients' best therapeutic interest for the therapist to assume more responsibility for client behavior than absolutely necessary. However, if the husband were to include the therapist in a delusional system with the wife and therapist plotting against him, the therapist must conclude that the husband's competence to act responsibly is impaired and accordingly must act on his client's behalf.

We hope our most essential point is clear. The decision to implement protective steps on behalf of a client should not be based entirely on the assessment of client dangerousness. A mildly dangerous client who is incompetent may require as much therapeutic direction as an extremely dangerous client who is also competent and responsible—both dimensions require careful consideration.

What Are the Legal Issues?

A legal review of this case illustration raises the following issues for consideration:

1. In the event of violence, are there other foreseeable victims in the environment where the violence is most likely to occur?

2. Can the danger in this situation be considered imminent?

3. Does the therapist have a duty to protect the wife from potential harm by her husband?

4. Are there any professional standards of care applicable to this situation?

5. Does the state in which this incident occurred have any legal statutes indicating that clinicians have a legal duty to protect innocent victims from harm by their dangerous clients?

6. If a legal duty does not exist, what are the prospects of being sued for a breach of confidentiality if a warning is used, particularly if no harm occurs after a warning is given?

7. How can therapists discharge their legal duty to protect innocent victims from harm by dangerous clients?

The next few sections discuss the clinical management of potentially dangerous clients that takes these legal considerations into account. The most pressing issues that should govern the management of clinical cases are defined by two inescapable conclusions from the assessment process. First, any method of predicting violence will produce at least as many false positives as true positives. Threats of violence are simply more common than actual violent behavior, and, consequently, practicing clinicians consistently overpredict dangerousness (Monahan, 1976; Roth & Meisel, 1977; Steadman & Cocozza, 1974).

Second, because of the high frequency of errors in predicting violence, any clinical decision to respond to predicted violence must rest on (1) acceptance of undeniable facts that most predictions of violence will be wrong and (2) basing any course of action on a risk/benefits analysis of the consequences of both accurate and inaccurate predictions.

The case management procedures we discuss are designed to reduce the risks to client welfare when predictions are wrong and to protect the integrity of the therapeutic relationship, the safety of innocent victims, and the personal well-being of the therapist.

CASE MANAGEMENT

Virtually every clinician is aware of the effects of *Tarasoff* and the problems inherent in a duty to warn. Interventions other than warning are less often discussed. Our discussion is based on the assumption that there are numerous ways of protecting third parties; warning the victim is only one of many possible interventions. We therefore discuss the case management of dangerous clients with regard to:

1. Forming a new therapeutic alliance with informed consent
2. Clinical strategies and alternatives
3. Clinical illustration

Forming a New Therapeutic Alliance

Once a clinician determines that a client is at risk for violence, we suggest that the therapy process stop until a new therapeutic alliance is discussed and formed. Regrettably, we cannot say much more about the point at which a client can be considered "at risk"; we have already discussed the areas of inquiry that should be covered in making such an assessment. No cutoff scores or patterns of responses settle this question—this is clinical judgment in its purest form.

So, after a clinician has made a proper assessment and determined that a particular client is at risk for violence, we suggest that: the clinician openly and candidly discuss with the client reasons for concluding that the client is at greater-than-average risk for violence compared to other clients. Many potential therapeutic benefits can be suggested to justify such an approach. But our purpose, at least initially, is more limited and specific: to form a therapeutic alliance with the client that is dedicated, at least in part, to helping the client understand and then control those factors that could harm the client as a result of the harm the client could inflict on others.

The first step in forming this new therapeutic alliance is to determine the degree to which the client can "own up" or "agree" with the clinician's estimates of the client's "potential" dangerousness. If the client and therapist share similar concerns about the client's potential for violence, then the next steps in forming a therapeutic alliance are relatively easy; they include such fundamental factors as (1) agreeing on therapeutic goals; (2) intensifying treatment; (3) setting ground rules about the client's use of alcohol, drugs, or weapons; (4) team-building conversations between the therapist and client about their mutual commitment to prevent any violent acts by the client; and (5) clarifying options and procedures that might be followed if the client starts to lose control. At the end of this process, a working therapeutic alliance exists if the client and therapist mutually agree on estimates of violence and therapist and client role expectations when dangerous situations arise and share a commitment to reducing the client's potential for violent acts.

If the therapist and client do not share similar conceptions about the client's potential violence, then a meaningful therapeutic alliance cannot be formed. The client and therapist must now very carefully and precisely consider, discuss, review, and evaluate each other's opinions. The goal is to find common ground for future therapeutic work. But this process should not be confused with psychotherapy, which would be an unfortunate mistake for both client and therapist. This process is really a form of pretherapy clarification that gives both the client and therapist the information they need to determine if they can find a mutually acceptable basis for a therapeutic relationship. These discussion, evaluation, and review processes should continue until the therapist and client acquire a mutually understood and acceptable purpose for psychotherapy or discontinue their dialogue.

A New Therapeutic Alliance and Informed Consent. The actual legal/ethical principles that govern the new therapeutic relationship we just described are fundamentally different from those that govern more traditional therapeutic relationships. Confidentiality is more readily compromised because of the growing influence of the *Tarasoff* doctrine, and client welfare is more easily sacrificed for the benefits of social welfare. In clinical cases that involve potential violence, the therapist is literally a double agent. Therapists have legal obligations to the society in which they live, and they have legal/ethical obligations to the clients they serve. Regrettably, these dual obligations can conflict with each other. The only possible solution to this confusing and ambiguous state of affairs is for all relevant parties to have the same understanding about the rules and expectations that govern therapeutic relationships.

To this end, we suggest that once a therapeutic alliance is formed, the therapist accept the responsibility for reemphasizing and informing the client fully and completely of the (1) limits of confidentiality in the therapist/client relationship, (2) therapist's obligation to protect innocent third parties and some of the more common means that could be exercised in meeting this duty, (3) inherent fallibility of the procedures for assessing risk, and (4) therapist's prior experience with potentially dangerous clients. Anything less is an ethical violation of serious proportions. A client simply cannot make an informed decision about willingness to participate, or continuing to participate, in therapy without knowing and being reminded of the limits to confidentiality and the treatment plan that currently prevail when dangerousness might be involved. These rules are so unusual that it is easy to understand why a client could angrily turn on a therapist if these rules were not made clear and the client unexpectedly found the therapist breaking assumed confidences and protecting the welfare of others at the possible expense of the client!

Informed Consent and Individual Competence.   A therapeutic alliance based on informed consent is also a way for the therapist to establish and demonstrate the client's level of competence and personal responsibility. Please remember that the typical courtroom assumption is that clients "are children in the hands of parentally responsible children" (Gutheil et al., 1986, p. 124), which almost automatically creates the expectation that a good therapist is one who makes many responsible decisions on behalf of less responsible clients. While the validity and therapeutic folly of this view are obvious to most clinicians, it is nevertheless a psychological reality in many courtrooms. Obviously then, the more clients demonstrate their capacity, or lack of it, for meaningful and responsible participation in the therapeutic process, the easier it becomes to determine how responsible they are for their conduct outside the consulting room.

Thus, forming a new therapeutic relationship serves three important functions in the therapeutic process. First, it helps clarify the limits of confidentiality and other risks to the client as a result of participating in therapy. Second, it helps identify the client's level of personal competence, which is an important consideration in selecting the types of clinical interventions that will be most useful for client care. Third, it provides documented evidence that can be used in a courtroom to justify a clinician's judgment about the client's capacity to understand personal issues, make important choices, and be held personally accountable for conduct outside the courtroom. (The issues of informed consent and competence are more fully discussed in Chapter 6.)

Clinical Interventions

Up to this point, we have suggested two essential steps for minimizing the opportunities for legal liability when dealing with potentially dangerous clients. First, we provided conceptual guidelines for the assessment of dangerousness that are based on the most current research findings. Second, we suggested a way of restructuring the therapeutic relationship so that it reflects the legal/ethical realities of our time. Before proceeding with our discussion of basic clinical strategies for dealing with clinically dangerous clients, we wish to remind the reader of the most consequential implications of the *Tarasoff* doctrine for clinical practice:

1. One of the most fundamental criticisms of *Tarasoff* is its legal foundations. Latham (1975) and Griffith and Griffith (1978) pointed out that the therapist has *no right to control* the client (outpatient treatment) since the client/therapist relationship is not a custodial one. There are cases where the courts have ruled that physicians must warn third parties in noncustodial relationships (for example, *Jones v. Stenko*), but these cases involved a

contagious disease. Invoking this general rule for psychotherapists is inappropriate because the physician, unlike the psychotherapist, can reliably diagnose contagious diseases and predict the consequences for those who come into contact with the disease. Psychotherapists are not able to reliably predict dangerousness or its particular consequences.

2. The inability to predict dangerousness creates another dilemma for the therapist (Griffith & Griffith, 1978). If therapists underestimate the probability of violence and do not warn when they should, they are at risk for failing to protect the innocent victim. If they overpredict dangerousness and warn a potential victim when such action is not warranted, they are at risk from two other sources. First, the client could sue for breach of confidentiality. Second, the innocent victim could sue for the creation of unnecessary stress and anxiety. The ambiguities inherent in the *Tarasoff* doctrine create *a number of double-bind dilemmas for the clinician.*

3. The mere introduction of information that may compromise the *fiduciary relationship that binds the client and therapist in a common cause may undermine the entire therapeutic process.* Confidentiality, trust, and honesty are essential ingredients for any effective psychotherapeutic relationship. A client may be unwilling to fully disclose personal dilemmas in the absence of a confidential relationship in which the therapist's silence is assured both legally and ethically. Ultimately, this unfortunate state of affairs may actually increase public violence by creating conditions that would virtually preclude the potentially violent clients from seeking treatment.

Nevertheless, and no matter how undesirable the current legal doctrines may first appear, the doctrines are still the general context within which clinical intervention takes place with potentially dangerous clients. With these considerations in mind, we now outline a range of clinical responses to dangerous clients as well as several of the more preferred options.

Common Clinical Strategies. A recent study (Botkin & Nietzel, 1987) provided empirical data with which the development of a comprehensive standard of care for the treatment of homicidal or assaultive clients was begun. Based on their review of existing literature and a survey of practicing psychotherapists, these investigators identified 46 clinical interventions that had been used or suggested to manage dangerous clients. These interventions were then rated by a national sample of 101 practicing psychotherapists on the following three dimensions: (1) frequency of use, (2) perceived effectiveness with clients, and (3) perceived effectiveness for protecting innocent victims.

These 46 clinical interventions were then statistically collapsed into the following nine categories based on the internal consistency of the ratings:

1. *Hospitalization.* Voluntary or involuntary hospitalization as the primary intervention.

2. *Diagnosis/referral to others.* Consultation, referral, assessment, or differential diagnosis as the primary intervention.

3. *Confidentiality.* Breaching confidentiality to warn the police, victim, or others as the primary intervention.

4. *Management of environment.* Reducing alcohol consumption, removing weapons, getting family members to stay with the client, or having the client stay away from the potential victim as the primary interventions.

5. *Involve others in treatment.* Involving family, significant others, or the potential victim in the treatment process as the primary intervention.

6. *Build rapport.* Building rapport or increasing affiliation between therapist and client as the primary interventions.

7. *In-session behavioral strategies.* Cognitive/behavioral, social learning, assertiveness training, contracting, and other similar behavioral strategies as the primary interventions.

8. *In-session evocative strategies.* Development of insight, exploration of affective states, or the use of cathartic techniques as the primary interventions.

9. *Contingency setting by therapist.* Interventions that made continuing therapy contingent on successfully completing specific requirements for managing dangerousness.

A factor analysis of these nine categories was performed to determine their underlying factor structure. A three-factor solution, based on the scree plot test, accounted for approximately 70% of the variance.

Factor I: Protecting Victims.   Factor I included the following subscales with loadings greater than .5: breaching confidentiality, management of environment, involve others in treatment, and contingency setting by therapist. Botkin and Nietzel (1987) suggested that this factor represents interventions intended to protect potential victims.

Factor II: Therapy as Usual.   Factor II included the following subscales with loadings greater than .5: management of environment, build rapport, in-session behavioral strategies, and in-session evocative strategies. This factor was labeled "therapy as usual" and represented interventions primarily directed at treating the client through typical therapeutic procedures as a means of reducing the danger of violence.

Factor III: Diagnosis/Referral.   Factor III included two subscales with loadings greater than .5: hospitalization and diagnosis/referral to others. This factor was labeled involvement of medical or other specialists in caring for the client.

While Botkin and Nietzel (1987) reported numerous findings, the most pertinent results for our discussion are summarized in Table 4-1. The data in this table summarize how practicing psychotherapists rate each of the nine categories of clinical interventions with regard to (1) frequency of use, (2) perceived effectiveness with clients, and (3) perceived effectiveness for protecting innocent victims.

Table 4-1   Preferred Interventions for Managing Dangerous Clients*

Subscale	Factor	Use	Rank Order of Intervention	
			Effectiveness	Protective
Breach confidentiality	I	4	7	2
Involve others in treatment	I	9	8†	6†
Contingency setting by therapist	I	8	9†	7†
Management of environment	I, II	3	3	2
Build rapport	II	2	2	4
In-session behavioral strategies	II	7	4	5
In-session evocative strategies	II	6	5	8†
Hospitalization	III	1	1	1
Diagnosis/referral to others	III	5	6	9†

*Based on Botkin and Nietzel (1987).

†Overall mean was below 5 (midpoint) and thus represented interventions generally rated unfavorably.

Generally, the usefulness of the case management procedures parallels different levels of client dangerousness. The procedures described in "therapy as usual" appear to be most useful with low levels of dangerousness. As dangerousness increases, however, therapists must exercise more initiative and responsibility for client welfare with interventions such as voluntary or involuntary hospitalization and warning potential victims or the police. Herlihy and Sheeley (1988), as well as Gross, Southard, Lamb, and Weinberger (1987), developed decision trees that graphically demonstrate the increased therapist activity and direction required as client dangerousness increases.

For the purposes of our discussion, we discuss case management procedures that match three levels of client dangerousness and competence: (1) mild, (2) moderate, and (3) severe.

Mild: Therapy As Usual.   Clinical interventions for the mildly dangerous fit into Botkin's and Nietzel's (1987) "therapy as usual" category. Our assumption is that most clinicians have listened to angry clients make meaningless threats. Typically, clinicians approach this type of anger with traditional therapeutic techniques such as catharsis, insight, interpretation, problem solving, and communication skills. Occasionally the clinician may include those who are the target of the anger in future sessions, particularly if they are family members. In general, however, the therapist helps clients explore the meaning and origin of their anger as well as develop more appropriate methods for expressing it.

Table 4-2 summarizes a number of treatment techniques for managing this level of dangerousness. In reviewing these techniques, however, it is important to remember that as the level of client dangerousness increases, the clinician must start considering more clearly defined and controlling therapeutic steps.

Table 4-2   Therapy as Usual

In-Session Evocative Strategies
  Discuss motivation and consequences of actions.
  Use gestalt "empty chair" for expression of emotions.
  Discuss the plan of action and consequences.
  Explore the self-punitive implications of the client's actions.
  Encourage ventilation of hostile emotions.
  Explore underlying frustrations, including nonviolent ways of achieving goals.
  Explore options.
  Focus on exactly what the client says she or he is going to do and how the client
    feels.
  Remain nonjudgmental.

In-Session Behavioral Strategies
  Contracting nonviolence.
  Assertiveness training.
  Cognitive awareness of triggering events.
  Direct instructions delaying aggressive actions.
  Explore precipitating behaviors and emotions and create ways to avoid them.
  Encourage client to focus on positive elements of the situation.
  Extinguish hostility and reinforce nonhostile attitudes.
  Use RET to eliminate irrational thinking concerning the dangerousness.

Build Rapport
  Give phone number and instruct client to call in a crisis.
  Establish personal bond and then express disapproval of violence.
  Take all threats seriously.
  Communicate collaborative nature of the relationship (working together to prevent
    violence).

Moderate: Intensifying Treatment.   Although it may seem a bit unusual at first glance, we suggest that moderate levels of client dangerousness pose the greatest risk of liability to practicing clinicians, for several reasons. Remember, this is the first stage at which clinicians start earnestly considering the methods they may use to discharge their duty to protect innocent victims. The methods could involve involuntary hospitalization or breaching confidentiality, potentially liable actions if they are not based on sound clinical judgment and evidence. But more importantly, no matter how careful the clinician may be, errors of clinical judgment are more likely at moderate levels of dangerousness. Extreme deviations are generally easier to recognize and respond to in almost any clinical activity. And the same is true of client dangerousness. Extremely high or low levels of dangerousness are usually easier to recognize and respond to than moderate levels, which is why the assessment of client competence is such a crucial consideration at moderate levels of dangerousness. Let us explain and illustrate this point more fully.

Cases involving severe dangerousness will almost automatically require hospitalization or breaching confidentiality—failure to do so is an invitation to be held liable for negligence. Similarly, cases of mild dangerousness hardly ever involve breaching confidentiality or involuntary hospitalization—any attempt to usurp the client's prerogatives on these matters requires extraordinary justification if a lawsuit is to be avoided or was once filed.

But moderate levels of dangerousness are another matter entirely. There are no clearly demarcated guidelines or suggestions for case management at this level, which is precisely why client competence is the crucial consideration in case management decisions at this level: It is more reliably assessed and more relevant to clinical decision making. In general terms, we suggest the following procedures, which, if faithfully followed, substantially reduce the risk of liability in this dangerous area of clinical work:

1. At moderate levels of dangerousness and low competence, the clinical considerations involved with severe levels of dangerousness are probably the most applicable.

2. At moderate levels of dangerousness and high competence, the clinical considerations involved with mild levels of dangerousness are probably the most applicable.

3. At moderate levels of dangerousness with moderate competence, intensifying treatment is probably the most reasonable approach provided that the clinician can seriously consider
   a. Having the work on the case supervised by a colleague
   b. Carefully documenting the basis and evidence involved in all clinical decisions
   c. Obtaining a second opinion on all case management decisions
   d. Seeking legal consultation and review of case management decisions.

Clients who can satisfy the usual criteria for being considered at least moderately competent fit best into a case management strategy we call *intensifying treatment.* That is, when clients demonstrate an acceptable capacity to understand the meaning and consequences of their behavior, are willing to take appropriate self-regulating steps, such as calling the therapist in an emergency, and understand and participate in the therapeutic process in a meaningful way, they demonstrate their capacity to be held legally responsible for their own behavior outside the consulting room. These are the conditions under which moderately dangerous clients may be managed through intensifying treatment and other outpatient strategies.

If a client fails to demonstrate these attributes, the therapist may want to start discussing if the client needs hospitalization. Remember, the Botkin and Nietzel (1987) survey indicated that clinicians rate hospitalization as the preferred method for handling dangerousness on all three of their dimensions (frequency of use, effectiveness, protection). In one respect, this is not a surprising result because such intervention gives potential victims maximum protection and requires little or minimum breach of confidentiality. It also transfers the most libelous clinical responsibilities from the therapist to the hospital. Hospitalization is also the case management strategy Gross, Southard, Lamb, and Weinberger (1987) and Herlihy and Sheeley (1988) suggested where danger is imminent; when danger is not imminent, they suggest intensifying treatment. Clearly, hospitalization has much to recommend it from a case management point of view.

However, hospitalization of dangerous clients may be more psychologically desirable for the clinician than it is legally feasible. Wexler (1981) astutely pointed out that most clients who threaten to kill are afflicted with characterological disorders, not psychotic disorders. Therefore, attempting to commit these individuals will fail under most state statutes because (1) they do not have a "severe mental illness," and (2) short-term hospitalization is seldom beneficial to clients with problems rooted in characterological deficiencies. Additionally, unwarranted attempts at involuntary hospitalization are themselves libelous acts that should be of concern to clinicians.

The respondents in the Botkin and Nietzel (1987) survey also rated several of the more traditional psychotherapeutic techniques rather favorably. *Building rapport* was the clinical intervention rated second for effectiveness and frequency of use and rated fourth for protecting innocent victims. The logic behind these high ratings seem rather straightforward and is probably an expression of faith in the therapeutic process by practicing therapists. Presumably, the stronger the therapeutic relationship, the more carefully and candidly violent impulses can be explored and ameliorated.

But this logic has serious shortcomings. If there is a disproportional number of characterological disorders among the clients who threaten to kill (and there probably is), then relationship issues are probably not the most important considerations in the treatment process. Rather, it is the ability of the therapist to help the client become more self-regulating by setting contingencies, enforcing limits, and providing differential reinforcement and punishment. There are ample "expert witnesses" who would make this point on the witness stand.

Furthermore, the link between the quality of the *therapeutic relationship* and *protecting innocent victims* is tenuous at best, particularly in a hostile legal environment. The value of this intervention represents a leap of logic that psychotherapists are more willing to make than lawyers would be willing to tolerate.

Finally, *management of the environment* rated third on clinical effectiveness and frequency of use, fourth on protecting innocent victims. This intervention includes reducing alcohol consumption, removing weapons, getting family members to stay with clients, and keeping the client away from potential victims. Several observations about these activities should be made. First, they may be easy to do. Second, they are interventions that non-mental health professionals (judges, lawyers, juries) can readily understand as responsible protective steps. Third, they are inherently helpful. On these grounds alone, it seems appropriate to include them in any treatment plan irrespective of any other treatment considerations.

There are other important reasons, however, for seriously considering these interventions. When Botkin and Nietzel (1987) compared the ratings of clinicians considered "experts" with less experienced clinicians, they uncovered two additional points. First, experts rated *management of environment* and *involving others in treatment* as more useful of all three dimensions. *Building rapport* and *in-session behavioral strategies* were also rated as more effective and used more frequently. Collectively, these four categories suggest that the expert is more likely to take a directive role managing dangerous clients. The expert takes more responsibility for the therapeutic relationship, the client's environment, in-session behavior, and involving others in treatment. The potential involvement of others in the treatment process, particularly potential victims, is an important element to notice: This category was ranked "least likely" to be used overall, while experts saw it as a useful and preferable intervention.

We suggest, therefore, that management of the environment take precedence over hospitalization whenever possible for moderately dangerous clients. The problem with this approach is that the client remains unrestrained, which makes the client's level of demonstrated competence a paramount consideration. It would be difficult to justify asking clients to give up weapons, participate in behavioral contracting, stay away from alcohol and drugs, or evaluate the risk and benefits of any therapeutic procedure without a demonstrated ability to be at least moderately self-regulating. Table 4-3 on page 78 lists other possible methods of intensifying treatment.

In those cases where warnings may appear necessary, we suggest that attempts be made to have clients accept responsibility for this process or be deeply involved in it. To the degree the client will act responsibly in warning potential victims (see Table 4-4), the integrity of the therapeutic relationship can be preserved, allowing the therapist to continue in the primary fiduciary duties to the client.

Severe: Protecting Potential Victims.   With some clients, there comes a point of imminent and reasonably predictable danger that requires the therapist to shift focus from the client's therapeutic welfare to potential victim's protection. This is the point at which the potential victim, the police, and perhaps relevant others should all be warned (see Table 4-4 for a list of possible management methods). If the client appears to meet the criterion for involuntary commitment, then these procedures should be initiated.

Interestingly, Botkin's and Nietzel's (1987) survey indicated that clinicians do not look favorably on these steps. Breaching confidentiality to warn the police or the victim is seen as one of the more useful ways of protecting victims; it is, however, rated rather low for treatment effectiveness in treating the client and frequency of use. Many clinicians appear to see breaching client confidentiality useful only as a last resort (see Table 4-4).

Table 4-3 Intensifying Treatment

Managing the Environment

Ask a relative to stay with the client.

Commit the client, to avoid contact with the potential victim.

Encourage placing weapons in a safe place.

Attempt to eliminate or reduce alcohol or drug consumption.

Increase the frequency of sessions.

Involve Others in Treatment

Encourage the client to invite the potential victim to treatment.

Notify significant others and give helpful suggestions.

Discuss with family members or others how they have contained the client's violence in the past.

Involve the victim in family therapy if victim is a family member.

Diagnose/Referral

Refer to a physician for medication.

Obtain complete physical, neurological, competency, and personality evaluation.

Carefully assess client cognitive functioning, controls, and willingness to resolve problems in therapy.

Consult with colleagues who have experience with violent clients.

Hospitalization

Seek hospitalization.

Have client hospitalized by family members.

Seek voluntary hospitalization if possible.

Contingency Setting

Give full disclosure of steps you will take if the client becomes dangerous.

Tell client you cannot be the therapist if strong consideration of violence continues.

As a last resort, tell clients that if he or she does not seek hospitalization, therapy will terminate and family members will be notified that hospitalization is recommended.

Table 4-4 Protecting Potential Victims

---

1. As a final recourse, tell the client you believe she or he will commit the violent act and that you will do everything you can to stop it.
2. Be firm about your willingness to break confidentiality if necessary.
3. Set a limit within which the client must take positive actions or else notify police and victims.
4. Break confidentiality and notify targets and family members.
5. Notify other treating professionals.
6. Notify police.

SUMMARY

We reviewed the conceptual and empirical literature on the assessment of dangerousness. The technical problems involved in accurately predicting violence are monumental, and we have little reason to be optimistic about their resolution in the near future. However, we can assess the personal, environmental, and combined factors that indicate a higher-than-average risk for violence. While this level of assessment does not allow us to predict with any degree of functional accuracy the specific individuals who will actually commit violent acts, it does help us identify the types of people most often involved in violence.

In general, future violence is best predicted from past violence and an understanding of the environmental "triggers" associated with it. Even though a higher level of professional modesty regarding our ability to accurately predict violence is called for, it is still an essential clinical activity. We reviewed the conceptual considerations and empirical evidence that are most useful in guiding this evaluation.

We also identified and discussed the more pressing pitfalls that can accompany clinical work with potentially dangerous clients. We outlined the steps involved in developing a new therapeutic alliance with clients once the therapist judges the clients at higher-than-average risk for violence. This alliance is based on two primary sets of considerations. First, the therapist and client have a mutually accepted and shared understanding of the primacy of preventing the client from being harmed as a result of the harm they may inflict on others. Second, the client is fully informed of the legal obligations imposed on the therapist as a result of current legal doctrines. Only after the client fully understands and accepts the dual nature of the therapist's obligation to the client, potential victims, and society in general does the actual process of therapy continue. Otherwise, it must be responsibly terminated.

Additionally, we identified and discussed the perceived value of a full repertoire of clinical interventions that can be used with dangerous clients. Generally, the choice of therapeutic interventions can be based on two underlying considerations: levels of client dangerousness and competence. The more dangerous and/or the less competent the client, the more direction and responsibility the therapist exercises in case management.

Generally, practicing clinicians view hospitalization as the intervention of choice, and for good reason. This option has a number of benefits to recommend it. We suggested, however, that this practice may be more desirable than feasible for a variety of different reasons. Improving the therapeutic relationship is also a commonly accepted and valued practice when working with dangerous clients. We noted, however, that this practice may have little to recommend it in a hostile, legal environment, where it may be rightly or wrongly viewed as insufficient. Finally, we discussed the value of the therapist attempting to manage the client's environment by removing weapons, reducing alcohol consumption, or having family members stay with potentially dangerous clients. We suggested that these interventions are beneficial both legally and therapeutically and should be seriously considered in addition to any other treatment considerations.

CLINICAL ILLUSTRATION

We have three reasons for presenting the following in-depth case analysis of a dangerous client. First, it illustrates the underlying complexity of the legal and ethical issues involved in clinical work with dangerous clients. As you will see, continuous review and evaluation of the appropriateness and adequacy of case management procedures are called for. Second, the therapist had a lawyer on retainer during the entire treatment process. Reading these consultation dialogues will provide an informative review of the form and substance legal issues take in a real case. Third, it is important to illustrate the applications of the principles we introduced in this chapter.

Emergency Care

It was about 8:00 in the evening. The therapist had just finished what he assumed was the last session of the evening. As he prepared to lock the reception area, the door opened, and a middle-aged man walked in, looked around, and then asked if a doctor was available. There was nothing particularly unusual about him—he dressed neatly, did not appear overly distressed, and gave the impression of being coherent and deliberate. He certainly did not appear ready to commit a murder.

Even though the therapist was anxious to go home, he asked the stranger what he wanted. The man replied that he was on the verge of a very important decision and felt he should talk with somebody about it. He did not know where else to go, so he came to the clinic. The therapist assumed that the man was maybe filing for a divorce, possibly quitting his job, or even perhaps disappearing without a trace. The therapist decided to talk with him, thinking this might be an important conversation for the client. He usually would not accept walk-ins without an intake evaluation, but in this situation it seemed that an exception to the rule would be both proper and potentially profitable for the client.

Once seated in the consulting room, the therapist started the conversation by asking what the stranger, Brad, had on his mind. With only the slightest hint of nervousness, Brad cleared his throat and said he was thinking about killing Helen this evening. She was his supervisor at work, and he reported that she had been insulting him publicly for about 9 months. For whatever reason, it appeared that she had crossed the line this afternoon. The therapist asked how he was going to kill her. Brad pulled a razor-blade knife from his jacket pocket and said he was going to slice her face open and then pour acid on the wounds. He opened a small paper bag to show the therapist a small bottle of muriatic acid.

Two hours later, it was clear to the therapist that this client was not mentally ill in the legal sense of the term. His comprehension of right and wrong was unimpaired, as was his understanding of the consequences of his behavior. His level of dangerousness was more difficult to assess. He reported no history of violent behavior in his past. He also came to the clinic to talk instead of proceeding directly to Helen's home. Furthermore, he now thought it would be best if he had several sessions with the therapist before deciding what to do. However, the fact that he was carrying a knife and a bottle of acid deeply troubled the therapist. Even though the client complied to surrendering his weapons with little hesitation when asked to do so, the therapist knew that they could be easily replaced at a dozen or more stores. The therapist suspected that the catharsis the client experienced by openly expressing his anger toward Helen had substantially reduced his capacity for actual violence.

At this point, the therapist really did not know what to do. Involuntary hospitalization was not feasible. The client may have actually been dangerous, but he certainly was not mentally ill. (Both conditions were required for involuntary commitment in the state where this situation occurred.) Additionally, the client showed a real interest in seeing the therapist in order to "talk" this problem out, and he had agreed to not see Helen before another session the next morning. On the other hand, the client's anger was based on a long history of perceived mistreatment and accumulated rage, and he had the means to inflict a heinous form of violent retribution. It was simply not possible to predict whether this relatively quiet man was about to explode or whether he would sink back into his relatively private world of psychic frustration. The therapist felt that any attempt to warn the potential victim at this point would seriously jeopardize the fragile therapeutic alliance that had been forming during the last 2 hours. This would destroy the best and, perhaps, the only opportunity that this individual might have to learn how to cope with his suppressed feelings of anger without committing a violent act.

The therapist quickly decided to call the attorney the clinic had on retainer for situations such as this. For the first 15 minutes of the conversation, the therapist carefully reviewed the events that had transpired the preceding hour. The remainder of the conversation is transcribed below. The footnotes included throughout the dialogue provide insights into legal issues that would have important practical implications if facts about the clinical case were slightly different.

Questions About the Therapist/Client Relationship

ATTORNEY: OK, I think I have a general picture of your problem. Before I make any recommendations, however, I need to ask you a number of more specific questions. I want you to understand that these first few questions are important because they will define the nature of the relationship between you and the client. The whole premise of liability is the existence of a special relationship between you and the client that allows you the *right or ability to control* the client. If we do encounter legal action, the first issue may be demonstrating the presence or absence of a special relationship. Are you ready?

THERAPIST: That's very puzzling to me. I don't see how I ever have control over an outpatient client. What do you mean by *control*? Furthermore, my understanding is that a special relationship or fiduciary duty for my client was established the minute I invited the client into my office to talk.

ATTORNEY: The special relationship I'm referring to is distinct from your fiduciary duty to the client. Your fiduciary duty stems from your obligations to the client because of your expertise and his position of reliance on your skill. The special relationship I'm referring to is based on your right or ability to control the client's conduct. The presence of this ability or right to control is the legal basis for holding a therapist liable for his client's actions.

THERAPIST: I still don't understand. I can't see that I ever have the power to *control* a client's conduct.

ATTORNEY: The law does not require this control in absolute terms. The fact is that most therapists have a unique relationship with their clients that results in sufficient influence which the law recognizes enough control to hold them legally liable for their client's acts.

THERAPIST: Are you saying that I can be held liable for my client's behavior whether I can actually control his behavior or not?

ATTORNEY: Yes. Because of your special relationship with your clients, you have a legal duty to either control the behavior of your dangerous clients or to protect innocent parties. Are you ready for my questions now?

THERAPIST: Go ahead.

ATTORNEY: OK, I will start with questions about your relationship with the client. The person we're dealing with was not an inpatient, the person was an outpatient—is that right?

THERAPIST: That's right.[2]

ATTORNEY: And exactly how long have you been seeing this client?

THERAPIST: As I said earlier, I never saw him before tonight—this was our first meeting. Is the special relationship that you're talking about established in the first visit?

ATTORNEY: Probably. It will likely hinge on the content of the session. Courts have given little guidance as to what is required to find this "special relationship," but it is reasonable to believe that it does not suddenly appear at some point; rather, it exists along a continuum. It is reasonable to assume that the relationship moves along this continuum as the therapist gains influence

---

[2]Where the client is an inpatient, the degree of control the therapist exercises is greatly enhanced and the "special relationship" more readily found. While RESTATEMENT (SECOND) OF TORTS Section 315 is relied on for finding a special relationship between therapist and patient in the outpatient context, courts have relied on RESTATEMENT Section 319 in the context of negligent releases. As an example of a relationship imposing liability, Section 319 provides: "One who takes charge of a third person whom he knows or should know to be likely to cause bodily harm to others if not controlled is under a duty to exercise reasonable care to control the third person to prevent him from doing such harm."

over the client and knows, or should have known, about the client's potential to harm others.[3]

THERAPIST: Are you saying that because this was a walk-in emergency and I had to make assessments and judgments quickly that the basis for my liability could be minimized?

ATTORNEY: Maybe. It will depend on the content of your conversation with the client and what you should have been able to ascertain from your session with him according to your own profession's standards.

Questions About the Client's Communication to the Therapist

ATTORNEY: I'm going to ask a series of questions about what the client communicated to you that would suggest he might be dangerous. These objective facts, coupled with questions I will ask you later about your subjective assessment, will be the basis of my legal opinion about your obligation to control his behavior or issue warnings to potential innocent victims. These are important questions, and you will need to clearly differentiate facts from your opinions.

THERAPIST: OK, go ahead.

ATTORNEY: Did the client express any threats of violence?

THERAPIST: Yes.[4] He threatened to kill his employer.

ATTORNEY: In what context and manner were the threats expressed?

THERAPIST: Verbally.

ATTORNEY: No, that's not what I mean. I assume that in some situations you prod clients to express threats as part of their therapy or in expressing hidden feelings. What I need to know is if this client's threats can be understood or explained as anything other than a present intent to harm.

THERAPIST: In other words, did I create the condition that provoked the threat?

ATTORNEY: Partly, but did the threat represent an intent to act?

THERAPIST: The threat was spontaneously volunteered, and at the time of the threat it was my opinion that he actually intended to harm his supervisor.

ATTORNEY: OK, how specific were the threats as to the time and manner in which they would be carried out?

THERAPIST: Extremely specific. He said he was going to kill her tonight by cutting her with a razor blade and pouring acid in the wounds. He indicated that

[3]Courts have largely evaded substantive analysis of the "special relationship" issue. Neither the RESTATEMENT nor judicial statements have made clear whether it is the frequency or the intensity of sessions that give rise to the "special relationship." Although unclear, it is reasonable to believe that the "special relationship" begins to appear as the patient becomes increasingly subject to the therapist's influence. Both intensity and frequency of sessions are relevant to these criteria.

[4]If the patient has not communicated express threat of violence, it should be determined if behavior that may indicate violent intent has been exhibited and to further determine the regularity and intensity of that behavior.

he stopped by the clinic because he wanted to talk to someone before taking such drastic action.

ATTORNEY: Did he give you the name of the victim?

THERAPIST: I didn't ask specifically.

ATTORNEY: Were you in a position when he left your office to readily ascertain the victim's identity?

THERAPIST: Yes,[5] but not from specific information he gave me.

ATTORNEY: If anything unpleasant happens tonight, you need to understand that the law will hold you accountable for what you *should* have found out as well as what you actually knew.

THERAPIST: Oh, great!

ATTORNEY: Do you know where the victim lives?

THERAPIST: No, not specifically. It's probably a couple of blocks from here.

ATTORNEY: Were there any other things that he described that would allow you to specifically know when or where the victim would be attacked?

THERAPIST: Well, at a general level, it was clear that she lives within a mile or two of here and that the client could be there in 5 or 10 minutes in a car. I know enough about the potential victim to get her name from the company she works for, and I assume I could get her address from a phone book.

ATTORNEY: You understand this is not what I wanted to hear from you!

THERAPIST: Why don't you just wait and comfort me later!

ATTORNEY: What provoked his anger?

THERAPIST: His anger was a result of several years of frustration with his boss at work. Apparently an incident took place today that seems to be the straw that broke the camel's back.

ATTORNEY: What I need to know is if his anger was caused by a person, a relationship, or some event.

THERAPIST: It seems to be the result of his growing frustration over the way his boss supervises his work.

ATTORNEY: Are the factors that provoked his anger likely to continue? Are they likely to get worse? Also, is his agitation likely to get worse if the factors remain constant?

THERAPIST: Your question is not answerable. At this point, I would assume that the problems that provoked his anger will continue, but I have no way of knowing that. In fact, if I spoke with his supervisor, I might hear an entirely different version of the whole story. You must remember this was an unexpected walk-in emergency.

---

[5]When the victim is specifically identifiable, it is also important to determine whether persons closely related to the potential victim are likely to be harmed by the threatened attack. The therapist's duty to protect may extend to persons foreseeable near the victim, such as children of the victim, who may be endangered by the patient's violence.

If the victim's identity is not readily identifiable, the inquiry shifts to a broader examination of whether a group or class of persons is foreseeably endangered. If a class or group can be identified, the size of the group is important. The policy justifications for issuing warnings are attenuated when the size of the group undermines the utility of the warning.

ATTORNEY: Well, is he going to work tomorrow!

THERAPIST: I can't answer that question for him!

ATTORNEY: Then we better assume that he is going to work and that the same type of incident could recur!

THERAPIST: Why would we assume that when we really don't know!

ATTORNEY: Because you may have a legal duty to control this client or protect potential victims, and I would prefer to assume a worst case scenario.

THERAPIST: Right!

ATTORNEY: OK, you don't know then if the setting that created his anger will continue, nor do you know if it will intensify?

THERAPIST: No, I do not know, but it would seem very reasonable to assume that things will continue just as they have been in the past or get worse.

ATTORNEY: If I understand this situation correctly, the facts of the case are as follows: (1) this is a new walk-in client, (2) who is threatening to kill his employer, (3) because of growing frustrations over the way his work is supervised, (4) who has a lethal weapon in hand, (5) who has a clearly identified victim in mind, and (6) who stopped in your office to talk to you before actually going through with such drastic plans. Have I left anything out?

THERAPIST: No, that seems to have covered everything so far.

ATTORNEY: OK, and you are in a position to foresee the client's opportunity to act?

THERAPIST: That's right.

Questions About the Therapist's Clinical Assessment

ATTORNEY: Alright, then, the next series of questions will focus on your knowledge about the client and your ability to predict whether he will carry out the threat. The most important criterion for imposing liability is foreseeability of harm. I will use this information, together with the facts you've just described, for two purposes: To determine whether a legal duty to a third party has been triggered and to ensure that your actions conform to applicable professional standards. Do you know if the client had a prior history of violence?

THERAPIST: It depends on what you mean by *history* and *violence*. If you ask if he has had fights with his wife, the answer is yes. If you want to know if he has spanked his children harder than he may have meant to, the answer is yes. You are using terms that don't have clear clinical definitions.

ATTORNEY: Let me ask the question another way: "Do you know about his propensity for violence?"

THERAPIST: Most of the time he is a quiet, shy, retiring person. No one would assume him to be a violent person.

ATTORNEY: Does he have any history of actually harming other people?

THERAPIST: Not that he reported to me. He does, however, have a history of accumulating frustrations up to a point of exasperation and then blowing off a lot of steam.[6]

ATTORNEY: How does he blow off the steam?

THERAPIST: Verbally—he denied any prior physical violence.

ATTORNEY: How much do you know about the frequency, magnitude, or recency of these episodes?

THERAPIST: They're irregular and infrequent.

ATTORNEY: What do you mean by infrequent?

THERAPIST: According to his report, he can go for several months and appear to be a shy, quiet, retiring person.

ATTORNEY: How much do you know about the magnitude of the episodes that he has had?

THERAPIST: He reported what I would consider moderate, occasionally intense levels of anger. During these episodes, he yells and screams and appears to be in a different state of mind.

ATTORNEY: Do you know if the client has an arrest record?

THERAPIST: No. What do you mean by "know"?

ATTORNEY: Did you ask him if he has ever been arrested?

THERAPIST: No.

ATTORNEY: OK, let me advise you that it's more important that you have asked the questions than that you know what the correct answers were. You can't be held accountable for his deceit, but you may at some point be held accountable for questions that you should have asked but didn't. OK, was the client's attitude hostile or threatening when he left your office?

THERAPIST: Compared to what? When he came in?

ATTORNEY: Was his demeanor threatening compared to an average person?

THERAPIST: You legal guys kill me! You ask these questions as though you really believe they have answers. You're using an imaginary reference point that is meaningless!

ATTORNEY: In your professional opinion, did you believe he would actually harm the intended victim?

THERAPIST: No, not when he left. After we had talked for about 30 minutes, he calmed down a great deal and became very accommodating and reasonable.

ATTORNEY: If avoiding legal liability is your goal, then your decision to take action to detain your client or issue warnings tonight will hinge entirely on the reasonableness of your assessment that the client was not dangerous when he left your office. Tell me everything relevant concerning your assessment that he was not dangerous when he left your office.

THERAPIST: Like many upset clients, he immediately started to calm down after he had the chance to ventilate a lot of pent-up feelings. Once he started calming

---

[6]Where the patient has no history of violence directed toward other people, it becomes relevant to determine if the patient has any history of expressing violence toward property. If so, it is important to determine if the destruction of property is an indirect way of hurting the property owner.

down, he unhesitantly surrendered his razor-blade knife and bottle of acid at my request and agreed to go directly home. He also indicated that he would not go by the intended victim's home for any reason or make any attempt to harm her this evening. He clearly understood the consequences that would follow if he did make any attempt to harm the intended victim. He was also eager to meet with me again in the morning to discuss the problem and nonviolent solutions in more detail. Essentially, the client seemed to quickly return to his more typical and less threatening demeanor once he vented his pent-up feelings.

ATTORNEY: The legal issue is not the accuracy of your professional opinion, but whether or not you have satisfied the standards of your profession in gathering information and arriving at a conclusion. What professional standards apply to assessing dangerousness in these situations and did you follow them?

THERAPIST: I hate to say this to you again, but your question is almost meaningless in a clinical context!

ATTORNEY: Look, it may be a meaningless clinical question, but it's a fundamental legal question.

THERAPIST: You seem to get angry when I challenge the relevance of your questions!

ATTORNEY: Gratuitous analysis of my emotions won't reduce your legal fees.

THERAPIST: But it may make you a better attorney!

ATTORNEY: Touché. Now, back to my question please.

THERAPIST: OK, let me put it this way. There is no empirically demonstrated method or information that allows one to predict dangerousness with any degree of accuracy. The psychological and legal literature on this point is abundantly clear. So I have no idea what standard of care could possibly be violated! Given this, what on earth is the legal relevance of your question?

ATTORNEY: It is still of fundamental importance. The legal system will *impose* a standard of care on you in this situation, and your conduct will be measured against that standard.

THERAPIST: And where is the standard of care coming from? What is it based on, and why on earth is the legal system dictating what it is?

ATTORNEY: The standard may be arbitrary and may even be ill-founded, but the role of the legal system is to determine fault and negligence when innocent parties are harmed as a result of deviations from professional standards.

THERAPIST: Do you realize what you are saying to me? This is absolutely crazy! This is nothing more than semantic nonsense. I just told you there is no standard to deviate from. How can you disregard such fundamental conceptual realities and not call your legal analysis mythology?

ATTORNEY: In the final analysis, what the court deems prudent and reasonable is the standard.

THERAPIST: I object to the legal system imposing clinical standards they are not qualified to make or understand.

ATTORNEY: Objection overruled. I understand that you may not like the rules of the game, but your objections won't change any of the rules! You still need to know and tell me what information a reasonable and prudent psychologist would have gathered in this situation and what conclusions these data would suggest.

THERAPIST: OK. One could not possibly form a reasonable conclusion about the possibilities of future violence without taking a detailed history of past violence. In other words, in the absence of demonstrated violence in the past, it is unreasonable to make any predictions of violence in the future. Additionally, there are a number of demographic considerations that could be related to violent behavior. And finally, a number of personality characteristics could be associated with violent behavior. I made detailed inquiries into all these areas and found virtually no evidence to suggest the likelihood of future violence. The only substantive evidence about this man's intent to harm anyone was his verbal threats, which appeared to be the result of a temporary and heightened state of frustration. Once that frustration was partially alleviated, his threats decreased.

ATTORNEY: Do you have any reason to assume that what you witnessed, the flux in his behavior, was just part of an ongoing up-and-down pattern of behavior?

THERAPIST: I can't say for sure. On the basis of a 1-hour sample, I think this is a low-profile, quiet guy who got his fuse lit. He came in and unloaded his pent-up feelings and then returned to a quiet, low-profile, more reasonable sort of fellow again.

ATTORNEY: The reason I'm asking you about this is because if he commits harm to someone, and after the fact it turns out that his emotions are continually in a state of flux and what you witnessed was just part of that pattern, then it would have been important for you to have known that.

THERAPIST: Well, I can't be sure what a complete diagnostic workup might reveal. On the basis of his verbal reports, it seems entirely reasonable to see him as a person who is usually more on the shy and retiring side. It is entirely possible, however, that a more sophisticated diagnostic evaluation would reveal different conclusions.

ATTORNEY: OK, in your opinion do you think that the client was capable of or was, in fact, exercising deliberate judgment?

THERAPIST: When he came in, I would say he definitely was not. After 20 to 30 minutes he started to, and when he left he seemed well in control and very rational.

ATTORNEY: What things did you consider that would indicate that he would continue to exercise deliberate judgment and be rational after he left?

THERAPIST: My clinical opinion is that after I helped him pull the fuse on a lot of the emotions he was feeling, he returned to what was his more typical, psychological state.

ATTORNEY: Was that opinion based on anything more than all the things you have already mentioned?

THERAPIST: Yes.

ATTORNEY: What?

THERAPIST: Twenty years of clinical experience has revealed a pattern in which many people express their pent-up emotions and then return to their more typical and moderate level of psychological tension?

ATTORNEY: Do they continue to remain calm after that happens?

THERAPIST: Well, certainly for a short period of time. I scheduled him to come right back in the morning so I could do a more complete diagnostic workup.

ATTORNEY: Do you know or did you find out if he uses alcohol or drugs?

THERAPIST: I didn't ask him that specifically because I knew he wasn't under the influence at the time he came in. I didn't ask him if he ever had or if he ever would.

ATTORNEY: Have you consulted anyone about this problem?

THERAPIST: Of course.

ATTORNEY: Who?

THERAPIST: You.

ATTORNEY: No, I mean another clinician.

THERAPIST: You need to be more specific with your questions!

ATTORNEY: You learn quickly.

THERAPIST: I know.

ATTORNEY: Have you consulted any other clinicians about this problem?

THERAPIST: No, I called you immediately.

ATTORNEY: A professional consultation is always invaluable in situations like this.

Attorney's Recommendations

THERAPIST: OK, so what, if anything, do you recommend we do tonight?

ATTORNEY: Based on what you have told me, let me summarize the primary legal issues and my evaluation of them. Because of the content of your session and your apparent influence with the client, you probably already have established a special relationship sufficient to impose a legal duty on you to control your client or protect people whom you are specifically aware of from serious threats of harm.

THERAPIST: So that special relationship can be established in just a single hour visit?

ATTORNEY: In this situation I'm confident that it was. Your description of the session indicates two important factors that I believe suggest the presence of the special relationship: First, your ability to influence the client's behavior is evident, and second, the specificity of the threats expressed to you in that session.

THERAPIST: Would it have been wise for me to have been less influential for my own sake?

ATTORNEY: *No!* You don't want to do that either. That would be a breach of your fiduciary duty to the client, which is a more clearly defined source of liability.

THERAPIST: I understand.

ATTORNEY: The presence of a specific threat, a specific victim, and a lethal weapon clearly suggests that this was a serious threat and that you may have to take action to restrain the client or protect the victim.

THERAPIST: Doesn't that depend on the probabilities of him. . . .

ATTORNEY: It does, but we're looking at a client who has expressed specific threats and came to you with a weapon in hand. And if he goes to the corner market, gets another razor blade, and kills her tonight, the jury is going to know these facts and some two-bit plaintiff's attorney is going to be convincing the jury that no reasonable clinical assessment overrides these objective facts.

THERAPIST: Are you telling me to issue a warning?

ATTORNEY: No, but I want you to understand the considerations; another of which is that if you do issue a warning and the client is in fact not dangerous, then you've breached your fiduciary obligations to the client.

THERAPIST: In other words, it's as important to be equally prudent in predicting violence or the absence of it.

ATTORNEY: Precisely!

THERAPIST: So, all things considered, what is it that you are recommending that I do about this case tonight?

ATTORNEY: OK. Under the situation you've described and your clinical assessment that actual violence is unlikely, I would recommend that you do nothing special tonight. This opinion, of course, is based on the assumption that you have not deviated from the routine a competent therapist would have followed in gathering data and drawing conclusions from that data. Your fiduciary obligations to your client are already clearly established and issuing imprudent warnings would breach that fiduciary duty. Your duty to the third party is triggered when you determine that your client poses a serious threat of violence to another, and I don't sense that you believe a serious threat is present.

THERAPIST: That's my opinion.

ATTORNEY: Well, I'm not so concerned that your opinion is correct, just as long as if it's wrong it's not negligently wrong. Even if the client does carry out harm, retrospect will not be permitted to influence what you should have done. The important thing is that other competent therapists would have gathered similar information and reached similar clinical conclusions given that information.

THERAPIST: But competent therapists would disagree about how to go about assessing danger and about what conclusions can be drawn from the same data.

ATTORNEY: What will matter is that the method you followed and the conclusions you drew represent acceptable professional practice in the general sense of the term.

THERAPIST: And that would be determined by the court.

ATTORNEY: That's right—based on evidence presented to the court by qualified psychological experts.

THERAPIST: So you don't want me to call anyone tonight.

ATTORNEY: That's right. When you see him in the morning, perform the diagnostic workup you described and reassess his dangerousness. Make notes of your assessment from tonight's and tomorrow's sessions. If we find that you've incorrectly assessed his danger tonight or if his danger increases in the future, then we will have to either issue warnings to the police and the victim, start commitment proceedings, or both.

THERAPIST: Have we covered everything we need to talk about tonight?

ATTORNEY: Everything except my bill.

THERAPIST: And what are you charging for this consult?

ATTORNEY: You really don't want to know that right now!
THERAPIST: It sounds like you don't really want to say right now!
ATTORNEY: Good grief!
THERAPIST: Good night.

REFERENCES

Botkin, D. J., & Nietzel, M. T. (1987). How therapists manage potentially violent clients: Toward a standard of care for psychotherapists. *Professional Psychology: Research & Practice, 18*(1), 84–86.

DeLeon, C. H. (1961). Threatened homicide: A medical emergency. *Journal of the National Medical Association, 53,* 467–472.

Givelber, D. J., Bowers, W. J., & Blitch, C. L. (1984). *Tarasoff, myth, and reality: An empirical study of private law in action.* 1984 WIS. L. REV. 443, 467.

Griffith, E. J., & Griffith, E. H. (1978). Duty to third parties, dangerousness, and the right to refuse treatment: Problematic concepts for psychiatrist and lawyer. *California Western Law Review, 14*(2), 241–274.

Gross, B. H., Southard, M. J., Lamb, H. R., & Weinberger, L. E. (1987). Assessing dangerousness and responding appropriately: Hedlund expands the clinician's liability established by Tarasoff. *Journal of Clinical Psychiatry, 48*(1), 9–12.

Gutheil, T. G., Bursztajn, H., & Brodsky, A. (1986). The multidimensional assessment of dangerousness: Competence assessment in patient care and liability prevention. *Bulletin of the American Academy of Psychiatry and Law, 14,* 123–129.

Hellman, D. S., & Blackman, M. (1966). Enuresis, fire-setting, and cruelty to animals. A triad predictive of adult crime. *American Journal of Psychiatry, 122,* 1431–1435.

Herlihy, B., & Sheeley, V. L. (1988). Counselor liability and the duty to warn: Selected cases, statutory trends, and implications for practice. *Counselor Educator and Supervision, 28,* 203–215.

Hyman, S. E. (1984). *Manual of psychiatric emergencies.* Boston: Little, Brown.

Kozol, H. L., Boucher, R. J., & Gawfalo, R. F. (1972). The diagnosis and treatment of dangerousness. *Crime and delinquency, 18,* 371–392.

Kutzer, D. J., & Lion, J. R. (1984). The violent patient. In S. Saunders, A. M. Anderson, C. H. Hart, & G. M. Rubenstein (Eds.), *Violent individuals and families.* Springfield, IL: Charles C Thomas.

Latham, J. A., Jr. (1975). Torts-duty to act for protection of another-liability of psychotherapist for failure to warn of homicide threatened by patient. *Vanderbilt Law Review, 28,* 631–640.

Litwack, T. R. (1985). The predictors of violence. *The Clinical Psychologist, 38,* 87–91.

Meehl, P. (1954). *Clinical versus statistical prediction: A theoretical analysis and a review of the evidence.* Minneapolis: University of Minnesota Press.

Meloy, J. R. (1987). The prediction of violence in outpatient psychotherapy. *American Journal of Psychotherapy, XLI,* 38–43.

Monahan, J. (1978). The prevention of violence. In J. Monahan (Ed.), *Community mental health and the criminal justice system.* New York: Plenum Press.

Monahan, J. (1981). *Predicting violent behavior: An assessment of clinical techniques.* Beverly Hills: Sage Publications.

Mulvey, E. P., & Lidz, C. W. (1984). Clinical considerations in dangerousness prediction. *Clinical Psychology Review, 4,* 379–401.

Roth, L. H., & Meisel, A. (1977). Dangerousness, confidentiality, and the duty to warn. *American Journal of Psychiatry, 135,* 508–511.

Skodol, A. E. (1984). Emergency management of potentially violent patients. In E. S. Bassach & A. W. Birk (Eds.), *Emergency psychiatry: Concepts, methods, and practices.* New York: Plenum Press.

Skodol, H., & Karasu, T. (1977). Emergency psychiatry and the assaultive patient. *American Journal of Psychiatry, 135,* 202–205.

Sonkin, D. J. (1986). Clairvoyance vs. common sense: Therapist's duty to warn and protect. *Victims and Violence, 1,* 7–22.

Soreff, S. M. (1984). Violence in the emergency room. In B. S. Comstock, W. E. Fann, A. D. Pokorny, & R. I. Williams (Eds.), *Phenomenology and treatment of psychiatric emergencies.* New York: Spectrum Publications.

Steadman, H. J. (1982). A situational approach to violence. *International Journal of Law and Psychiatry, 5,* 171–186.

Steadman, H. J., & Cocozza, J. J. (1974). *Careers of the criminally insane.* Lexington, MA: Heath.

Tarasoff v. Regents of University of California. 529 P.2d 553, 118 Cal. Rptr 129 (1974).

Wexler, D. B. (1981). *Mental health law-major issues.* New York: Plenum Press.

5

Suicidal Clients: Legal Duties

Ι n the mental health professions, some high-risk situations occur that expose the professional to heightened risks of liability. High risks include the duty to control dangerous clients, the emerging duty to warn and protect third parties from potentially dangerous clients, and the added care and precaution required in the treatment of suicidal clients.[1] While suicide is not a tragedy exclusively reserved for the mental health professions, the therapist's liability for such tragedies is being recognized with increasing frequency. The subject therefore demands special consideration by mental health professionals in all disciplines.

The law's view toward suicide itself has evolved over the past 200 years. In eighteenth century England, those who died by suicide were viewed as "self-murderers" and buried under a public highway with a stone placed over the face and a stake driven through the heart. Any estate the decedent accumulated while living was forfeited to the crown rather than passed on to heirs.[2] Today, no such legal sanctions are placed on the burial or estate of those who take their own lives. In fact, by the end of the nineteenth century, American courts were occasionally compensating the suicide victim's relatives and heirs.[3] As tort law has developed in the twentieth century, recovery of damages by surviving relatives and heirs has gained even greater acceptance, although still statistically infrequently.[4]

Throughout this chapter, be aware of two important caveats. First, suicide cases tend to be very fact-dependent. In fact, "no general rules can be deduced from the cases. Close distinctions must be drawn to allow for even slight differences in the facts and it is difficult to lay down any hard and fast general rule that can be made to apply to any considerable number of cases."[5] Second, the vast majority of client suicide cases result in a finding of no liability. Therefore, while this entire chapter is devoted to a therapist's liability when the client commits suicide, keep in mind that liability is the exception, not the rule. However, exceptions do exist, so therapists have been and will continue to be found liable for client suicide.

---

[1]*See,* J. Smith, Medical Malpractice: Psychiatric Care 62 (1986).

[2]Comment, *Civil Liability for Suicide: An Analysis of the Causation Issue,* 1978 Ariz. St. L. J. 573, 573 n.1 [herinafter Comment, *Civil Liability for Suicide*].

[3]*Id.* (citing, *Mutual Life Ins. Co. v. Terry,* 15 Wall. 580 (1873)).

[4]*Id.*

[5]12 Am. Jur. Proof of Facts 131 (1962). Consider also the comments of one scholar: "A brief review of various cases reveals much contradictory law or contradictory application of law." Perr, *Suicide Responsibility of Hospital and Psychiatrist,* 9 Clev-Mar L. Rev. 427, 428 (1960).

Liability judgments against therapists for the suicide of a client can be very costly. For example, in *Pisel v. Stamford Hospital,*[6] a client, who unsuccessfully attempted suicide, brought suit against the hospital and the staff psychiatrist and received a $3,600,000 judgment.[7] In short, while it is not *probable* that a therapist will be sued and found liable for a client's suicide, the prudent therapist understands that such an outcome is certainly *possible* and that it can be both professionally and financially devastating.

FAILURE TO PREVENT SUICIDE

The law imposes on certain classes of people an affirmative duty to prevent the suicide of another.[8] When the duty is breached, liability will be found. Therefore, before liability can be found for failing to prevent suicide, three questions must be answered:

1. Does the defendant have a duty to prevent suicide?
2. What is the scope of that duty?
3. Was the duty breached?

Duty Created Because of a Special Relationship

Certain special relationships, such as that which exists between a therapist and a suicidal client, create the existence of the duty to prevent suicide.[9] The rationale for such a duty is that (1) the therapist is placed in a superior position as the client's caretaker, and (2) the client relies on the therapist's special knowledge, training, and experience to recognize and treat suicidal tendencies.[10] Therefore the duty to prevent suicide may arise when the therapist or hospital undertakes to care for the health and safety of its clients.[11]

It is important to note that the creation and continued existence of a duty to prevent suicide arise by operation of law. In other words, the duty does not depend on a specific client request to prevent a contemplated suicide. Neither does the duty depend on an implied contract of rehabilitation between the therapist and client; the duty exists because the therapist has special knowledge regarding the client's suicidal tendencies and ability and undertaking to control the client's

[6]180 Conn. 314, 430 A.2d 1 (1980).
[7]This judgment was upheld by the Connecticut Supreme Court. *Id.*
[8]Schwartz, *Civil Liability for Causing Suicide: A Synthesis of Law and Psychiatry,* 24 VAND. L. REV. 217, 237 (1971).
[9]Comment, *Civil Liability for Causing or Failing to Prevent Suicide,* 12 LOY. L.A.L. REV. 967, 987 (1979) [hereinafter Comment, *Causing or Failing to Prevent Suicide*].
[10]*Id.* at 990.
[11]*See* Swenson, *Legal Liability for a Patient's Suicide,* 14 J. PSYCHIATRY & LAW 409, 413 (1986).

behavior. As a result, the act of suicide, although intervening in the chain of causation, neither supercedes the therapist's duty nor displaces the therapist's liability.[12]

Some commentators suggest that the duty to prevent suicide should never be imposed in the outpatient context.[13] They suggest that hospitalization would be an absolute prerequisite to finding liability, reasoning that when the client commits suicide, the duty breached is one of control and watchfulness, and only in the hospital setting can the client be continually watched and adequately controlled.[14] Despite these commentators, however, the courts have found a duty and imposed liability on treating therapists in both the inpatient and outpatient settings.[15]

Finally, the therapist should be aware that the duty to prevent suicide can be created in a single consultation—a series of visitations is not a prerequisite to the creation of the special relationship. For example, in *Farrow v. Health Services Corp.*,[16] Chester Farrow suffered from cervical spondylosis after he accidentally struck his elbow against the side mirror of his pickup truck. Chester ultimately underwent surgery to correct this condition. On returning from the recovery room, however, he became confused, disoriented, and suffered from hallucinations. When the conditions persisted, psychiatric help was requested. Dr. Moench, the staff psychiatrist, saw Chester that evening, where in the course of 1 hour he completed the examination and report. Less than 8 hours later, Chester attempted suicide by jumping through his sixth-floor window. As a result of the fall, Chester was rendered a quadriplegic.

Chester sued the hospital, the treating physician, and Dr. Moench. Both the hospital and the treating physician obtained summary judgment in their favor and were therefore dismissed from the case. The action, however, went to trial against Dr. Moench, wherein the jury found him not liable.

On appeal, the Utah Supreme Court determined that a jury instruction which Chester had requested should have been given. The court, accordingly, reversed the judgment of no liability and remanded the case for a new trial. Although the Utah Supreme Court opinion focused primarily on whether Dr. Moench breached a duty to Chester Farrow, implicit in the decision is the finding that Dr. Moench had a duty to prevent this suicide attempt. Therefore, the creation of the duty to prevent suicide may arise from a single 1-hour examination![17]

---

[12]*See* Comment, *Causing or Failing to Prevent Suicide, supra* note 9, at 987; *see, e.g., Brandvain v. Ridgeview Inst., Inc.,* 188 Ga. App. 106, 372 S.E.2d 265 (1988), *judgment aff'd by, Ridgeview Inst., Inc. v. Brandvain,* 259 Ga. 376, 382 S.E.2d 597 (1989).

[13]*See e.g.,* Perr, *supra* note 5, 432; Schwartz, *supra* note 8, at 245.

[14]Perr, *supra* note 5, at 432.

[15]*See Bellah v. Greenson,* 81 Cal. App.3d 614, 146 Cal. Rptr. 535 (1978), for a case demonstrating that therapist's can be liable for the suicide death of an outpatient.

[16]604 P.2d 474 (Utah 1979).

[17]This does not mean, however, that every time a therapist meets and examines a new client, the special relationship creating the duty will exist. The quality and intensity of the examination as well as revealed intentions through client communications will be considered in determining whether the duty was created. Likewise, whether the client was hospitalized or not will be an important factor.

Scope of the Duty—Foreseeability

The therapist's duty to prevent suicide does not extend to every conceivable case. Liability will exist only if the risk of suicide was foreseeable, so liability will never attach unless the plaintiff can show, usually through expert testimony, that the suicide should have been reasonably anticipated. In this sense, failure to prove foreseeability will absolutely preclude recovery and is therefore a major element.[18] Practically, however, demonstrating foreseeability is a minor hurdle that is very easily satisfied.

The law considers a suicide foreseeable if the client (1) has a history of suicidal tendencies, (2) is being treated for suicide prevention, or (3) exhibits suicidal tendencies while being treated for something else.[19] When none of these elements are present in a given case, the plaintiff must show that the therapist was professionally negligent in failing to recognize the client's suicidal tendencies.

Breach of Duty to Prevent Suicide

Standard of Care.   Even though a therapist is under a duty to prevent a foreseeable suicide, the mere fact that the client subsequently takes his own life does not make liability automatic. To be liable, the therapist must also be found to have deviated from acceptable professional standards and practices. These standards have been defined to include the following requirements:

> (1) He [the therapist] must possess the degree of professional learning, skill, and ability which others similarly situated possess; (2) he must exercise reasonable care and diligence in the application of his knowledge and skill to the client's case; and (3) he must use his best judgment in the treatment and care of his client.[20]

The standard of care required of therapists and the rest of the medical profession is uniquely derived within the legal system. Normally, judges, aided by the litigants' adversarial arguments, define the standards of acceptable conduct. If actions fail to meet those judicially mandated standards, liability will be found. In malpractice cases, however, the customary practices of the treatment specialty play the dominant role in establishing the standard of care, giving the profession the special privilege of setting its own standards of care by adopting treatment practices. The reason for such deference is a recognition that judges and lawyers lack expertise when judging another profession and therefore fear the injustice of imposing liability based on an uninformed judgment.[21]

---

[18]"The most important single factor in determining the liability of a hospital for failing to prevent the suicide of a client is whether the hospital authorities in the circumstances could reasonably have anticipated that the client might harm himself." *Bornman v. Great Southwest Gen. Hosp., Inc.*, 453 F.2d 616, 621 (5th Cir. 1971); *accord, Keebler v. Winfield Carraway Hosp.*, 531 So. 2d 841 (Ala. 1988).

[19]*See* Comment, *Causing or Failing to Prevent Suicide, supra* note 9, at 992; *Keebler v. Winfield Carraway Hosp.*, 531 So. 2d 841, 845 (Ala. 1988).

[20]*Stone v. Proctor*, 259 N.C. 633, 131 S.E.2d 297, 299 (1963).

[21]Furrow, Malpractice in Psychotherapy 23–24 (1980).

Breach of the Standard of Care. The duty to prevent suicide is breached when the therapist's judgment and actions fall below the level of skill exercised by others in the medical community. This requirement does not mean, however, that the therapist is obligated to adopt the most widely accepted treatment method. Courts recognize that even therapists of great repute may disagree as to the most appropriate form of treatment in a given case. Therefore, when several methods of treatment are accepted by the medical community, the therapist is free to select and implement any one of them.[22] Liability will be found only when the therapist implements clearly unacceptable treatment methods. In other words, choosing a wrong or unpopular course of suicide prevention is not what makes the therapist liable—negligently choosing wrong is what creates liability.

Liability Prevented Through "Reasonable" Care. No doubt a client determined to commit suicide will eventually succeed regardless of whether the client is in the protective confines of a mental institution or simply an outpatient. Even the most well-developed precautionary plan implemented by the most competent professionals and staff will not thwart the client who wants to die. Establishing liability, therefore, is not simply a question of whether the doctor failed to prevent a client from committing suicide; rather, the threshold question is whether the doctor exercised reasonable care in the evaluation and treatment of the client under the circumstances. If reasonable care was exercised, then liability will not be found even if a suicide attempt was successful.[23]

NEGLIGENTLY CAUSING SUICIDE

Some situations do not occasion a duty to prevent suicide. For example, if a client poses no inherent, independent foreseeable risk of suicide, then there is no duty to prevent suicide. Nevertheless, such clients occasionally commit suicide. Although the plaintiff will likely try to state a cause of action for failing to prevent the suicide, the action will fail unless the suicide was foreseeable. Therefore the plaintiff will also plead a cause of action based on general negligence.

To prove malpractice under a negligence theory, the plaintiff must still show that the therapist owed a duty of care to the client and that the duty was breached. However, the plaintiff must additionally demonstrate that the treatment the therapist furnished eventually caused the client to commit suicide.[24] Therefore, while subtle legal differences distinguish the duty involved in a failure to prevent suicide case from the duty in a negligence case, the major distinction between the two theories is causation.

[22]Perr, *supra* note 5, at 432; Swenson, *supra* note 11, at 416; Waltzer, *Malpractice Liability in a Patient's Suicide,* 34 AM. J. PSYCHOTHERAPY 89, 90 (1980).

[23]J. Smith, *supra* note 1, at 506, *citing, Vistica v. Presbyterian Hosp. & Medical Center,* 67 Cal. 2d 465, 432 P.2d 193, 62 Cal. Rptr 577 (1967).

[24]*See, e.g.,* Furrow, *supra* note 21, at 26; Swenson, *supra* note 11, at 419.

Duty to Refrain from Causing Suicide

The duty of the therapist under a negligence theory is slightly different from the duty in a failure to prevent suicide case. If a therapist has a specific duty to prevent suicide, she has just that: an affirmative duty to *prevent* a foreseeable suicide. On the other hand, all therapists have a general duty to diagnose and treat in a nonnegligent manner—that is, while all therapists are not obligated to protect their clients from suicide, all therapists are obligated to *refrain from causing* suicide. Therefore a therapist has a duty to refrain from revealing confidential communications that would be so damaging as to lead the client to commit suicide. Further, the therapist must avoid negligently prescribing lethal quantities of medication to suicidal or depressed clients.[25]

Scope of Duty—Foreseeability

Foreseeability is still a necessary element in actions based on general negligence. However, the foreseeability that is relevant in negligence actions differs from that involved in duty to prevent cases.

To establish liability in a duty to prevent case, the plaintiff must show that the client's suicide was foreseeable *independent of* any interaction with the therapist. On the other hand, to establish liability in a negligence action, the plaintiff must prove that the client's suicide was foreseeable *because of* the therapist's involvement with the client. Thus situations may arise in which a suicide was not foreseeable in a duty to prevent context but was foreseeable in an action based on general negligence.

To illustrate, a client who is receiving counseling for a sexual disorder and has no prior suicidal history may be greatly embarrassed and humiliated if the therapist divulges confidential information. If the client's despair causes him to commit suicide, the client's survivors may have a cause of action based on a negligence theory, but not a duty to prevent theory, because the client posed no foreseeable risk of suicide absent the therapist's breach of confidence.

Breach of Duty As a Proximate Cause of Suicide

As indicated, the major difference between a failure to prevent case and a negligence theory case is causation. To prove negligence, the plaintiff must establish that the therapist's acts or omissions were the proximate cause of the suicide.[26] That is, although a treatment decision is substandard, even negligently

---

[25]Schutz, Legal Liability In Psychotherapy: A Practitioner's Guide to Risk Management 67 (1982). According to the author, the duty to refrain from causing suicide is also breached when the therapist gives "clear directives for action that lead to a suicide; and, far more subtly, the fostering of dependence in a patient to the extent that a suicidal crisis is precipitated when therapy is, or is about to be, terminated." *Id.*

[26]Furrow, *supra* note 21, at 26.

substandard, liability will not attach unless the treatment has a direct causal link to the suicide.[27]

Since the immediate cause of death in a suicide is the client's own conduct, the suicidal act always intervenes between the therapist's negligence and the client's death. Intervening acts, however, are classified as either dependent or independent. A dependent intervening act is one that does not happen in the absence of some other act. Consequently, if a client's act of suicide is deemed dependent on the therapist's negligent act, the therapist's act will be considered the legal cause of the suicide. An independent intervening act, on the other hand, is one that would occur in spite of the therapist's negligence. Therefore an independent intervening act supersedes the therapist's conduct as the cause of the suicide, thus relieving the therapist from liability.[28]

Whether the client's act of suicide is deemed an independent or dependent intervening act often focuses on whether the suicide was "voluntary." If the suicide is truly voluntary, the client will be found completely responsible for her own actions and the therapist accordingly will be found not liable. Conversely, if the client's suicide is somehow deemed involuntary, the court will assess whether the defendant is blameworthy.

"Involuntary," as used in this legal context, however, has a slightly different meaning than nonlawyers are accustomed to. The law considers a suicide involuntary and therefore will impose liability if the therapist's negligent act either (1) brings about insanity in the client, which prevents the client from realizing the nature and risk of the act, or (2) causes the client to have an irresistible impulse to commit suicide.[29]

This view agrees with that furnished by the RESTATEMENT (SECOND) OF TORTS:

> If the [therapist's] negligent conduct so brings about the delirium or insanity of [the patient] as to make the [therapist] liable for it, the [therapist] is also liable for harm done by the [patient] to himself while delirious or insane, if [the patient's] delirium or insanity
>
>   (a) prevents him from realizing the nature of his act and the certainty or risk of harm involved therein, or
>
>   (b) makes it impossible for him to resist an impulse caused by his insanity which deprives him of his capacity to govern his conduct in accordance with reason.[30]

Negligence That Prevents Client from Realizing the Nature of the Suicidal Act.   Under this test, liability may attach if the negligently inflicted injuries produce a state of mind that prevents the client from appreciating the nature and risk of suicide. In other words, if the client does not know what he is doing when he acts to take his own life, the suicide will be deemed an involuntary act

---

[27]Swenson, *supra* note 11, at 419.

[28]*See* Comment, *Causing or Failing to Prevent Suicide, supra* note 9 at 974.

[29]Swenson, *supra* note 11, at 419.

[30]RESTATEMENT (SECOND) OF TORTS Sec. 455 (1965).

caused by the therapist's negligence, not the result of free will.[31] The test was applied in *Daniels v. New York, N.H. & H.R. Co.*[32] wherein recovery was denied because the decedent arguably understood the nature of his suicidal act when he locked his bedroom door, presumably to exclude others, before strangling himself.[33]

The "Irresistible Impulse" Test.   The alternative test advanced by the RESTATEMENT imposes liability if the client commits suicide in response to an "uncontrollable" or "irresistible" impulse—that is, this test allows recovery even when the client knew his act would cause his own death but, as a result of emotional distress caused by the therapist's negligent conduct, was unable to control himself.[34]

Differing opinions exist as to whether evidence of suicide planning negates liability under an irresistible impulse theory. For example, in other contexts, courts have found an irresistible impulse negated by evidence that the suicide victim left a note,[35] the victim purchased ammunition for the purpose of killing himself,[36] or the victim was merely efficient in the manner he cut his own throat.[37,38] Conversely, other courts have found that even though evidence established that the decedent contemplated suicide for hours,[39] days,[40] or weeks,[41] such action did not, by itself, prove the absence of an irresistible impulse.[42]

Ultimately, however, the existence or absence of an irresistible impulse will depend on the testimony presented at trial because the issue is one of fact.[43] This means that the jury, not the judge, determines whether the suicide was committed under the delusion of an irresistible impulse.[44] Expert testimony therefore is a critical factor in irresistible impulse cases.

Broadening Liability Through the "Substantial Factor" Test.   Because it is impossible to question the deceased suicide victim regarding her state of mind when she took her own life, an irresistible impulse is understandably difficult to prove. Consequently, because some jurisdictions felt that this evidentiary burden of proof placed an undue hardship on the victim's survivors and worked to preclude recovery in many otherwise close cases,[45] the "substantial factor" test was

---

[31]Comment, *Causing or Failing to Prevent Suicide, supra* note 9, at 979.

[32]183 Mass. 393, 67 N.E. 424, 426 (1903).

[33]*See* Comment, *Causing or Failing to Prevent Suicide, supra* note 9, at 979.

[34]*See* Schwartz, *supra* note 8, at 227.

[35]*Jones v. Traders & Gen. Ins. Co.*, 140 Tex. 599, 605–606, 169 S.W.2d 160, 163–164 (1943).

[36]*Long v. Omaha & C.B. St. Ry.*, 108 Neb. 342, 351, 187 N.W. 930, 933–934 (1922).

[37]*Brown v. American Steel & Wire Co.*, 43 Ind. App. 560, 88 N.E. 80 (1909).

[38]Schwartz, *supra* note 8, at 227.

[39]*Burnight v. Industrial Acc. Comm'n*, 181 Cal. App. 2d 816, 5 Cal. Rptr 786 (1960).

[40]*Fuller v. Preis*, 35 N.Y.2d 425, 322 N.E.2d 263, 363 N.Y.S.2d 568 (1974).

[41]*Orcutt v. Spokane County*, 58 Wash. 2d 846, 364 P.2d 1102 (1961).

[42]*See* Comment, *Civil Liability for Suicide, supra* note 2, at 587–588.

[43]*Id.*

[44]Technically, the "fact-finder" determines the facts of the case. In jury cases, the jury is the fact-finder; in nonjury cases, the fact-finder is the judge.

[45]*See* Schutz, *supra* note 25, at 77.

developed, which allows recovery if the therapist's negligence is merely a substantial factor in the client's suicide. Under this test, the suicide victim's survivors need not prove that the therapist's negligent treatment was the sole precipitating cause of the client's suicide but only a substantial contributing factor.

Whether a treatment decision is a factor in a client's suicide and whether the factor is "substantial" is determined by (1) comparing the client's pre- and posttreatment mental states, (2) considering the length of time the client was treated in a negligent manner, and (3) analyzing events that intervened during the treatment period.[46]

EVIDENTIARY CONSIDERATIONS IN CLIENT SUICIDE CASES

Expert Testimony

Expert testimony is almost always required to determine whether a chosen treatment method conformed to the appropriate standard of care. However, because psychotherapy is a field in which different therapists subscribe to different schools of thought, disagreements within the field can be very relevant.[47]

For example, a therapist who belongs to a nondirective psychoanalytic school of thought would not want treatment decisions scrutinized by an expert witness who subscribes to directive or behavioral-modification techniques. As a general rule then, a therapist who follows a particular professional philosophy is judged by the standards of that school of thought. Consequently, the testimony of an expert from another school is inadmissable, unless the witness also happens to be an expert in the standards of the defendant's school of thought *and* limits testimony to a discussion of only those standards subscribed to by the defendant's school.[48]

Res Ipsa Loquitur

The American system of legal justice is premised on the belief that the person claiming injury (the plaintiff) bears the burden of proving what is claimed and that the defendant will not be found liable unless the plaintiff proves each element of the cause of action. Thus the system requires the plaintiff to affirmatively prove the defendant's liability, not the defendant to prove lack of liability. Practically, this means that if the plaintiff fails to establish each element of the cause of action, the defendant must be found not liable even though the defendant fails to produce a shred of evidence.

[46]*See* Swenson, *supra* note 11, at 420.
[47]Furrow, *supra* note 21, at 25.
[48]*Id.*

The law, however, contains a doctrine, *res ipsa loquitur,* that can turn the presumption of innocence on its head. This tort doctrine literally means "the thing speaks for itself"; it permits a plaintiff, who is unaware of the exact circumstances that led to an injury, to demand an explanation from the defendant.[49]

Within the client suicide context, the doctrine has been applied by some jurisdictions when circumstances surrounding a client's suicide are unclear.[50] The doctrine has the effect of creating a *presumption* that the client's suicide would not commonly happen in the absence of negligence. Therefore, unless the therapist comes forward with evidence to rebut this presumption, the jury is justified in concluding the suicide in fact resulted from therapist negligence.[51]

There is no doubt the *res ipsa loquitur* doctrine is a very beneficial plaintiff's tool. The doctrine effectively puts the therapist in the awkward position of having to establish a negative (nonnegligence) rather than simply "neutralizing" specific allegations of negligence the plaintiff offers. However, a plaintiff can invoke the doctrine if, and only if, three essential elements are satisfied:

1. The event is of a kind that ordinarily does not occur in the absence of negligence.

2. Other responsible causes, including the conduct of the plaintiff and third persons, are sufficiently eliminated by the evidence.

3. The indicated negligence is within the scope of the defendant's duty to the plaintiff.[52]

At first blush, the *res ipsa loquitur* doctrine seems irrelevant in the client suicide context. Regarding the first factor, suicide is certainly a kind of accident that can, and usually does, happen in the absence of third-party negligence. As to the second factor, it seems almost impossible to exclude the victim as at least partly responsible for her or his own death, for suicide is by definition an intentional act. The third factor is usually analyzed in terms of whether the defendant was in exclusive control of the instrumentality of harm.[53] Accordingly, it is hard to understand how the psychotherapist is in *exclusive* control of the instrumentality of harm when the client personally carries out the act, many times in absolute seclusion.

While the *res ipsa loquitur* doctrine has been applied in only a handful of client suicide cases,[54] the fact that it has been applied at all is indicative of how far some courts will go to provide the victim's survivors a channel for recovery.

---

[49]J. Smith, *supra* note 1, at 117.

[50]Furrow, *supra* note 21, at 43.

[51]*E.g., Maki v. Murray Hosp.,* 7 P.2d 228, 231 (Mont. 1932).

[52]RESTATEMENT (SECOND) OF TORTS Sec. 328D (1965).

[53]*See, e.g.,* D. Dobbs, Torts and Compensation: Personal Accountability and Social Responsibility for Injury 175 (1985).

[54]*See also, Meier v. Ross General Hosp.,* 71 Cal. Rptr 903, 445 P.2d 519 (1968); *Pietrucha v. Grant Hosp.,* 447 F.2d 1029 (7th Cir. 1971); *Vistica v. Presbyterian Hosp. and Medical Center,* 67 Cal. 2d 465, 432 P.2d 193 (1967).

CONCLUSION

We attempted to find common themes and analyses in the legal materials regarding a therapist's liability for client suicide, but the fact is that the state of the law remains a ragbag of undifferentiated data from which no certain conclusions can be drawn. Notwithstanding this lack of clarity, however, courts are finding hospitals and therapists liable for literally millions of dollars.

Perhaps the best protective measure against being found liable is a good set of meticulous, accurate records. Judges and juries will often empathize with the uncertainty involved in the decisions a therapist has to make but will nonetheless want to be satisfied that a "thoughtful" decision/diagnosis was made. The therapist who can explain and support decisions with copious records will be in an improved position to have a judge or jury side with him even though his decisions ultimately proved wrong. The absence of such records, however, may make the judge or jury assume the worst and can therefore be devastating.[55]

In addition to maintaining good records, the therapist may want to implement the following suggestions:[56]

1. Bargain with the client, if possible and credible, for a promise to refrain from committing suicide and to call the therapist or a suicide crisis hotline if suicidal impulses become strong.

2. Increase the frequency of therapy sessions and have telephone contact with the client between sessions.

3. Maintain adequate staff supervision during all client activities.

4. Periodically collaborate with colleagues, soliciting their opinions regarding the client's condition, treatment, and care.

5. Obtain permission to contact the client's close friends and relatives and ask them to provide support between therapy sessions.

6. Ask the client to be voluntarily hospitalized. Otherwise, consider involuntary commitment. If a decision is ultimately made to not involuntarily commit the client, document the fact that consideration was given and the reasons why a decision was made to not commit.

Implementing these suggestions will not ensure that the psychotherapist will avoid the courtroom, but they will help reduce the risks associated with client-inflicted injuries. Further, these sound practices will help establish that a reasonable attempt was made to control the client and thus will be a viable defense if the therapist is ever hauled into court because of a client's suicide.

---

[55]*See* Klein & Glover, *Psychiatric Malpractice,* 6 J. LAW & PSYCHIATRY 131, 144–145 (1983).
[56]*See* J. Smith, *supra* note 1, at 74; Schutz, *supra* note 25, at 72–73; Swenson, *supra* note 11, at 417.

6

*Suicidal Clients: Clinical Duties**

Our analysis of the legal literature suggests that three primary clinical legal duties apply to case management procedures with suicidal clients:

1. To exercise the ordinary skill and care of a reasonable professional in *identifying* those clients that are higher-than-average risks for suicide.

2. To exercise the ordinary skill and care of a reasonable professional in *taking affirmative steps to prevent* the suicide of clients who are at risk for suicide.

3. To exercise the ordinary skill and care of a reasonable professional in helping clients *overcome their suicidal tendencies.*

Essentially, these duties pertain to questions of (1) accurate diagnosis, (2) taking affirmative steps to prevent a suicide once a client's level of suicide risk is identified, and (3) generic considerations in the psychological treatment of clients with suicidal tendencies. Because of the vast amount of literature available on each topic, we discuss the most nuclear considerations for defining or defending a standard of care for suicidal clients: (1) assessment of suicide risk, (2) clinical management of suicidal clients, and (3) an applied illustration of legal principles with a suicidal client.

ASSESSING SUICIDE RISK

Any attempt to accurately assess suicide risk must not lose sight of three fundamental propositions (Hawton, 1987). First, the actual base rates for suicides are so low that even the most optimistic belief about our professional skill in predicting suicides will include a large number of false positive predictions. For example, if clinicians could predict suicide with 80% accuracy (which they cannot even come close to), 8 out of 10 suicidal individuals could be successfully classified. However, if 10 suicides per 1000 was the actual suicide base rate (and it is really more like 5 in 100,000) and 1000 people were assessed, 192 nonsuicidal people would be inaccurately diagnosed as suicidal. These 192 people would presumably lose their civil liberties, run up expensive hospital bills, suffer public exposure,

*Thanks are extended to Ben Ogles for his fine work in the development of this chapter. He was recently awarded his doctorate from the Clinical Training Program at Brigham Young University and is currently employed as an assistant professor of psychology at Ohio University in Athens.

and so forth. Few would argue that even this most optimistic rate of false positive predictions is unacceptably high. In reality, however, the actual rate of false positive predictions would be enormously higher than in our example, and clinicians' predictive accuracy and the base rate for suicide would be considerably lower in the general population than in our example. The result, obviously, is an extremely low base rate for suicide that virtually precludes accurate prediction case by case.

Second, factors that affect suicide potential can change rapidly—for example, the risk of suicide for a chronically depressed, middle-aged male may be only moderate, but in the event of additional, unexpected stressors such as losing a loved one or a job, the risk can immediately become severe. Accurate prediction of suicide is not really feasible without a reasonable understanding of the stressors an individual will encounter in the immediate and long-term future. And information about most of these psychologically important events will never be available in advance of their actual occurrence!

Third, the characteristics that define suicide risk generally have been derived from studies using clients who were receiving psychological treatment at the time of their suicide attempt. These studies "actually identify factors which predict the risk of suicide for clients while they are receiving treatment" (Hawton, 1987, p. 145). The hazards of individual predictions from group data and overgeneralization are well known and need not be repeated here. Nevertheless, it would be unfortunate if we failed to notice that our primary data sets about suicidal clients usually represent clients who have attempted suicide in spite of treatment and that the implications of this observation alone are potentially staggering. It suggests that our primary indicators of suicide risk may be completely confounded with (1) poor treatment strategies, (2) psychonoxious therapists, (3) unusually strong suicidal urges, and (4) an extreme or uncommon form of suicidal preoccupation.

In spite of the difficulties of assessing suicide risk, however, practicing clinicians are regularly required to evaluate the risk of suicide in a variety of clients and situations. Two sets of relevant information regularly guide this evaluation. The first set consists of empirical data that identify and describe personality and environmental characteristics which are used to differentiate high and low levels of suicidal risk. The second set is information obtained during client interviews. This information is useful for inferring the intensity and seriousness of clients' correct intent to kill themselves. We review the empirical results first.

EMPIRICAL FINDINGS

Studies spanning several decades of research have repeatedly reported demographic and personality characteristics that help identify suicide attempters and completers (Bongar, Peterson, Harris, & Aissis, 1989; Prentice, 1974). The most significant results are as summarized.

Sex

Women are more likely to attempt suicide than men by a ratio of at least 2:1. Men, however, are much more likely to successfully kill themselves if they make an attempt (Walker, 1983).

Age

Suicide risk and age are positively correlated, although suicide rates for children and adolescents are increasing (Slaby, Lieb, & Tancredi, 1986).

Do not underestimate the general importance of the sex and age findings. When a man is middle-aged or older and becomes suicidal, any attempt will almost always be lethal; a gunshot to the head seldom leaves a margin for recovery. Conversely, when a relatively younger female reports suicidal feelings, most attempts will involve ingestion of an overdose of some kind of drug that is seldom lethal. Of course, other considerations with individual cases can modify the applicability of these general patterns, but these two factors are sufficiently important and revealing to warrant special comment.

Marital Status/Isolation

Social isolation and loneliness are predominant themes in the lives of suicide attempters and completers (Comstock, 1984; Hawton, 1987). Singles have a higher rate of attempted and completed suicides, particularly divorced, widowed, or separated individuals who are living alone (Walker, 1983; Urbartis, 1983).

Loss

Recent losses such as the loss of loved ones, employment, or social status increase the risk of suicide (Comstock, 1984). A family history of suicide is also suggestive of future attempts by other family members.

The categories of marital status/isolation and loss reveal the possibility of loneliness and despair being underlying issues for suicidal clients. The loss of "meaningfulness" inherent in many of the specific losses that have been empirically identified suggests the important role of "loneliness" in our understanding of suicide and suicidal risk. However, in the assessment of suicide potential, we doubt that it is the loss of any specific relationship, loved one, or position of power that is the underlying concern; rather, it is the underlying feeling of "meaninglessness" and/or "hopelessness" these events create that is at the heart of the assessment question.

Previous Attempts

Approximately 50 to 80% of those who commit suicide made previous attempts (Slaby, Lieb, & Tancredi, 1986), but about 1% of those who attempt suicide will try again successfully within a year of their first attempt (Hawton, 1987). Once a suicide attempt has been made, the risk of additional attempts remains higher than average for at least 8 years. The more severe the initial attempt, the greater the risk of future attempts (Pierce, 1984).

Psychopathology

The following populations are at higher-than-average risk for suicide: (1) depressives, (2) substance abusers, (3) alcoholics, (4) homosexuals, and (5) schizophrenics (Slaby, Lieb, & Tancredi, 1986; Motto, 1980). Hopelessness, which may or may not be linked to any specific disorder, has been empirically linked to suicide (Beck, Steer, Kovacs, & Garrison, 1985). Some researchers have suggested hopelessness as the most essential element in suicide (Beck, Rush, Shaw, & Emery, 1979). Of those seriously contemplating suicide, about 50% are depressed, 30% are alcoholic, and 5% are schizophrenic (Hawton, 1987).

Behavioral Clues

The following behaviors are indicative of suicide risk: (1) disposal of property, (2) self-neglect, (3) no future plans, (4) severe insomnia, (5) impaired memory, (6) command hallucinations, (7) preoccupation with "anniversary reactions," (8) radical shifts in behavior, and (9) economic problems (Hawton, 1987; Hyman, 1984; Slaby, Lieb, & Tancredi, 1986).

Physical Illness

Recent surgery, chronic disease or pain, and terminal illness all increase the risk of suicide (Hyman, 1984).

Emerging Pattern

When all eight variables are considered collectively, a picture of the modal suicide attempter begins to emerge. Our hypothetical person is most likely isolated, lonely, and depressed. Additionally, the person may have suffered an emotional, social, or physical loss recently. If the person is an older male, the seriousness of the situation is probably acute. It would not be uncommon for an individual in these circumstances to turn to alcohol or drugs to find relief from feelings of hopelessness and despair but fail to find any enduring relief. As their suicidal impulses become more compelling, suicide attempters may give clues to those around them as trying to cry out for help. These verbal and nonverbal cues include disposing of property, nonlethal suicide attempts, and talking about the meaninglessness of life.

The more of these indicators an examiner finds in a person's life, the more substantial the basis for inferring the possibilities of life-threatening behavior by the client.

PSYCHOMETRIC SCALES

Several psychometric instruments have been developed to help practitioners evaluate suicide risk. The advantages of these assessment scales are that they provide a standardized procedure for assessment, are based on normative data, and usually have demonstrated acceptable levels of reliability and validity. The instruments we describe are generally held in high professional regard. They all contain varying degrees and mixtures of the empirical factors identified over the years through the research just discussed, but they have different purposes and psychometric properties.

Hopelessness Scale

The Hopelessness Scale (Beck, Weissman, Lester, & Trexler, 1974) is a 20-item scale developed to measure a client's self-reported pessimism. The items are True-False statements, with an overall internal consistency of .93 using coefficient alpha. Several validity studies have been done using the scale, with limited positive results.

Suicidal Ideations Scale

Beck, Kovacs, and Weissman (1979) developed the Suicide Ideation Scale to quantify and assess suicidal intention. The 19-item scale has a high internal consistency rating (.89, coefficient alpha) and moderate correlations with clinical ratings of suicide risk. The instrument significantly discriminated between depressed outpatients and hospitalized depressed clients with suicidal ideation. Beck, Kovacs, and Weissman (1979) recommended using the instrument for research and as a data-gathering technique for clinical practice.

Suicide Intent Scale

The Suicide Intent Scale (Beck, Schuyler, and Herman, 1974) was developed to assess the level of *suicide intention for clients with a recent suicide attempt.* The scale includes 20 items covering the circumstances and self-report reactions and thoughts concerning the attempt. In addition, the clinician rates variables associated with the reliability of the client's report.

Risk Estimation for Suicide

The Risk Estimation for Suicide (Motto, Heilbron, & Juster, 1982) was created to estimate the general risk of suicide in adults during the 2-year period following the assessment. The 12-item scale is administered by a clinician, who rates each of the 12 risk factors, which include age, occupation, recent losses, and weight or sleep changes. The scale then sums the items for a total score estimate of risk. Reliability and validity data as yet have not been reported.

Risk/Rescue Rating Scale

The Risk/Rescue Rating Scale (Weissman & Worden, 1972) was developed to quantify and describe the seriousness or *lethality of suicide attempts.* Clients are evaluated on five risk factors (agent used, impaired consciousness, lesions/toxicity, reversibility, and treatment required) and five rescue factors (location, person initiating rescue, probability of discovery, accessibility to rescue, and delay until discovery). Two scores are produced to give estimates of the total risk and rescue. Reliability and validity data are unavailable as yet.

Reasons for Living Inventory

The Reasons for Living Inventory was developed to assess the client's *will to live* (Linehan, Goodstein, Nielsen, & Chiles, 1983). The scale consists of 47 items from 6 categories or reasons for living, including coping beliefs, responsibility to family, child-related concerns, fear of suicide, fear of social disapproval, and moral objectives.

Suicide Prevention Center Assessment of Suicide Potentiality

This scale, developed at the Los Angeles Suicide Prevention Center (Lettieri, 1974), was designed to be used by a rater to assess a client's *suicide potential.* Data are gathered from 10 general areas of suicide risk: age, sex, symptoms, stress, acute versus chronic, plan, resources, medical status, communication, and reaction of significant others. While instruments are useful for gathering data and as research tools, the ability to predict suicide remains hampered by low base rates.

CLINICAL INTERVIEW

It is not unusual for clients to report suicidal thoughts to their therapist. In fact, many clients seem to have considered the possibility of suicide at one time or another, as have most people. But having suicidal thoughts is not the same as actively planning to implement them. Because of the fundamental difference between thinking about suicide and actively planning one, an important part of any suicide assessment is estimating the intensity and imminence of a client's intent to kill himself. While the demographic variables we already discussed can alert the clinician to the possibilities of suicide, a client's actual intent to destroy herself may be best determined in an interview with a skilled clinician since it allows more flexibility than the self-report questionnaire data. The following seven areas (A to G) of inquiry are generally accepted as the most promising indicators of a client's intent to commit suicide.

Premeditation and Specificity of Suicide Plans

While suicide at times may be an impulsive act, many suicides are carefully planned and quite deliberate. The level of premeditation and specificity of a suicide plan are clear indicators of real intent and are more promising for prediction and management than those indicators that are more clearly compulsive. Usually, information about specific suicidal plans is obtained rather easily from most clients. A calm and deliberate review of suicidal plans can reveal the care and specificity with which suicidal preparations have been made. For example, a client who has carefully acquired and meticulously prepared lethal doses of poison for ingestion is a more immediate and higher risk than one who would "overdose on everything" in the medicine cabinet.

Availability of Means

A suicide attempt requires that a person inflict serious harm on herself—usually by ingestion, shooting, jumping, asphyxiation, cutting, or hanging. Even though suicides may be carefully planned in advance, the actual attempt may be a more impulsive act. In general, the more available the means for self-destruction in the client's immediate environment (guns, drugs, poisons), the greater the risk of a suicide plan being implemented.

Lethality

The more lethal the method described in the suicide plan, the greater the risk of a successful suicide. Nevertheless, two considerations are important in this stage of the assessment. The first is rather obvious and straightforward. A gun is more lethal than most poisons, and most poisons are more dangerous than barbiturates, and most barbiturates are more dangerous than aspirin. And so it goes. In addition to these factual realities, however, is the client's understanding of the lethality of the method he plans to use. A client who takes three extra sleeping pills, fully expecting to never wake up again, is telling us a great deal about the seriousness of his suicidal intent. And *it is more important to understand the intent of the client than to assume that the risk is lowered because the client is misinformed about the lethality of his plan.*

Timing and Location: Risk/Rescue Ratio

Another revealing consideration in determining suicidal intent is the planned timing and location of the suicide. An attempt at a time and place where the possibilities of being rescued are high does not pose the same risk as an attempt that will take place when the possibility of being rescued is low. Some suicide attempts are planned so that rescue is almost inevitable; these attempts are a cry for help and expressions of the client's profound ambivalence about dying. As mentioned, a risk/rescue scale has been developed (Weissman & Worden, 1972) for the evaluation of previous attempts in order to evaluate actual suicidal intent. This measure may be useful for evaluating client plans as well.

Mental Status

Clients whose perceptions and thinking are disorganized, disoriented, or confused while making suicidal statements are at substantial risk for suicide completion (Hatton & Valente, 1984). In addition, these clients cannot meaningfully and responsibly participate in the therapeutic process. In these cases, involuntary hospitalization is usually necessary.

Client Competence

In Chapter 4, we discussed the role of client competence in the case management of potentially violent or dangerous cases. In most important respects, all these considerations apply to the suicidal client as well. In general, we suggested that as the client's level of competence decreases, the need for the therapist to initiate more decisive acts (hospitalization, managing the environment, and so forth) to protect client welfare correspondingly increases. Again, we remind readers that the greatest risk of incurring liability is at moderate levels of suicide risk because of assessment limitations, which is why the assessment of client competence is such a crucial matter at moderate levels of suicide risk. Remember, cases involving severe suicide risk almost automatically require hospitalization or breaching confidentiality. On the other hand, mild levels of risk hardly ever involve breaching confidentiality or involuntary hospitalization because of the suicide risk alone. But a moderate level of suicidal risk is another matter entirely—case management guidelines are not nearly as clear or easy to justify. Client competence is more reliably assessed and more relevant to clinical decision making.

Pain, Perturbation, and Press

Schneidman (1988), whose long-term contributions to the assessment and understanding of suicide are hallmark, suggested the following 10 factors that he believes are common to all suicide attempts:

1. The *purpose* of suicide is to seek a solution.
2. The *goal* of suicide is relief from "intolerable mind content."
3. The *stimulus* in suicide is psychological pain.
4. The *stressor* in suicide is frustrated psychological needs.
5. The *emotion* in suicide is helplessness.
6. The *cognitive state* in suicide is ambivalence.
7. The *perceptual state* in suicide is constriction with lack of choices.
8. The *action* in suicide is regressive.

9. The *interpersonal act* in suicide is communication of intention.

10. The *consistency* in suicide is with lifelong coping patterns.

He summarized these 10 factors in "a theoretical cubic model of suicide" (Schneidman, 1988). The dimensions of the cube are pain, perturbation, and press. *Pain* is the amount and level of psychological pain the individual is experiencing. *Perturbation* is the amount of constriction, lack of choices, or "proclivity for irreversible action" (p. 8). *Press* is everything that is done to an individual, including family influence, genetics, situational pressures, and chance events. The implications for assessment and treatment that are derived from Schneidman's model are quite obvious: (1) suicidal intent increases relative to the pain, perturbation, and press the client experiences, and (2) case management is focused on relieving the pain, providing alternatives, and reducing the negative press. Clients with less pain, more choices, and less negative press will not choose suicide as the only way out.

Formulating Estimates of Suicide Risk

A number of different scales have been developed to help integrate information from different sources into a single estimate of suicide risk (Hatton & Valente, 1984; Litman, 1974). We summarize one such scale to demonstrate the utility of these guides. Based on the *Comprehensive Mental Health Assessment Guide,* a table of suicide risk, with ratings from 1 (no risk) to 4 (very high immediate risk), was developed. Each type of risk is summarized below:

Low risk: Involves threats with no plans, no previous attempts, no alcohol/drug problem, and satisfactory social supports.

Moderate risk: Includes threats with low lethal plan or consideration of high lethal attempt with no specific plan, history of low lethal attempts, drug use for stress relief, ambivalence about life and death.

High risk: Described as current high lethal plan, available means, previous attempts, drinking problem, depressed, and wanting to die.

Very high risk: Includes all the high-risk criteria plus impending loss or social crisis, using alcohol to excess, or a history of high lethal attempts.

Each category is further discussed as one of three types of suicidal behavior:

Type I: Suicidal behavior is described as verbal threats with no specific plan or means of carrying out a plan. Additionally, any attempt that involves no physical danger to life or clearly provides for rescue is classified as type I suicidal behavior.

Type II: Suicidal behavior includes threats with available means and a potentially lethal plan. Additionally, attempts that include the potential for physical harm (not fatal) or do not provide for rescue are classified as type II behavior.

Type III: Suicidal behavior includes threats or attempts in which the client anticipates a fatal outcome. Typically, the client has ambivalent feelings about death but tends to favor dying. In type III behavior, clients are at risk for suicide on both a short- and long-term basis.

Suicide is the most frequent form of psychological emergency practicing clinicians will face (Schein, 1976). As we already pointed out, lawsuits over suicide cases usually evolve around two central issues. The first issue is the foreseeability of a suicide attempt or accurate diagnosis of suicide potential. The second issue is causation, or the use of appropriate case management procedure, that appropriately balances the benefits of the least restrictive form of treatment with the client's need to be protected from potential harm. With these two considerations in mind, the importance of forming a reasonable clinical opinion about suicide risk is obvious. Failure to meet professional standards in assessing suicide risk is negligence, and a faulty assessment can also lead to faulty case management.

These are certainly consequential judgments for both the client and the therapist. And this is precisely the point at which therapists should remember that legal negligence is defined in terms of falling below professional standards of care, not being right or wrong in predictions. When judgments about suicide risk are based on the most relevant information known about suicide risk, it is extremely difficult to demonstrate professional negligence—even in those unfortunate circumstances when clients successfully kill themselves. Professional negligence is a failure to collect and carefully consider all the clinically relevant information about suicide assessment and prediction. We already identified and discussed the information that is considered relevant to the assessment of suicide. With this information in hand, the accuracy of clinical predictions becomes quite secondary to the care and thoroughness with which it was collected and considered in malpractice cases, so the primary considerations involved in any clinical opinion about suicide risk should be formally summarized in the clinical record. This record normally includes a summary of the assessment data collected and the objective and subjective factors that influenced their interpretation.

The following case helps illustrate the clinical process and considerations involved in formulating estimates of suicide risk. Norman was a 48-year-old white male who had suffered from chronic and relatively severe depression for the past 4 years. During this time, he had been essentially unemployed except for occasional part-time work. He was intelligent, slightly obsessive, and extremely self-punitive about his perceived failures as a provider, father, and husband. He exhibited no obvious signs of a thought disorder or conceptual disorganization. He was, however, extremely despondent and totally lacking in self-confidence. His wife had been seriously considering a divorce. About 2 weeks earlier, Norman left home in the car with a gun. Before his departure, Norman talked with three people about his despair and feelings of hopelessness. No one has seen or heard from him since.

It was at this point that the family called the therapist who had worked with Norman 11 years earlier. He knew them well because of his prior contacts with Norman, which had lasted about 14 months. During this time, Norman was treated for depression and had made substantial progress. Norman's treatment was terminated prematurely, however, because the therapist moved to another state. Norman did not continue in therapy with another therapist, but his improved condition lasted for about 4 years. He then started into a gradual decline over a 5-year period that gradually led to his current desperate condition.

A little over 2 weeks after Norman's disappearance, he called home, much to everybody's relief. He was several thousand miles from home and was wandering aimlessly about the country in his car. He had no purpose or goal in his travels. He was still considering shooting himself, particularly in the early morning hours when he was laying in his car unable to sleep. His wife pleaded with him to return home, but he refused. She informed him that she had contacted his former therapist, in whom Norman had substantial trust and confidence, and that the therapist could see him if he would travel to his new location. Norman left immediately for a 1300-mile trip and arrived 2 days later.

After an evaluation interview, the therapist started considering Norman's situation carefully. A number of factors painted an unhappy prognostic picture. Norman was an older male who (1) had lethal means for any suicide attempt, (2) was socially isolated, (3) was in the midst of a potential divorce, (4) reported feelings of severe depression and hopelessness prior to disappearing, and (5) was not likely to be rescued from any suicide attempt. In spite of the severity of each of these considerations, it was equally obvious that Norman was not intent on killing himself immediately, based on (1) his resisting his suicidal impulses for over 2 weeks while driving around alone; (2) his having no specific time, date, or plan for killing himself; (3) his showing no signs of mental disorganization, hallucinations, or delusions; (4) his substantial hope over the prospects of seeing his old therapist; (5) his ability to travel 1300 miles in 2 days for his scheduled appointment; and (6) his religious beliefs, which prohibited suicide. During the interview, Norman demonstrated a clear grasp of the life-and-death issues involved in his current situation, but he did not believe hospitalization would do him any good in the long run—an important point with which the therapist could not disagree.

Based on all these considerations, the therapist understood that Norman's situation was a dangerous one at best. The most objective predictors of suicide risk were not in Norman's favor, but the more subjective ones were. He had not yet killed himself in spite of opportunity, lethal means, significant family losses, and social isolation. Nevertheless, he was still a high suicide risk, and his situation could deteriorate rapidly, depending on family support, financial problems, and unemployability. But Norman's religious views had demonstrated their power in the equation for Norman's survival, as did his ability to still be goal-directed and self-regulating, as evidenced by his ability to quickly traverse several states to meet with a therapist he believed in.

The ultimate conclusion seemed fairly clear to the therapist. Norman had an extremely high suicide potential. No compelling evidence suggested that a suicide attempt was imminent now, although it could be later—particularly if therapy did not go well. Furthermore, it appeared that Norman's best interests would be best served with outpatient care as long as it was justifiable to do so. Balancing the risks and benefits of outpatient care suggested the value of not attempting to hospitalize Norman against his will and to proceed with outpatient care with all the precautionary steps outlined in the later case management section of this chapter. Ultimately, the therapist believed that Norman belonged to a class of clients with an extremely high risk of suicide. But the therapist was equally aware that most clients in Norman's risk category would not kill themselves. Whether Norman would be among those few who would actually kill themselves was not known, but case management precautions that acknowledged his high-risk status would have to be taken. Thus carefully calculated judgments about the need for hospitalization, outpatient treatment, Norman's long-term potential for recovery, and appropriate precautions for outpatient care would be subject to continual review. After reviewing all these facts, the therapist outlined in considerable detail in the clinical record all the data and risk/benefit analyses involved in his decision about Norman. The therapist fully realized that errors of clinical judgment are inevitable with high-risk clientele like Norman, but basing these judgments on limited, irrelevant, or erroneous information could be potentially libelous, which is why rigorous record keeping is essential with high-risk clients.

SUMMARY

We summarized the empirical and clinical interview materials most relevant to the assessment of suicide risk and found that a number of demographic, personality, and environmental characteristics can alert us to the increased possibilities of suicide in some clinical populations. These characteristics are particularly important to the assessment process because they are the best "nonverbal" correlates of suicide risk. Their role is to alert the clinician to the dangers of suicide when the client is reluctant, unwilling, or unable to discuss emerging suicide wishes. But a client's actual wish to die is probably best assessed in a clinical interview, in which the best indicators of imminent suicide intent are (1) specificity of plan, (2) lethality of means, (3) availability of means, (4) client's mental status, and (5) the risk/rescue ratio of the suicide plan. Finally, we discussed a method of integrating all these different types and sources of information into a single estimate of suicide risk.

CASE MANAGEMENT

Common Concerns

Before introducing the case management considerations we consider optimal for different levels of suicide risk, let us present several clinical concerns common to all types of suicidal behavior.

Underlying Dynamics.   Case management with suicidal clients must be based on some substantive understanding of the meaning and functioning of suicidal behavior for each client, for two reasons. First, suicide threats are dramatic and extreme events that require well-conceived responses from the practitioner, so this is not the time or place for trial-and-error learning. Second, there are two separate and distinct phases of responding to suicidal threats. The first phase is crisis management in cases of acute suicide risk. Here, the therapist's task is to simply help keep the client alive until the crisis passes, whether by hospitalization, medication, or giving support and reassurance. The fact that many of these interventions actually enhance dependency or other forms of pathology is a secondary consideration.

But as the acute risk starts to subside, the second phase of treatment begins: identifying and dealing with the client's enduring and underlying personality style, whatever it may be.

The best empirical evidence and commonly accepted clinical belief indicate that hopelessness, depression, despair, and mental disorganization are some of the best single predictors of suicide. Clearly, one important dimension of suicide risk is affective and mood disturbances of all subtypes, particularly depression (Clark, 1988). These outward symptoms, however, can be a function of different underlying personality and biochemical dynamics (Maltsberger, 1988). Even though the assumed etiology of mood disorders is probably diverse and certainly controversial, the most common personality style assumed to lie beneath these symptoms is probably the dependent personality (Millon, 1969), with its enduring disposition to please and placate others and avoid interpersonal conflict. In fact, this may be the most common personality configuration associated with suicidal behavior. And when it is operative, client anger toward self and others is most likely interjected, allowing this conflict-avoidant personality to continually seek reassurance from others while accruing more internal self-hatred.

If this is only a partially valid construction of one of the most common personality components associated with suicidal behavior, it is no surprise to find suicide threats as one of the bargaining chips in the equation of interpersonal affection and affiliation. The fact that a suicide threat may have strategic value does not diminish its potential validity, and the fact that suicide threats are almost always dramatic events does not alter the underlying meaning and function of the behavior: controlling, manipulative, and a generic plea for help and attention. That the suicidal behavior is itself irrational and self-defeating in every imaginable way is only a demonstration of the client's desperation.

Thus we see the possibility that the emotional support and encouragement therapists frequently offer may be useful in getting a suicidal client through a crises in the short run but are self-defeating interventions in the long run, only reinforcing the client's already pathological reliance on others for emotional support. Additionally, most therapeutic steps in which client compliance is rewarded by therapist approval runs the same risks—the client successfully seduces the therapist into a temporarily pleasing and conflict-avoidant relationship.

We hope this illustration clarifies the necessity of two important points in the treatment of suicidal clients. The first point is to work toward acquiring an understanding of the meaning and function of suicidal behavior in each client; the second is to consistently respond to suicidal clients in a style that is a logical extension of the therapist's conceptual understanding of the client. Even though the therapist's understanding of any client will necessarily be incomplete to some degree, clinical intervention needs to be anchored to a stable theory about suicide rather than the occasionally dramatic machinations of an unstable and dangerous client. Again, trial-and-error learning can have disastrous consequences in this situation.

Establishing a Therapeutic Alliance. Developing and maintaining a therapeutic relationship with a suicidal client is a crucial and difficult task. In terms of risk management, a high-quality therapeutic relationship is required for the following therapeutic functions.

Informed Consent. At some point, clients at moderate to severe levels of suicide risk need to clearly understand and proceed in therapy with the understanding that their therapist has a duty to take affirmative steps to prevent what may reasonably be considered an imminent suicide attempt. This action could involve breaching confidentiality, involuntary hospitalization, or including family members or others in the treatment process. While these issues may have been briefly discussed early in therapy, they need to be reinforced at this time of crisis because they are all sensitive and delicate topics that can lead to fundamental disruptions in the therapeutic process and relationship and so must be discussed in an atmosphere of professional trust and excellent rapport. Otherwise, the client's more typical patterns of defense and denial are sure to appear in the form of feeling betrayed, abandoned, or deceived—all unwelcomed and dangerous feelings for suicidal clients.

Establishing Levels of Competence. It is important to remember that when charges of professional negligence are filed against a therapist, the typical courtroom assumption is that clients are "little children in the hands of parentally responsible therapists" (Gutheil, Busztajn, & Bradsky, 1986). In the courtroom, this literally means that clients are assumed to be incompetent until the therapist introduces documented evidence to the contrary. One of the better ways of assessing clients' capacity to understand and responsibly respond to important life issues is to watch them try to do so during the therapeutic process. This is particularly true during the process of obtaining a client's informed consent about the ground rules governing the therapeutic process. For example, a client's capacity to adhere to informed choices—based on an accurate understanding of the nature of the treatment process, the role expectations of the client and therapist, and the conditions and reasons for compromises in confidentiality—is a way of accumulating documented evidence of personal competence, or the lack of it, both legally and psychologically. This information is paramount in establishing legal liability of clients for their conduct outside the consulting room as well as helping the therapist identify the level of control they need to exercise in case management decisions. An open, trusting therapeutic relationship is necessary for this level of therapeutic dialogue.

Clients who are unable or unwilling to participate in a meaningful therapeutic relationship may warrant special clinical consideration. It has been suggested (Simon, 1987) that one of the more ominous signs of genuine suicidal intent may be the client's lack of involvement in a therapeutic alliance. While this
observation alone should not be overweighted in any suicide assessment, it can
be an important red flag indicative of the client's suicidal intent.

Relationship Building with Suicidal Clients.   It is not uncommon for
some clients to try and discuss their suicidal impulses during their first therapy
session. This seems a difficult undertaking for most clients for several reasons—
all of which are perfectly understandable. Let us discuss these relationship difficulties and possible responses.

Clients seldom have clear expectations about psychotherapy. Research data
from a variety of areas in psychology have taught us that ambiguity and uncertainty, particularly in areas of personal importance, breed anxiety and worry, and
that is exactly what many clients experience during their first relatively ambiguous
therapy hour. Clients, with their varied stereotypes and mythical expectations of
therapists, really do not know what to expect if they candidly tell a therapist about
their suicidal concerns. Some are profoundly afraid that they will be immediately
hospitalized and pronounced insane; others fear that they may frighten their
therapist and be rejected as a client. And still others need assurance that the therapist
is able to handle their problems before they divulge them.

All these relationship restraints are primarily a function of the client being placed in a situation that requires high psychological risk taking in a trusting
interpersonal relationship which has not been experienced or earned. At best, this
is a very difficult situation for most clients, and one in which the therapist's relationship-building skills will be taxed. The therapist's most central task is to start
building professional credibility.

The client may not be the only one uncomfortable in this situation; we
know of few therapists who find any comfort in dealing with seriously suicidal
clients. In fact, Deutsch (1984) stated that clinicians reported working with suicidal
cases as the most stressful clinical work. In today's legal environment, such clients
can also arouse high levels of litigation anxiety, in addition to concern for the
client's safety. And anxiety affects therapists the same way it does clients: At low
levels, it may enhance performance, but after that its effects on performance are
seldom pleasing. Again, these are not the optimal conditions for developing a new
therapeutic relationship.

Because of these potential relationship-building obstacles, we suggest that
the relationship-building activities proceed with the following three guidelines
in mind:

1. Resist the natural temptation to be reassuring to new clients. Enduring
credibility comes from being honest and deliberate in professional judgment and behavior. Most clients understand the seriousness of their prob-

lems, and any attempt to respond to them in overly reassuring ways is seldom useful. Besides, many suicidal clients present themselves in ways carefully calculated to elicit reassurance. Under these conditions, it is most inappropriate to respond with superficial reassurance.

2. Help clients recognize and legitimize their ambivalent feelings about confiding in a therapist through empathic understanding and reality testing. Openly acknowledge the validity of their concerns when doing so is appropriate. Also, try and help clients understand that you understand the basis for their affective ambivalence about talking openly with a stranger. And finally, do not press for a decision. Instead, focus on the anxiety that surrounds clients' fear of therapy, and try to facilitate clients' expressions of their own thoughts and feelings.

3. Do not contribute to the expectation that clients should be comfortable in the early stages of relationship building. Suicidal clients are worried, distressed, and depressed, and usually for good reasons. Very little is going to happen in the early stages of psychotherapy to improve this unhappy state of affairs. In fact, a number of things could make it worse. It is better for clients to have realistic expectations about the distress or improvement they may experience in the first few weeks of therapy than to be surprised or disappointed.

Routine Precautions.   There are a number of compelling reasons to consider outpatient care for many moderately suicidal clients. Remember that in the absence of clear signs of an imminent suicide attempt, it may be difficult to hospitalize clients against their will. Additionally, the client's long-term well-being may be best served by not hospitalizing them. Appropriate case management considerations require that the therapist recognize the risk of suicide and balance this risk with the benefits of the least restrictive and appropriate form of treatment and protection of the client.

When a therapist elects to treat suicidal clients on an outpatient basis, no matter what the reason, a number of routine precautions should be meticulously implemented. All these rather mechanical steps can help minimize risks associated with outpatient care resulting from limited contact.

1. Being able to provide 24-hour contact and coverage

2. Being able to increase the frequency of therapy sessions as needed

3. Having accurate information about important anniversary and holiday reactions

4. Giving clients limited supplies of antidepressants or other medications

5. Considering routine consultations with professional colleagues

6. Employing the use of telephone check-ins by the client during periods of stress and turmoil

Clinical Interventions

Conceptual Dimensions.   Recently, Kramer (1982) used a multidimensional scaling approach to identify the conceptual dimensions underlying clinical work with suicidal clients. This methodological approach required the following three steps in data collection and analysis:

1. A random sample of practicing clinicians was asked to identify the clinical interventions they believed useful with suicidal clients. The result was a list of 51 treatment techniques (after a minor reduction of items by raters) based on conceptual similarities.

2. A new sample of psychologists was asked to rate the degree of similarity/ dissimilarity between all possible combinations of the 51 treatment techniques that had been identified. These ratings were then analyzed by using multidimensional scaling methods. Essentially, this process consists of transforming ratings of item similarity into two or more dimensions of euclidean space. The closer the items are placed in this conceptual space, the more similar their ratings. After all the items are located in the conceptual space, they are interpreted much like factor analysis results—that is, the common conceptual properties that seem to bind items together are identified. It was found that four conceptual dimensions seemed to adequately account for the results of the multidimensional scaling results.

3. Two expert judges identified the most appropriate conceptual names for the four properties that were identified.

Figure 6-1 summarizes the most essential information about the four underlying conceptual dimensions that practicing clinicians use to think about the management of suicidal clients. As can be seen, the four primary conceptual dimensions include focus of treatment, emotional needs, affective facilitation, and emotional distance.

Focus of Treatment.   The focus of treatment interventions can vary from mobilizing the client's internal resources to maximizing the use of the environmental resources surrounding the client. This dimension is essentially one that describes clinical interventions which vary with respect to their emphasis on internal or external control and/or influence of client behavior.

Naturally, clinical activities that define and illustrate various points along this continuum differ from each other substantially. At one end of this continuum, the therapist will impose a great deal of structure and control over the client's environment and treatment. This action could include involuntary hospitalization, having the client surrender weapons, or arranging for constant companionship with family or friends. The other end of this continuum would involve encouraging introspection of exploring the meaning and function of psychic pain or client response styles. Here, clinical interventions are designed to mobilize client internal resources and facilitate client independence and personal responsibility.

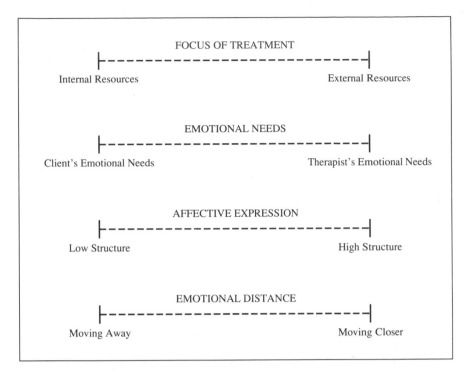

Figure 6-1   Primary conceptual dimensions of interventions with suicidal clients (summarized from Kramer, 1982).

A complete menu of clinical interventions from these four conceptual dimensions and their use as case management techniques with clients at different levels of suicide risk are discussed in the next section of this chapter. For now, we wish to point out that focusing clinical interventions on the client's internal or external resources is only one of the primary dimensions along which case management procedures vary with suicidal clients.

Emotional Needs.   This dimension describes different steps therapists can take to accommodate their emotional needs or the client's emotional needs. Clinical interventions designed to accommodate client emotional needs include activities such as exploring client guilt, anger, hopelessness, or anxiety. They could also include more structured activities such as having the client chart daily mood swings or the environment cues associated with the onset of depressive moods. Therapists can take a number of steps to maintain their own emotional well-being when working with suicidal clients, including limiting the number of high-risk cases they accept and having regular consultation and supervisory sessions with colleagues on high-risk cases.

Even though each conceptual dimension is being described in bipolar terms, remember that none of these dimensions automatically suggest clinical suitability of its interventions for different levels of client risk. In fact, as client risk increases, a therapist may well choose to select a number of different clinical interventions from different points along these conceptual dimensions. The use of one of these clinical interventions does not automatically preclude the use of another. For example, it could be that as suicide risk increases, therapists will increase their level of attention to accommodating both their emotional needs and those of the client. A more complete menu of clinical interventions along this continuum is identified and discussed shortly.

Affective Facilitation.   This dimension represents a continuum that describes different levels of therapist-imposed structure for the purpose of facilitating client affective expression. One end of this continuum is interventions that are nondirective and supportive and include activities such as probing, open-ended questions, and reflective listening. Open-ended exploration of client affect is typified by the less controlling forms of therapy that enhance personal expression and individuality. More structured approaches for facilitating client affective expression could include guided fantasies about death, anger, or predicting what significant others will be doing 6 months after the client's death. The suitability of clinical interventions along this continuum for different levels of client risk are discussed shortly.

Emotional Distance.   This dimension refers to the degree in which the therapist moves toward or away from the client's emotional distress. One end of this continuum is anchored to high levels of therapist involvement and usually appears in the form of the therapist being more involved and responsive to the client's distress. In this sense, this dimension is similar to the second dimension (emotional focus) because it attempts to respond to the client's emotional pain and experience. However, this dimension refers to the amount of distance or perceived attachment between therapist and client, whereas the emotional needs dimension refers to active focusing on the client's versus the therapists's needs. In short, even when therapists focus on their own needs, we hope they will not become too distanced from the clients. When they become overly involved, there are interventions or actions they can take to provide an adequate amount of distance. The other end of this continuum is anchored to the therapist maintaining more distance from the client's emotional turmoil.

Case Management Considerations

As is now apparent, practicing clinicians see most clinical interventions with suicidal clients varying with respect to (1) treatment focus on internal or external sources of client influence, (2) the importance of attending to client and therapist emotional needs, (3) expression of affect as a result of open versus structured interventions, and (4) the amount of emotional distance or involvement between the therapist and client. Obviously, these are robust and relevant conceptual dimensions for classifying and describing a wide range of clinical interventions.

Table 6-1 lists a number of therapeutic tasks and techniques that illustrate both ends of these bipolar dimensions. The table summarizes a variety of actual clinical interventions corresponding to the four conceptual dimensions practicing clinicians identify when they think about suicidal client case management.

Please notice the unmistakable relationship between clinical interventions along these dimensions and case management considerations most suitable for

Table 6-1   Therapeutic Tasks by Dimension

Internal Resources	*External Resources*
Encourage the patient to generate other solutions.	Initiate commitment proceeding through family.
Increase client's insight into mode of coping and explore reasons for mode.	Manage substance usage.
	Encourage voluntary committment if possible.
Identify and label source of guilt and anger. Devclop assertiveness skills to deal with these emotions.	Assess the extent of depression. Consider medications or ECT.
Empathize and reflect the client's perception of endless struggle.	Help relieve client isolation.
	Monitor medication amounts.
Encourage proper sleep and eating habits.	Remove weapons, medications, and so on from client's environment. Enlist help of others if possible.
	Moderate the client's support systems.
	Make the risk known to all concerned parties if client remains in outpatient treatment.
	Obtain a medical consultant.
	Arrange for 24-hour companionship.
Patient's Emotional Needs	*Therapist's Emotional Needs*
Encourage short-term goal setting.	Consult with colleagues.
Constantly reevaluate suicide risk.	Recognize that the patient is ultimately in control.
Help the patient problem solve. Have client chart behaviors, images, and words that precede suicidal ideation.	Therapists generally should not treat more than two high-risk patients on an outpatient basis at any given time.
Take extra precautions on anniversaries and holidays.	
Be especially careful when providing posthospitalization, follow-up treatment.	

Table 6-1 *(continued)*

Affective Expression: Low Structure	*Affective Expression: High Structure*
Provide space and encourage ventilation of feelings.	Take clients through detailed guided fantasy about their deaths. Focus on feelings of survivors.
Help the client recognize and express anger more effectively.	Include important others in therapy, and facilitate communication.
Encourage the client to share feelings with others.	Encourage physical and social activity. Help the patient experiment with own mood-altering behavior.
Provide hope.	Activate happier memories as a way of increasing distance from current pain. Convey that good and bad times come and go—nothing is permanent.

Emotional Distance (Moving Closer)	*Emotional Distance (Moving Away)*
Identify and label patient's irrational beliefs and cognitive distortions.	Help the client use religious resources and additional social support.
Explore the patient's motives. Question faulty assumptions.	Obtain a commitment to postpone suicide while therapy continues: Secure a promise to give treatment a chance.
Recognize the underlying motive.	
Increase the frequency of sessions.	
Encourage daily telephone contact.	

clients at different levels of suicide risk. As suicide risk increases, there is a consistent and corresponding shift in the need for the therapist to focus on environmental control, more structured affective expression, managing the distance in the therapeutic relationship, and attending to client as well as therapist emotional needs. The general trend is clear: As client dangerousness increases, there is a corresponding increase in the need for the therapist to exercise more initiative and control for provocative interventions to protect client welfare. Let us now discuss the applicability of these general therapeutic principles with regard to minimal, mild, moderate, and severe levels of suicide risk.

Minimal.   When suicide risk is minimal, the only action needed is to document that an assessment has been completed and that the client is at minimal risk. The procedures and evidence to support this conclusion should be summarized in the clinical record.

Mild.   In general, mild levels of suicide risk do not require drastic deviations or alterations in one's general management style. For the most part, it is therapy as usual, except for additional emphasis on meticulous record keeping, periodic reviews of the client's suicidal ideation and impulses, and an occasional consultation and review of case progress with a colleague. With therapist preference, clinical interventions and management can stay at low levels of control and structure. Consideration of therapeutic distancing, focusing on the client's emotional needs, and facilitating affective expression remain at usual levels. If the client's level of hopelessness or suicidal ideation increases, the therapist should seriously consider discussing with clients their more enduring coping strategies and try to minimize the isolation of excessively withdrawn clients.

Moderate. As the level of suicide risk increases, there is usually a corresponding need for the therapist to exercise greater control over the therapeutic process. In addition, the therapist should increase attention to both client and personal emotional needs and the facilitation of client affect and maintain appropriate levels of distance in the relationship. This may take the form of more emphasis on solving immediate day-to-day problems, affective expression, and client emotional needs. In some cases, clients will need greater protection, and the therapist may exercise more direct control over relieving isolation, removing weapons, drugs or alcohol, and establishing nonsuicidal contracts. Also, as suicide risk increases, it usually becomes more important and appropriate for the clinician to seek consultation with other professionals and start considering the wisdom of minimizing the number of additional high-risk clients accepted. This is also time to start considering and assessing the value of hospitalization for some clients.

Severe. This level of suicide risk requires that the therapist act decisively to protect clients from suicidal impulses. Specific action should be taken to maintain appropriate levels of distance and provide for client and therapist emotional needs. Interventions aimed at managing external resources and facilitating expressions of affect should be carefully chosen and implemented.

Therapists frequently choose hospitalization for clients at this level of risk, although not every case demands this level of control and structure. Encouraging appropriate eating and sleeping habits, along with developing daily schedules, can help establish a sense of direction for some clients. Crucial consideration for using resources in the client's environment, such as around-the-clock companionship, may be the only alternative to hospitalization. Removing weapons or intoxicants and establishing social contacts is also important.

Clients who are disoriented, disorganized, psychotic, or delusionally depressed may be unable to work cooperatively with the therapist. Such cases require the therapist's complete control and directiveness. Hospitalization or 24-hour home care is usually mandatory at this level of risk.

SUMMARY

The clinical management of suicidal cases should be a function of the severity of suicide risk. In general, as the suicide risk increases, the more active and directive the therapist should become, with involuntary hospitalization as the terminal point in this process. Movement along other treatment dimensions should also correspond to changes in the severity of suicide risk.

CLINICAL ILLUSTRATION

Earlier in this chapter, we introduced the case of Norman, a 48-year-old white male with a long history of depression and suicidal tendencies. As you may recall, Norman's situation appeared close to desperate at the time he appeared at his therapist's office. Naturally, the therapist was very concerned about the prospects of a suicide because Norman (1) was socially isolated; (2) was seriously depressed, with pronounced feelings of hopelessness; (3) had lethal means available for a suicide attempt, (4) was on the verge of being divorced, and (5) was not likely to be rescued in the event of a suicide attempt. After this preliminary interview, the therapist called his attorney; their conversation went as follows:

INTRODUCTION TO SITUATION

Questions About Foreseeability of Suicide

THERAPIST: Hello counselor, this is your favorite therapist calling again. I hate to say this, but I need your help again. It looks like it might be a serious suicide case tonight.

ATTORNEY: You guys must run ads to attract high-risk clients. Are you having a special this week?

THERAPIST: No, but high-risk cases always gravitate to the best therapists. Is the same true for attorneys?

ATTORNEY: You seem to be feeling rather spry this evening—shall we get down to business?

THERAPIST: OK, these are the essential facts of the situation: (1) I have a client who is at substantial risk for suicide, (2) who will not consent to hospitalization, (3) whose optimal chances for recovery would be reduced by hospitalization, and (4) many clinicians would disagree on the need for hospitalization in this case, and also on the appropriateness of outpatient care.

ATTORNEY: So you have a case that is admittedly at risk for suicide and you're unsure of the legal liabilities associated with both hospitalization and outpatient treatment.

THERAPIST: That's right.

Questions About Foreseeability of Suicide Risk

ATTORNEY: I'm going to ask you a series of questions to determine if the *risk* of suicide by this client could reasonably be anticipated. Legally, I'm talking about the concept of foreseeability. Before a therapist can be held liable for a client's suicide, the therapist must have known or according to professional standards, should have known, that the risk of suicide was present. Did I understand you to say that this client is clearly at risk for suicide?

THERAPIST: He's certainly a higher risk than the typical client I see. As a matter of fact, I would judge the risk to be substantial. Nevertheless, it is imperative that you understand that even at this level of risk, very few clients will actually make a suicide attempt. About 10 years ago I saw this client, and at that time he was equally suicidal. At that time he had acquired lethal means and expressed serious intent to harm himself, but he never actually implemented his suicidal plans.[1]

ATTORNEY: Nevertheless, the fact that you see him as a high suicide risk clearly suggests foreseeability.

THERAPIST: What you're saying is not necessarily true; it may even be illogical. The most likely outcome of this case is no suicide attempt. The statistical evidence will bear out this point over and over. In light of this statistical evidence, it is most reasonable to suggest that a suicide attempt is not foreseeable. You must understand that "high-risk" is a relative term; in this case, the risk of a suicide attempt is higher than with most clients but still remains very low.

ATTORNEY: Will suicide prevention considerations be involved in the treatment of this case?

THERAPIST: Absolutely.

ATTORNEY: Then a court will find the risk of suicide foreseeable.

THERAPIST: You know this sounds like the same circular conversation we had last night [see Chapter 4]. I'm telling you that the probabilities of this person actually attempting suicide are low. And what you're telling me is that because these low probabilities exist, a suicide attempt is foreseeable. What you seem to be saying is that the remotest possibility of suicide equals foreseeability. In reality, low probabilities clearly suggest the absence of foreseeability. Do you understand why you're confusing me?

ATTORNEY: Nevertheless, the law says that if you are using suicide prevention considerations in your treatment plan, a subsequent suicide is foreseeable.

THERAPIST: Even when the suicide prevention considerations are employed as precautions?

ATTORNEY: That's right.

THERAPIST: That level of semantic elasticity allows words to mean anything you want them to mean. The improbable is now foreseeable and the probable is disregarded. That's not the way a reasonable person's world works.

ATTORNEY: It may appear that way, but "foreseeability" is a legal term of art whose meaning is different from the social vernacular.

---

[1] If the response to this question is "yes," then additional issues come into play. For example, the recency and number of previous attempts must be determined. If the most recent attempt was quite some time ago, then an issue may be raised as to whether the circumstances that precipitated those previous attempts have since recurred without a suicide attempt, thereby demonstrating a new tolerance to previously threatening circumstances.

THERAPIST: Whoa! You are totally misunderstanding my point and unintentionally verifying it. Your definition of foreseeability makes *everything* foreseeable.
That makes the word completely meaningless and allows courts to apply it
according to their whims and wishes. This would seem to permit the legal system
to justify *any* ruling by disingenuously asserting "foreseeability." Words with
infinite elasticity cannot have clear meanings.

ATTORNEY: When clinical decisions involve potential loss of life, lower probabilities will be used to establish foreseeability. Therefore, even though high-risk
cases rarely make actual suicide attempts, the fact that someone's life may be
at stake justifies a broader definition of foreseeability.

THERAPIST: So even though the specific probabilities of this client actually attempting suicide are extremely remote, the mere fact that I employ case management procedures for suicide prevention satisfies the legal definition of foreseeability?

ATTORNEY: That's right. But remember, a finding of foreseeability only represents the initial hurdle for establishing liability—a hurdle that is easily cleared.

THERAPIST: In essence, then, what you're telling me is that the law deems something foreseeable even if it's extraordinarily improbable?

ATTORNEY: Perhaps, but there's an important legal distinction I should explain
to you. It's important to distinguish between the foreseeability of a suicide attempt and merely foreseeing the risk of such an attempt. Courts recognize that
predicting a suicide attempt is all but impossible and therefore do not require
such a standard. However, anticipating a risk of a suicide attempt is certainly
within the therapist's ability. Merely diagnosing and treating the client for suicide
prevention is an admission by the therapist of a recognized risk of client suicide.
That makes it foreseeable.

THERAPIST: How important is foreseeability in establishing liability?

ATTORNEY: It is a major consideration without which liability can never be
found, but it is also easily established.

THERAPIST: OK, I'm clearly acknowledging the risk of a suicide attempt. Does
that have any legal implications beyond foreseeability?

ATTORNEY: Yes, it invokes an obligation on you to take affirmative steps to prevent a suicide attempt and reduce the suicide risk.

Questions About Preventing
Suicide (Legal Causation)

ATTORNEY: Now I'm going to ask you a series of questions about your affirmative duty to prevent a suicide attempt and/or reduce the suicide risk. All these
questions are related to the legal concept of causation.

THERAPIST: Before we start this, I need you to clarify what you mean by causation. I don't see how it would be possible for me to cause someone else's suicide.
People "suicide" themselves. I can't "suicide" them.

ATTORNEY: The question is not whether you "caused" the suicide in the normal sense of the word. Rather, if you could have prevented the suicide and didn't, the legal definition of causation in this context is satisfied.

THERAPIST: So, legally, my failure to prevent a suicide is considered a "cause" of the suicide?

ATTORNEY: Yes, as long as the threat of suicide is recognizable and was within your power to prevent by adhering to your profession's standards of care. What precautions will you be taking to diminish the risk of the client making a suicide attempt?

THERAPIST: If I treat him on an outpatient basis, there are a number of standard safeguards that are used to help minimize the chances of an actual suicide attempt. These include (1) increasing the number of sessions appropriately, (2) ensuring the client has telephone access to me, particularly in case of an emergency, (3) scheduling emergency sessions at any time the client has suicide impulses he finds difficult to manage, and (4) having the client literally sign a contract that he will not kill himself "accidentally" or "purposefully" before our next session.

ATTORNEY: Are these recognized methods of dealing with suicide clients?

THERAPIST: Yes.

ATTORNEY: Have you actually consulted your colleagues on these treatment decisions?

THERAPIST: Yes, and they are standard procedures and practices that are generally recognized and accepted in the profession.

ATTORNEY: Are there treatment methods that have been demonstrated to be more effective than others with this type of client?

THERAPIST: Probably not, although you would find a fair bit of controversy on this point. Practicing clinicians of different theoretical persuasions can have entirely different views and values about what constitutes the most essential considerations in dealing with suicidal clients. Essentially, however, there is no scientific evidence to support the views and values of any of these professional groups. I do think that most professionals would consider the use of psychotherapy and psychopharmacological medications as standard components to the treatment process.

ATTORNEY: Will your treatment include these?

THERAPIST: Of course!

ATTORNEY: Let me summarize what appear to be the most essential considerations in this case. First, you clearly recognize the risk of a suicide attempt with this client. Second, your opinion is based on assessment procedures consistent with accepted assessment practices. Third, in spite of the suicide risk, you judge this client an acceptable candidate for outpatient care. Fourth, you have selected outpatient care because the treatment gains associated with it outweigh the benefits and safety of involuntary hospitalization. Is that about it?

THERAPIST: Exactly. With that information, am I exposing myself to unreasonable risks of liability by treating this man on an outpatient basis?

Attorney's Recommendations

ATTORNEY: From the information at hand, I can make three important observations:

1. At least part of the treatment plan includes affirmative steps to prevent a suicide attempt. It is obvious, therefore, that the legal criteria for foreseeability are completely satisfied, and this element of liability will be easily met if a suicide ensues.

2. The suicide prevention procedures you will employ, although not universally agreed on, are safely within accepted professional practice. Although these relate to emergency procedures associated with suicide risk and not to your actual treatment plan, violations of clinical procedures provide the most direct path to liability.

3. As long as the procedure and substance of your assessment satisfies your profession's standards, and as long as the clinical precautions taken correspond to the suicide risk that you recognize, or should have recognized, you will be safe from liability. Liability will not result from incorrect assessment or treatment, but only from an assessment or treatment that is negligently incorrect. Remember, negligence results from deviation from recognized professional standards.

Based on these observations and your assessment of suicide risk, I would conclude that the treatment gains associated with outpatient care can reasonably be assumed to outweigh the rehabilitative and legal risks associated with involuntary commitment.

THERAPIST: Thank you counselor!
ATTORNEY: You bet. Will we be talking again soon?
THERAPIST: Probably. I have one case that is headed in the direction of an involuntary commitment that could get sticky.
ATTORNEY: Good grief!
THERAPIST: Good night.

REFERENCES

Beck, A. T., Kovacs, M., & Weissman, A. (1979). Assessment of suicidal intention: The scale for suicide ideation. *Journal of Consulting and Clinical Psychology, 47,* 343–352.

Beck, A. T., Rush, A. J., Shaw, B. F., & Emery, G. (1979). *Cognitive therapy of depression: A treatment manual.* New York: Guilford Press.

Beck, A. T., Schuyler, D., & Herman, I. (1974). Development of suicidal intent scales. In A. Beck, H. Resnik, & D. Lettieri (Eds.), *The prediction of suicide.* Bowie, MD: Charles Press Publications.

Beck, A. T., Steer, R. A., Kovacs, M., & Garrison, B. (1985). Hopelessness and eventual suicide: A 10-year prospective study of patients hospitalized with suicidal ideation. *American Journal of Psychiatry, 145,* 559–563.

Beck, A. T., Weissman, A., Lester, D., & Trexler, L. (1974). The measurement of pessimism, the hopelessness scale. *Journal of Consulting and Clinical Psychology, 42,* 861–865.

Bongar, B., Peterson, L. G., Harris, E. A., & Aissis, J. (1989). Clinical and legal considerations in the management of suicidal patients: An integrative overview. *Journal of Integrative and Eclectic Psychotherapy, 8,* 53–67.

Clark, D. C. (1988). Depression and suicide: Editor's commentary. *Suicide Research Digest, 11,* 2.

Comstock, B. S. (1984). Suicide-emergency issues. In B. S. Comstock, W. E. Fann, A. D. Pokorny, & R. L. Williams (Eds.), *Phenomenology and treatment of psychiatric emergencies.* New York: Spectrum Publications.

Deutsch, C. J. (1984). Self-reported sources of stress among psychotherapists. *Professional, Psychology, Research, and Practice, 15*(6), 833–845.

Gutheil, T. G., Bursztajn, H., & Bradsky, A. (1986). The multidimensional assessment of dangerousness: Competence assessment in patient care and liability prevention. *Bulletin of the American Academy of Psychiatry and Law, 14,* 123–129.

Hatton, C. L., & Valente, S. M. (1984). Assessment of suicidal risk. In C. L. Hatton & S. M. Valente (Eds.), *Suicide: Assessment and intervention* (2nd ed.). New York: Appleton-Century-Crofts.

Hawton, K. (1987). Assessment of suicide risk. *British Journal of Psychiatry, 150,* 145–153.

Hyman, S. E. (Ed.). (1984). *Manual of psychiatric emergencies.* Boston: Little, Brown.

Kramer, M. E. (1982). *Identifying the conceptual dimensions of suicide risk management.* Unpublished doctoral dissertation, University of Kentucky.

Lettieri, D. J. (1974). Suicide death prediction scales. In A. T. Beck, H. L. P. Resnik, & D. J. Lettieri (Eds.), *The prediction of suicide.* Bowie, MD: Charles Press Publications.

Linehan, M. M., Goodstein, J. L., Nielsen, S. L., & Chiles, J. A. (1983). Reasons for staying alive when you are thinking of killing yourself: The reasons for living inventory. *Journal of Consulting and Clinical Psychology, 51*(2), 276–286.

Litman, R. E. (1974). Models for predicting suicide risk. In C. Neuringer (Ed.), *Psychological assessment of suicide risk.* Springfield, IL: Charles C Thomas.

Maltsberger, J. T. (1988). Suicide danger: Clinical estimation and decision. In R. Maris (Ed.), *Understanding and preventing suicide.* New York: Guilford Press.

Millon, T. (1969). *Modern psychopathology: A biosocial approach to maladaptive learning and functioning.* Philadelphia: Saunders.

Motto, J. A. (1980). Suicide risk factors in alcohol abuse. *Suicide and Life Threatening Behavior, 10,* 230–238.

Motto, J. A., Heilbron, R. P., & Juster, R. P. (1982). Development of a scale for assessing suicide risk. *Proceedings of the 15th annual meeting of the American Association of Suicidology,* New York (pp. 164–166).

Pierce, D. W. (1984). Suicidal intent and repeated self-harm. *Psychological Medicine, 14,* 655–659.

Prentice, A. E. (1974). *Suicide: A selective bibliography.* Metuchen, NJ: Scarecrow Press.

Schein, H. M. (1976). Obstacles in the education of psychiatric residents. *Omega, 7,* 75–82.

Schneidman, E. S. (1988). Some reflections of a founder. In R. Mavis (Ed.), *Understanding and preventing suicide.* New York: Guilford Press.

Simon, R. I. (1987). *Clinical psychiatry and the law.* Washington, DC: American Psychiatric Press.

Slaby, A. E., Lieb, J., & Tancredi, R. T. (1986). *Handbook of psychiatric emergencies* (3rd ed.). New York: Medical Examination Publishing Co.

Urbartis, J. C. (1983). *Psychiatric emergencies.* New York: Appleton-Century-Crofts.

Walker, J. I. (1983). *Psychiatric emergencies, intervention, and resolution.* Philadelphia: Lippincott.

Weissman, A., & Worden, W. (1972). Risk-rescue rating in suicide assessment. *Archives of General Psychiatry, 26,* 553–560.

7

Informed Consent: Legal Duties

> A doctor might well believe that an operation or form of treatment is desirable or necessary, but the law does not permit him to substitute his own judgment for that of the patient by any form of artifice or deception.[1]

Informed consent refers to the right of individuals to be informed and make autonomous decisions about any treatments they receive. In this chapter we first introduce the theoretical underpinnings and legal foundation of informed consent. We then examine the doctrine's specific elements, focusing on the most critical and divisive legal issues. Finally, we examine the legal requirements for successfully implementing informed consent theory.

INFORMED CONSENT: LEGAL PROGENY OF NOBLE PARENTAGE

Informed consent is a relatively new and developing legal doctrine. Even though a legal fledgling, it is the progeny of one of the most deep-seated principles of democratic societies: the right of self-determination. Case law stemming back as far as 85 years illustrates judicial devotion to this principle. As stated in *Schloendorff v. Society of New York Hospitals:* "Every human being of adult years and sound mind has a right to determine what shall be done with his own body; and a surgeon who performs an operation without his patient's consent commits an assault, for which he is liable in damages."[2]

For many years, however, the right of self-determination has been honored more in theory than in practice. Only in the past 30 years has the right received meaningful support by courts and legislatures. The Supreme Court's 1976 disposition of the abortion cases is the most dramatic evidence of this shift. In acknowledging the primacy of a woman's right to terminate an unwanted pregnancy, the court rested its decision on the basic principle that every person has the right to determine what happens to his or her own body.[3] Informed consent is a result of the law's growing recognition of the importance of self-determination.

---

[1]*Natanson v. Kline,* 186 Kan. 393, 350 P.2d 1093, *reh'g denied,* 187 Kan. 186, 354 P.2d 670 (1960).
[2]*Schloendorff v. Society of New York Hosp.,* 211 N.Y. 125, 129–130, 105 N.E. 92, 93 (1914).
[3]R. Reisner, Law and the Mental Health System, 133 (1985) [hereinafter "Reisner"].

Informed consent consists of two elements. The first element is the duty to *disclose* information relevant to personal decision making; the second is a person's right to voluntarily consent to any treatments received. These elements are uniformly recognized as the backbone of the informed consent doctrine. Uniformity among jurisdictions swiftly disappears, however, as courts struggle to define what disclosure encompasses and what constitutes consent.

INFORMED CONSENT: CURRENT AND FUTURE APPLICATIONS IN PSYCHOTHERAPY

It is important to note that currently the only obvious applications of informed consent doctrine have been in the biomedical fields. So far there have been no reported cases in which violations of the informed consent doctrine in the practice of psychotherapy have been litigated.

Informed consent has not yet been applied to psychotherapy for three reasons. First, recovery of monetary damages under most tort theories requires a showing of physical injury. Even if a psychotherapy plaintiff clearly shows lack of informed consent, an equally clear demonstration of resultant physical injury is more difficult. For now, psychotherapy plaintiffs would seldom recover more than nominal damages.

A second reason explaining informed consent's limited application to psychotherapy is the legal requirement of factual causation and legal (proximate) causation in actions based in negligence. Factual causation requires a showing that an undisclosed risk materialized and that the injury is identifiable as a consequence of treatment. Legal (proximate) causation places further demands on the plaintiff: The plaintiff must show the absence of other superceding or intervening causes. In essence, legal causation requires a demonstration that the failure to inform was a *substantial* factor (not merely a contributing factor) leading to the injury. Pragmatically, this is a significant barrier to recovery in informed consent cases, as discussed in detail later in the chapter.

The final and perhaps most important reason for informed consent's limited application in psychotherapy is the nature of the psychotherapeutic process. In physical medicine, the patient/doctor relationship is important, but ancillary to treatment. A medical doctor may explain with detail and accuracy the nature of the operation, the medical procedure to be followed, and the expected extent of recovery. Information material to a medical patient's consent may be delivered independently of the doctor's personal relationship with the patient. The psychotherapeutic relationship is much different and has been artfully characterized as follows:

> The relationship itself is the subject matter of the treatment, and in this way it is distinguished from every other business or professional relationship. . . . When I go to a doctor for treatment of the flu, I depend on his ability to diagnose my symptoms and prescribe appropriate treatment. Successful treatment does not depend on our good relations (although they may be a factor in my improvement).

> But the essence of the contract for psychotherapy is the relationship between the psychotherapist and patient. . . . Without the interaction there would be no treatment. *The interaction is the essence of the contract.* . . . The therapist undertakes to provide an ongoing relationship to which he brings skill and knowledge, a regular time period during which this relationship will be delivered, and an appropriate milieu to foster its development. . . . The treatment is the skillful manipulation of the relationship to achieve certain mental states.[4]

This distinction not only explains why the doctrine of informed consent currently has limited application in psychotherapy, it also suggests the possibility that the mental health professions may be an unnatural environment for the doctrine of informed consent to flourish.

In spite of these considerations, legal trends are clearly moving in the direction toward greater emphasis on self-determination and informed consent and are already starting to have a pronounced effect on the mental health professions. As this change continues, the impact will become more obvious and substantial. For example, states are beginning to impose such statutory obligations on mental health professionals as the duty to disclose (1) the nature of procedures to be used in proposed treatment, (2) the probable degree and duration of improvement expected with and without treatment, (3) reasonable alternative treatments, and (4) the fact that the client has the right to accept or refuse the proposed treatment.

Historically, recovery of monetary damages has required that physical injury be demonstrated. This general principal is eroding, and its future is in doubt. In recent years there has been an increased tendency in many areas of law to compensate for nonphysical injuries. Significant monetary awards based on *intentional* infliction of emotional distress in the field of torts is a prime example. And most recently, courts have awarded significant monetary damages for *negligently* inflicted emotional distress without any showing of physical harm. Society and the law have become increasingly intolerant of wrongs without a remedy. Continuation of this trend will soon result in the psychotherapist's exposure to significant liability under the informed consent doctrine.

INFORMED CONSENT: EARLY CASES AND LEGAL FOUNDATIONS

Early Cases

The 1905 landmark case of *Mohr v. Williams*[5] established that a doctor was guilty of the intentional tort of battery if the doctor failed to obtain a patient's consent prior to providing medical treatment. Cases prior to the 1950s continued to emphasize the importance of bodily integrity but failed to materially advance individual protection from intrusive treatments whose purpose and consequence

---

[4]Tarhis, *Liability for Psychotherapy,* 30 Faculty L. Rev. 75, 77–78 (1972).
[5]*Mohr v. Williams,* 95 Minn. 261, 104 N.W. 12 (1905).

were unknown to patients. In 1957, a series of cases emerged recognizing the necessity of providing medical patients with information necessary for them to make an informed decision about treatment.[6] In the early 1960s, two cases, *Natanson v. Kline*[7] and *Mitchell v. Robinson*,[8] were decided that generally are viewed as having ushered in the modern doctrine of informed consent.[9]

Natanson and *Mitchell*, both decided within 2 days of each other, are especially significant because they asserted a willingness to impose malpractice liability without a finding of any negligence in medical procedure. Moreover, although neither patient was specifically informed as to the nature of the treatments provided, the patients' consent to treatment had been obtained in both cases. In *Natanson*, the patient received injuries from cobalt radiation treatment. The court ruled that the physician failed in a legal obligation to make disclosure to the patient. Failure of the doctor's legal obligation to provide information necessary for an "intelligent consent" was determined to constitute malpractice—without regard to how skillfully treatment might have been administered.[10]

In *Mitchell*, the patient suffered convulsive fractures of several vertebrae following insulin shock therapy. Mitchell consented to treatment but brought suit because he was not made aware of the attendant risks. In *Mitchell* the court stated:

> [T]he proper solution is to recognize that a *doctor owes a duty to his patient to make reasonable disclosure of all significant facts,* i.e., the nature of the infirmity (so far as reasonably possible), the nature of the operation and some of the more probable consequences and difficulties inherent in the proposed operation. It may be said that a doctor who fails to perform this duty is guilty of malpractice.[11]

The doctors in both *Natanson* and *Mitchell* were eventually found liable for breach of their obligations to give their patients an opportunity to render an informed consent.

These seminal cases provide the basic framework for all informed consent analysis, and by the might of these judicial decisions, informed consent became a force for health care providers to reckon with.

Legal Foundation: Negligence or Battery

With the informed consent doctrine now generally defined and illustrated in case law, we are ready to discuss its underlying legal foundations. Informed consent may be appended to one of two legal theories: negligence or battery. The doctrinal theory under which an informed consent action arises is of more than

---

[6]*See Lester v. Aetna Casualty Co.*, 240 F.2d 676 (5th Cir.), *cert. denied*, 354 Dis. 923 (1957). *Salgo v. Leland Stanford Jr. Univ. Bd. of Trustees*, 154 Cal. App. 2d 560, 317 P.2d 170 (1957).

[7]*Natanson v. Kline*, 186 Kan. 393, 350 P.2d 1093, *reh'g denied*, 187 Kan. 186, 354 P.2d 670 (1960).

[8]*Mitchell v. Robinson*, 334 S.W.2d 11 (Mo. 1960).

[9]*See* Comment, *The Doctrine of Informed Consent Applied to Psychotherapy*, 72 Geo. L. J. 1637 (1984) [hereinafter "Informed Consent in Psychotherapy"].

[10]*Natanson*, 350 P.2d at 1107.

[11]*Mitchell*, 334 S.W.2d at 18.

theoretical interest; it can have important implications for the litigants, stemming from the legal distinctions between battery as an intentional tort and negligence as an unintentional tort.[12]

Informed Consent Violations: When Is It Battery and When Is It Negligence? Informed consent actions may come under the heading of battery in three basic fact situations. In the first situation, the professional performs a procedure to which no consent, informed or uninformed, has been given.[13] In the second situation, performance of procedure is different than the one the patient authorized. Thus a dentist who extracts eight teeth but is authorized to extract only two may be subject to an informed consent action couched in battery.[14] In the third situation, the medical patient consents to performance of a procedure but the procedure is performed on a different part of the body than the patient had authorized.[15] Such was the situation in *Mohr v. Williams,* whereby a physician obtained consent for surgery on a patient's right ear but during the operation discovered a more serious defect in the patient's left ear and elected to perform the surgery on that ear instead, thus providing a basis for liability under a battery theory.

Remember that the presence of one of these three situations will not automatically append the informed consent action to a battery theory; jurisdictions may vary. Use of a battery theory is virtually precluded, however, if one of these three fact patterns does not apply.

Although negligence-based informed consent actions appear most prevalent, the potential for battery-based informed consent suits should not be underestimated. Moreover, whether an informed consent violation is construed as battery or negligence carries significant legal implications.

Negligence or Battery: Legal Consequences. Whether a jurisdiction brings informed consent under the aegis of battery or negligence has at least four important consequences for the litigants. First, the burdens of proof imposed on the parties will vary with the legal theory applied. In a battery action, it is easier for the plaintiff to recover without introducing expert testimony to establish the prevailing medical practice as to the scope of disclosure. Under a battery theory, the plaintiff may also be able to recover some damages without a showing of actual injury. Moreover, because the act of battery itself constitutes the tort, a showing of causation is unnecessary. Also, intentional torts are generally not subject to disclaimers, while ordinary negligence (but not gross negligence) may be effectively disclaimed. In negligence, the plaintiff is required to establish (1) a duty of disclosure, (2) breach of the duty to disclose, (3) actual injury, and (4) causation.

[12]For a more detailed discussion of the legal consequences of categorization, see Reisner, *supra* note 3, at 140–141.

[13]*See Hook v. Rothstein,* 316 S.E.2d 690 (S.C. App. 1984).

[14]*See Moore v. Webb,* 345 S.W.2d 239 (Mo. App. 1961).

[15]*See Mohr v. Williams,* 95 Minn. 261, 104 N.W. 12 (1905).

Second, the measure of damages may depend on which theory is utilized. Because battery is an intentional tort, the plaintiff may be able to recover punitive as well as actual damages. By contrast, recovery in negligence actions must bear a reasonable relation to the injuries actually suffered.

Third, as an intentional tort, an action in battery is generally subject to a shorter statute of limitations than an action couched in battery. Intentional torts (battery) generally possess a 1-year statute of limitations; unintentional torts (negligence) may vary from 2 to 5 years.

Finally, under the terms of most malpractice insurance policies, the defendant therapist or physician might not be covered if the action alleges battery since most insurance policies specifically exclude intentional torts.

ELEMENTS OF INFORMED CONSENT DOCTRINE

The specific elements of informed consent continue to change as the courts analyze them and they develop legally. This framework involves a two-tiered inquiry: (1) Is there proper and sufficient *disclosure* of relevant information to the patient, and (2) has the patient provided a valid *consent* to treatment?

Courts have agreed on only these two broadest elements of the informed consent doctrine. Within these two elements, and especially the duty to disclose, debate rages among jurisdictions as to the proper governing standards. Let us highlight these debates as we analyze the elements of informed consent.

Requirement of Disclosure

Informed consent case law requires that the disclosure requirement be analyzed under three prongs to determine if it is met. First, it must be determined if the disclosure duty applies. Second, if the disclosure duty applies, the required scope of disclosure must be determined. Finally, each situation must be analyzed to ascertain if it justifies one of the several exceptions to the disclosure duty.

Circumstances That Trigger the Duty to Disclose. Informed consent is not a doctrine of strict liability (liability without fault). Liability will not automatically attach for each undisclosed risk that materializes—for example, therapists or physicians have a duty to disclose only those risks known to them. Remember, however, that "nondisclosure of an unknown risk [may] . . . pose problems in terms of the physician's duty to have known of the risk and to have acted accordingly."[16] Moreover, as pointed out in the most recent informed consent decision, *Hondroulis v. Schumacher,*[17] the disclosure duty does not apply to risks that are not reasonably foreseeable, commonly understood, obvious, or already known

---

[16]*Canterbury v. Spence,* 464 F.2d 772, 787, n.84 (D.C. Cir.), *cert. denied,* 409 U.S. 1064 (1972).
[17]*Hondroulis v. Schumacher,* 546 So. 2d 466 (La. 1989).

to the patient. In addition, risks deemed minor by virtue of not causing substantial harm, discomfort, or pain are also excluded from the disclosure requirement.

With these exceptions, a client must be informed of the following: the risks, discomforts, and side effects of proposed treatment; the anticipated benefits of treatment; the prospects of success; the available alternative treatments and their attendant risks, discomforts, and side effects; and the probable consequence of refusing to be treated at all.[18] In general terms, courts have required all "material" risks to be disclosed. "Materiality" thus governs the scope of required disclosure, but jurisdictions vigorously disagree as to what standard governs materiality.

Standards Governing the Scope of Disclosure.   The standard a jurisdiction adopts to govern the scope of disclosure reflects how the competing interests of the client, the profession, and society are balanced.[19] A client's interest involves obtaining all information necessary for a meaningful decision on the proposed therapy. Professionals' interest centers on the ability to carry out professional functions efficiently and with minimum open-ended liability risks. The looser, or more uncertain, the legal standard, the more difficult it is for professionals to adhere to a standard of conduct that will eliminate the risk of liability. Finally, there is a broader societal interest in maximizing access to needed professional services: To access these services, costs must be reasonable. The greater professionals' liability exposure, the more burdensome the fee structures. Jurisdictions use one of two fundamental perspectives in determining the scope of required disclosure: that of the professional or that of the client.

Scope of Disclosure Governed by Professional Viewpoint.   Jurisdictions adopting a professional standard to govern the scope of disclosure hinge materiality on what a reasonable practitioner would disclose in the situation. The standard is well stated in *Hook v. Rothstein*:[20] "We . . . hold that the scope of a physician's duty to disclose is measured by those communications a reasonable medical practitioner in the same branch of medicine would make under the same or similar circumstances."[21] This is the standard that first emerged from *Natanson v. Kline,* in the early 1960s. By the early 1980s, approximately half the jurisdictions adhered to this approach,[22] but recent cases suggest that its popularity is declining.

The main argument for adopting a professional standard for determining materiality of risk disclosure is that judges and juries usually are not competent to judge whether or not a doctor has acted reasonably. While this is an attractive and workable approach for physicians, the standard breaks down when applied

[18]*Id.* at 469; *see also Informed Consent in Psychotherapy, supra* note 9, at 1642.
[19]Reisner, *supra* note 3, at 157.
[20]*Hook v. Rothstein,* 316 S.E.2d 690 (S.C. App. 1984).
[21]*Id.* at 698.
[22]President's Commission for the study of ethical problems in medicine and biomedical and behavioral research (1982). *Making Health Care Decisions: The Ethical and Legal Implications of Informed Consent in the Patient-Practitioner Relationship,* Vol. 3, Appendices, Appendix L, Washington, D.C. Government Printing Office (1982).

to psychotherapy because psychotherapy has not established its own professional standards.[23] Psychotherapy suffers from an obvious lack of consensus about the risks and benefits of even well-researched therapies.[24] Therapists often develop their own individual techniques that fit the personalities of both their clients and themselves. When a therapist's acts are unique, they cannot be meaningfully measured against the conduct of others. The lack of articulated professional standards among mental health professions results in judicial usurpation of the task of determining proper standards. Yet the very logic supporting the professional standard—that judges and juries are not competent to judge whether or not a physician or therapist has acted reasonably—defies this result. Thus, when professional standards are unclear, the judiciary ends up engaging in the very activity that adoption of the professional standard was intended to avoid.

The most recent trend of cases clearly reveals growing judicial dissatisfaction with the professional standard.[25] Indeed, five of the most recent jurisdictions to confront the issue have rejected the professional standard. Judicial dissatisfaction with the professional standard stems from a number of sources. First, allowing members of a profession to determine the governing standard effectively asks the fox to guard the chicken coop. If defined by the profession, the standard of materiality may be too low to satisfy the needs of clients to participate fully in the decision-making process. Second, the professional standard does not reflect an appropriate balancing between the client's interest in receiving information to furnish a basis of decision and the profession's interest in being able to carry out its professional function without undue risk of liability. Third, if litigation occurs, the professional standard requires that the *client* establish by expert evidence the governing standard of disclosure in the profession. Again, this is especially unattractive where professional standards vary or have not been clearly established. Finally, permitting professionals to determine what information is important to the client does not meet the objectives of informed consent doctrine. The meaning of self-determination is attenuated when an external source dictates what is material to the individual.

Scope of Disclosure Governed by Client's Viewpoint.   A growing number of jurisdictions, including five of the most recent jurisdictions to confront the issue, have adopted some form of a client-oriented materiality standard. Here the standard governing the scope of disclosure is determined from the client's perspective. The client's perspective may be evaluated from an objective and reasonable or a subjective approach.

Canterbury v. Spence[26] was the most important decision adopting the objective client standard to govern the required scope of disclosure. *Canterbury,*

[23]*Informed Consent in Psychotherapy, supra* note 9, at 1655.
[24]*See e.g.,* Lambert, Shapiro, & Bergin (1986); Rachman & Wilson, (1978).
[25]*See Hondroulis v. Schumacher,* 546 So. 2d 466 (La. 1989); *Largey v. Rothman,* 110 N.J. 204, 540 A.2d 504 (1988); *Arena v. Gingrich,* 84 Or. App. 25, 733 P.2d 75 (1987); *Smith v. Weaver,* 1225 Neb. 569, 407 N.W.2d 174 (1987); *Cheung v. Cunningham,* 214 N.J.Super 649, 520 A.2d 832 (1987); *Canterbury v. Spence,* 464 F.2d 772 (D.C. Cir.), *cert. denied,* 409 U.S. 1064 (1972).
[26]*Canterbury v. Spence,* 464 F.2d 772 (D.C. Cir.), *cert. denied,* 409 U.S. 1064 (1972).

the first case to depart from a professional standard governing the scope of disclosure, is especially significant not only because it adopted a client materiality approach but because it was handed down by the Federal Circuit Court of Appeals. This is the highest level an informed consent case has reached in the federal system; most informed consent cases originate under state law and never enter the federal system. Although federal authority is not binding in state court constructions of state law (informed consent arises under state common or statutory law), it is highly persuasive in jurisdictions confronting a similar issue for the first time.

Canterbury defines the breadth of required disclosure to include all risks that either singularly or in combination with other risks would be deemed significant by the *average* client in choosing whether to accept or forego treatment. The court stated:

> [T]he patient's right of self-decision shapes the boundaries of the duty to reveal. That right can be effectively exercised only if the patient possesses enough information to enable an intelligent choice. The scope of the physician's communications to the patient, then, must be measured by the patient's need, and that need is the information material to the decision. . . . [A]ll risks potentially affecting the decision must be unmasked.

> * * *

> The scope of the standard is not subjective as to either the physician or the patient; it remains objective. . . . In broad outline we agree that a risk is thus material when a reasonable person, in what the physician knows or should know to be the patient's position, would be likely to attach significance to the risk or cluster of risks in deciding whether or not to forego the proposed therapy.[27]

Under the objective client materiality standard, the jury determines what information would be significant to the average, reasonable client. The jury thus becomes the average, reasonable client in making this determination and the necessity of expert witnesses is therefore avoided.

Penetrating criticism may be levied against the objective client materiality standard. The primary fault of the objective standard is that it requires plaintiffs to prove that all reasonable persons in the same position would withhold consent—even though this particular plaintiff would have withheld consent and thereby avoided injury. This is the antithesis of the doctrine of informed consent, which is intended to afford plaintiff the *personal right* to decline treatment. This standard denies individuals the right to base consent on proper information in light of their individual fears, apprehensions, religious beliefs, and so forth. *Cheung v. Cunningham* artfully states the problem:

> We are not persuaded that there is justification for excluding from recovery under the aforementioned doctrine [objective patient materiality standard] all of those persons who because of their personal and individual traits might be classified as more cautious and circumspect than the hypothetical reasonably prudent person.

---

[27]*Canterbury*, 464 F.2d at 787.

Individuals are just that; different persons with different views and characters. Each is entitled to make a personal judgment as to what each will subject his or her body to after having had the benefit of such information as is reasonably necessary for that purpose. As stated in *Convoy,* "[i]ndeed, if the patient's right to informed consent is to have any meaning at all, it must be accorded respect even when it conflicts with the advice of the doctor or the values of the medical profession as a whole."[28]

While the client-oriented objective standard no doubt gives more weight to the client in balancing the competing interests, it must be questioned whether a standard that adopts a layperson's definition of materiality gives professionals adequate notice of what disclosure the law demands,[29] raising serious questions for both practice and effective supervision, training, and continuing education efforts. It is difficult to teach trainees what to disclose absent a concrete standard.

The standard most consonant with informed consent's objective of self-determination is the subjective client materiality standard. As we will explain, however, this standard carries burdensome evidentiary baggage.

Two of the most recent cases have adopted the subjective client material-ity standard.[30] Under this approach, "a risk is deemed material if it is likely to affect *that patient's* decision."[31] Under this rule, the principle problem is eviden-tiary in nature. A claimant's credibility must be closely scrutinized because of the possibility of both purposeful and unwitting deception. The question of whether or not the claimant would have refused treatment with knowledge of the risk is asked only after the injury has materialized. Resolution of the case now hinges on the answer to a hypothetical question directed to the party seeking recovery. The answer is no more than a guess, tinged by the fact that the uncommunicated hazard has in fact materialized.[32] This standard places ambitious expectations on the jury's ability to accurately make credibility determinations.

Although true to the objectives of informed consent, the subjective client approach may be criticized because it fosters the client's interest at great expense to the interests of the professional and society. The professional has no notice of the applicable disclosure standard until the client suffers the harm and answers the hypothetical question at trial. The great cost to professionals is eventually passed on to each person seeking professional services.

A partial solution to the evidentiary problems inherent in the subjective client materiality standard was forwarded by a recent case, *Arena v. Gingrich.*[33] The court, although adhering to the subjective client materiality standard, per-mitted evidence and argument about whether other clients, hypothetical or real, would have consented under similar circumstances. This evidence could be used

---

[28]*Cheung v. Cunningham,* 214 N.J. Super 649, 520 A.2d 832, 835 (1987).

[29]Reisner, *supra* note 3, at 156.

[30]*See Cheung v. Cunningham,* 214 N.J. Super. 649, 520 A.2d 832 (1987); *Arena v. Gingrich,* 84 Or. App. 25, 733 P.2d 75 (1987); *see also Scott v. Bradford,* 606 P.2d 554 (Okla. 1979).

[31]*Scott v. Bradford,* 606 P.2d 554, 558 (Okla. 1979).

[32]*See Cheung* 520 A.2d at 837 (Stern J., dissenting).

[33]*Arena v. Gingrich,* 84 Or. App. 25, 733 P.2d 75 (1987).

only for purposes of evaluating the credibility of the claimant. Here the subjective client standard governs, but the objective approach is used to help evaluate the client's claim. Combining the objective and subjective approach is an admirable attempt to assuage the evidentiary dilemmas of the subjective approach while remaining true to the spirit of informed consent. However, it must be questioned how effectively objective evidence may be used without subsuming the subjective approach.

The foregoing review of case law demonstrates the great variability in judicial approaches to balancing competing policies. The variety of positions and approaches reveals much about the way our judicial system works but provides few guidelines for practice. Practitioners seeking to find protection from legal storms by familiarity with black letter law will find that their knowledge provides only dilapidated shelter.

Exceptions to the Requirement of Disclosure.   Informed consent doctrine has grown out of the societal value accorded to individualism. Yet the individual's right to decisional autonomy must be balanced against the professional's interest and responsibility in promoting clients' health and welfare. Moreover, both individual and societal interests in health and welfare may become threatened if the "privilege" of self-determination is so unfettered that the right to consent becomes an absolute requirement, thus transforming the privilege into a burden.

The common denominator of the underlying competing interests is that the individual will make the "wrong" decision—a decision that, on balance, harms the individual, the profession, society, or all three.[34] Thus courts have placed some fetters on individuals' prerogative to choose for themselves, and exceptions to the informed consent requirements have been developed. In these situations, concern for the client's well-being is deemed to override the client's interest in autonomy. The exceptions include (1) emergencies, (2) therapeutic privilege, (3) waiver, and (4) incompetency.

Emergencies.   The requirement of informed consent may be suspended in emergencies involving the individual's welfare. As stated in the most recent informed consent decision: "[Disclosure] is not required when a genuine emergency arises because the patient is unconscious or otherwise incapable of consenting, and harm from a failure to treat is imminent and outweighs harm threatened by the proposed treatment."[35]

When a client is incapable of receiving information, or when the time taken for disclosure would harm the client's health, none of the interest promoted by informed consent doctrine is forwarded by its application; the client's health is not protected, and the client's interest in preserving individuality is not advanced.[36]

---

[34]Meisel, *The "Exceptions" to the Informed Consent Doctrine: Striking a Balance Between Competing Values in Medical Decisionmaking*, 1979 Wis. L. Rev. 413, 428 [hereinafter "Meisel"].
[35]*Hondroulis v. Schumacher*, 546 So. 2d 466, 470 (La. 1989).
[36]*Informed Consent in Psychotherapy, supra* note 9, at 1644.

The value of self-determination is illusory when one is incapable of decision. Since a reasonable person would consent to treatment in an emergency, if capable of doing so, the client's consent is implied.[37]

Case law poorly and inconsistently defines what circumstances constitute an emergency. At the most stringent extreme, an emergency requires that the person be

> . . . injured to the extent of rendering him unconscious, and his injuries of such nature as to require prompt surgical attention, [and] a physician called to attend him would be justified in applying such medical or surgical treatment as might reasonably be necessary for the preservation of his life or limb. . . .[38]

At the most liberal extreme, the informed consent requirement may be suspended because the patient was "suffering or [because] pain [would] be alleviated" by treatment.[39] The enormous gap between these definitions inhibits meaningful and useful application of the emergency exception, especially in psychotherapy, where the nature of an emergency may not be readily apparent or proved.

Additional ambiguity is introduced to the emergency exception by the requirement that relatives be used as an alternate source of consent. As stated in *Canterbury v. Spence*, "Even where a genuine emergency arises and the patient is incapable of consenting, [the professional] should attempt to secure a relative's consent, but if time is too short to accommodate discussion, the [professional] should proceed with treatment."[40] Again, the practitioner is left without meaningful instruction of what the law demands. In the face of such ambiguity, courts are more inclined, however, to defer to the attending professional's good faith judgment. Yet this general judicial inclination toward deference in the face of such ambiguity will be unsatisfying to each professional whose novel fact pattern is the source of new law or a new legal clarification.

A workable limitation on the emergency exception must focus on the purposes of informed consent doctrine. If the patient is incapable of giving consent or receiving information, because the patient is unconscious, not in contact with reality, or pain prohibits the patient's attention to conversation, none of the interests of informed consent doctrine are served.[41] In addition, the consequence to the patient's condition because of the time taken to explain information to a patient capable of receiving information and communicating consent must be considered. These factors should provide the framework for a more principled formulation of the emergency exception.

Therapeutic Privilege. Under the therapeutic privilege exception to informed consent, a professional may withhold some or all information while obtain-

---

[37]*See generally,* W. Prosser, The Law of Torts § 18 (4th ed. 1971).
[38]*Mohr v. Williams,* 95 Minn. 261, 269, 104 N.W. 12, 15 (1905).
[39]*Sullivan v. Montgomery,* 155 Misc. 448, 279 N.Y.S. 575 (City Ct. 1935).
[40]*Canterbury,* 464 F.2d at 788.
[41]Meisel, *supra* note 34, at 436.

ing a patient's consent if the communication itself would cause the patient's mental or physical condition to deteriorate. As stated in *Canterbury:*

> It is recognized that patients occasionally become so ill or emotionally distraught on disclosure as to foreclose a rational decision, or complicate or hinder the treatment or perhaps even pose psychological damage to the patient. Where that is so, the cases have generally held that the physician is armed with a privilege to keep the information from the patient.[42]

The general purpose of the therapeutic privilege is to free professionals from a legal requirement that contradicts their primary duty: to do what is beneficial for the client.[43] This privilege offers the dangerous potential, however, of legitimizing a professional's natural aversion to disclosing unpleasant information to the client.[44] It is precisely this fear that recently prompted the Supreme Court of Louisiana to warn: "This privilege must be carefully circumscribed, however, for otherwise it might devour the disclosure rule itself."[45]

The most important limitation on the therapeutic privilege is that it excludes the risk that the patient may choose to refuse medical care. Thus, "[t]he privilege does not accept the paternalistic notion that the physician may remain silent simply because divulgence might prompt the patient to forego therapy the physician feels the patient really needs."[46] The therapeutic privilege is thus limited to the harm that would come to a patient *simply from hearing the communication.*

The therapeutic privilege is especially important because its proper invocation is always measured by a professional standard. For a professional to successfully assert the exception, it must therefore be shown, by expert testimony, that reasonable professionals in a particular area of practice would have also foregone the communication for the patient's benefit.

Because the therapeutic privilege is measured by a professional standard, professionals may be able to circumvent the standard governing the scope of disclosure in jurisdictions having adopted patient-oriented materiality standards. Even if a patient proves that the information withheld would have altered his or her (or a reasonable patient's) decision, the professional may be able to invoke the therapeutic privilege as an exception to the disclosure requirement by showing that a reasonable mental health professional would have avoided disclosure. In this way, the exception to the disclosure requirement swallows the standard governing the scope of disclosure—the exception functionally determines the governing standard from the professional's viewpoint, rather than existing as a discreet exception to the patient-oriented standard. The result is that jurisdictions using patient materiality standards to govern the scope of disclosure have failed in their attempt to make the standard easier for patients to prove, because they have unintentionally introduced an extra hurdle to recovery. Now, not only must the plaintiff

[42]*Canterbury,* 464 F.2d at 788.
[43]Rice, *Informed Consent: The Illusion of Patient Choice,* 23 EMORY L. J. 503, 504 (1974).
[44]Meisel, *supra* note 34, at 461.
[45]*Hondroulis v. Schumacher,* 546 So. 2d 466, 470 (La. 1989).
[46]*Canterbury v. Spence,* 464 F.2d 772, 789 (D.C. Cir.), *cert. denied,* 409 U.S. 1064 (1972).

show individual materiality, but the plaintiff must also be prepared to refute proof offered by the physician that the lack of disclosure was within the professional standard. Jurisdictions having intended to adopt a client materiality standard should be especially disturbed by this possibility.

Waiver.   A limited number of cases acknowledge that clients may volitionally divest themselves of decisional authority as to therapy.[47] No cases have suggested that public policy or legal theory preclude a valid waiver of informed consent rights, yet legal decisions have offered very little guidance as to how the waiver doctrine should be applied to informed consent.

The judicially applied definition of waiver focuses on the "voluntary and intentional relinquishment of a known right."[48] Application of this definition to informed consent doctrine suggests that a medical patient must be informed of the following to execute a valid waiver.[49] First, the patient must know that the doctor has a legal duty to offer information about the treatment. Second, the patient must be aware of the legal right to decide whether or not to receive the treatment. Third, the patient must know that treatment cannot be rendered absent consent.

Imposing these requirements on execution of a valid waiver raises the question "How is a client to know these things?"[50] Given the fact that the professional is at risk of operating under an invalid waiver, the burden falls largely on the professional. Therefore, if the professional asserts the waiver exception, the elements of a valid waiver functionally become part of the disclosure duty itself.

What constitutes a voluntary waiver will no doubt become the subject of debate in the courts as the waiver exception becomes tested by application. In many instances, waivers may arise because of disclosures relating to the therapeutic process rather than disclosures relating to the right to information and the right to decide. Should delivery of information concerning risks, benefits, or alternatives of treatment that induces the patient to relinquish rights be viewed as rendering the waiver involuntary?[51]

Incompentency.   Individuals may be deemed incompetent to consent to treatment and thus be treated without their consent.[52] This exception is related to the emergency exception because it involves situations in which the patient is unable to effectively receive information and make a decision. The alternative of no treatment at all serves neither doctor and patient interest in preserving the patient's health nor the patient's interest in individualism.

Clearly, the threshold problem the incompetency exception raises is defining "incompetency." Clinically, there is no single, well-accepted definition of incom-

[47]*See, e.g., Kaimowitz v. Michigan Dept. of Mental Health,* 1 M.D.L.R. 147 (Cir. Ct. Wayne Co., Mich. 1976); *Holt v. Nelson,* 11 Wash. App. 230, 241, 523 P.2d 211, 219 (1974); *Cobbs v. Grant,* 8 Cal. 3d 229, 245, 502 P.2d 1, 12, 104 Cal. Rptr 505, 516 (1972).

[48]*See, Miranda v. Arizona,* 384 U.S. 436, 475–476 (1966).

[49]Meisel, *supra* note 34, at 454.

[50]*Id.*

[51]*Id.*

[52]*See Superintendent of Belchertown School v. Saikewicz,* 373 Mass. 728, 370 N.E.2d 417 (1977).

petency.[53] Despite the clinical difficulty of determining what constitutes "incompetency" (discussed later in the chapter), a judicially applied definition must focus on the objectives and competing interests in informed consent doctrine.

The notion that competence should be defined specifically within the legal context is supported by recent case law dealing with the rights of involuntarily committed patients to refuse treatment. Treatment of civilly committed patients without their informed consent is virtually routine in many institutions. Such procedures remained basically unquestioned through the 1960s and in conformity with the purpose of civil commitment: the restoration of mental health. Yet recent emphasis on patients' rights suggests that hospitalized patients may be unconstitutionally deprived of due process rights if informed consent prerogatives are automatically attenuated by institutionalization. Thus, regardless of the clinical standard of incompetence, a legal standard is required to permit meaningful application of the incompetency exception to informed consent.

Requirement of Consent

Consent to treatment, after required disclosure, is the second primary element of informed consent doctrine. Because conformity to disclosure standards has predominantly been the dispositive issue in case law, the consent element remains less developed legally. Yet, clearly, a valid consent requires that the consent be issued both voluntarily and with understanding.

Voluntary Consent.   Consent to treatment, after disclosure, confers legal rights to the professional. Because consent is a legally significant act, it will be given effect only if offered without force or coercion. Enforcement without consent would both recognize the legitimacy of force and make the state a partner to the coercion.[54] The policy behind the requirement of voluntary consent is thus clear. More difficult, however, is determining by what criteria the voluntariness of consent is to be judged. Because case law is relatively silent on this issue, we merely raise issues germane to the inquiry.

Voluntariness of consent in the informed consent context will rarely be viewed against a backdrop of physical coercion. Rather, voluntariness more frequently will be threatened because of the client's acute reliance on the professional. The unjustified promise of a particular benefit or the unwarranted caveat of particular repercussions may be deemed sufficient exercise of influence by the professional to threaten an otherwise voluntary consent. Here, voluntariness may be vitiated, not because of the technical absence of effective choice but because of the amount of influence generated from a relationship of deep-seated and uni-

[53]Meisel, *supra* note 34, at 440 (citing U.S. Dep't of HEW, *Protection of Human Subjects—Research Involving Those Institutionalized as Mentally Infirm: Report and Recommendations of the Nat'l Comm'n for the Protection of Human Subjects of Biomedical and Behavioral Research,* 43 Fed. Reg. 11,328, 11,345–11,346 (1978) ("[S]tatutory provisions for the adjudication of competency vary widely. . . . Court definitions of competency also vary).
[54]Reisner, *supra* note 3, at 174.

lateral reliance. The professional's status as an authority figure and ability to manipulate behavior through information control raise difficult questions as to when the influence becomes unacceptably coercive.

The solution tort law most typically adopts in this type of dilemma is to use an abstraction known as the "ordinary or reasonable man" as the focus of inquiry. This approach asks whether external forces or pressures are exerted on the "ordinary, reasonable man" of such magnitude as to override free will. One reason tort law uses this hypothetical person is because it offers a frame of reference for judges and juries to decide specific cases in a manner generally acceptable to society. Its primary disadvantage is that it offers the illusion of a real standard which in fact is contrived and fictional. The "ordinary, reasonable man" is quite a different person to each plaintiff, each defendant, and each juror.

In lieu of a well-defined, or more predictable standard, the guiding principle remains: The more a professional may be viewed as channeling a patient's decision by information control, manner of presentation, or even the professional's expectations, the more likely the voluntariness of the consent will be threatened.

Understanding Disclosure.   Courts and legal scholars agree that consent which merely follows disclosure is insufficient to satisfy informed consent requirements. The consent must be predicated by an understanding of the information disclosed. As stated by the court in the most recent informed consent decision in *Hondroulis v. Schumacher,* consent connotes the dual elements of awareness and assent: "To establish consent to a risk, it must be shown both that the patient was aware of the risk and that he assented to encounter it. Therefore, it is obvious that risk must have been understandably communicated before the element of awareness can be established."[55]

Unanswered by the requirement that consent result from understanding is whether the patent must have actual rather than imputed knowledge of the treatment being assented to. Consider the legal efficacy of a consent given by a patient who, unknown to the professional, fails to adequately understand correct and carefully delivered information. As with the governing standards of disclosure, courts follow either an objective or subjective approach in determining the patient's understanding.[56]

The objective approach focuses on the communication from the professional. If the communication is deemed adequate in the sense that an ordinary patient would understand the information provided, awareness is imputed without regard to the actual level of understanding. This approach was advocated in *Canterbury v. Spence:* "[T]he physician discharges the duty when he makes a reasonable effort to convey sufficient information *although the patient, without fault of the physician, may not fully grasp it.*"[57] This approach protects the professional to the extent a good faith attempt is made to explain treatment followed by receipt

---

[55]*Hondroulis v. Schumacher,* 546 So. 2d 466, 478 (La. 1989).
[56]Reisner, *supra* note 3 at 169.
[57]*Canterbury,* 464 F.2d at 780, n.15 (emphasis added).

of consent that the professional fairly believes stems from an understanding of the explanation.

Under the subjective approach, a client's consent is effective only if offered with *actual* knowledge and understanding of the professional's disclosure. In the event of litigation, a jury is required to determine whether the particular client understood what the professional explained. The following justification for this subjective approach has been offered:

> Even when the information presented is adequate . . . the consenting process may be nothing more than a "ritual" if the client remains "uneducated and uncomprehending." To avoid this result, the physician could be held responsible for taking reasonable steps to ascertain whether the information presented has been understood, so that if it has not he may supplement it as needed or may convey the same information in a manner more comprehensible to the particular patient.[58]

While at least four jurisdictions have followed this approach,[59] it has been rejected by the weight of legal opinion. *Hondroulis v. Schumacher* criticized the subjective rule because "to require the physician, absolutely, to use language which his client will in fact understand calls for clairvoyance."[60] Moreover, the subjective rule permits the client's testimony—susceptible to modification by hindsight—to control the issue of consent. The professional is also forced to bear the entire risk of the client's unspoken interpretive mistakes. Application of this rule ignores what the law has long recognized: Legal relationships based on communication cannot depend on the vagaries of parties' subjective intent.[61]

Minors. The rule that treatment may be administered only with the client's consent is generally deemed inapplicable in the case of minors. The legal incompetence of minors stems from two primary policies: (1) to protect children from their own inexperience and (2) to protect the interests of parents who bear financial responsibility for their children.[62] Because children are legally incapable of consenting to their own medical treatment, the substituted consent of a legal guardian is required. Three primary exceptions to the requirement of parents' substituted consent for minors exist; in these situations, no consent is required. First, in an emergency, when parents are unavailable, treatment may be rendered without parental consent. The other two exceptions apply to situations in which the interests of parents and their children may be in conflict. Thus a court may authorize treatment for a minor whose parents refuse medical treatment. In addition, treatments that are necessary and relatively risk-free may be rendered if parental

[58]Capron, *Informed Consent in Catastrophic Disease Research and Treatment,* 123 U. PA. L. REV. 340, 414 (1974).

[59]*See Gray v. Grunnagle,* 423 Pa. 144, 223 A.2d 663 (1966); *DiFillippo v. Preston,* 53 Del. 539, 173 A.2d 333 (1961); *Natanson v. Kline,* 186 Kan. 393, 350 P.2d 1093 (1961); *Bang v. Chas. T. Miller Hosp.,* 251 Minn. 427, 88 N.W.2d 186 (1958).

[60]*Hondroulis,* 546 So. 2d at 478.

[61]*See* J. Waltz & F. Inbau, Medical Jurisprudence, 165 (1971).

[62]Reisner, *supra* note 3, at 187.

consent would be withheld, thus obstructing the likelihood of obtaining the necessary treatment. This situation surfaces most frequently in circumstances requiring the treatment of minors for venereal disease, pregnancy testing, and drug dependency.[63]

FROM THEORY TO PRACTICE: HURDLES TO RECOVERY

The second part of this chapter reviewed the doctrinal components of informed consent. These components become the focus of inquiry in any informed consent cause of action. Yet a plaintiff who successfully shows professional behavior offensive to the requirements of informed consent has not completed the journey to recovery. If the informed consent action is based in negligence, the plaintiff will have to further demonstrate injury and causation. These elements offer unique evidentiary problems that the plaintiff must overcome. In many states, recovery is governed by state statutes that are the results of legislative rather than judicial balancing of the competing individual, professional, and societal interest in informed consent doctrine.

Causation

After a plaintiff shows that the informed consent doctrine applies and that the duty to disclose was breached by nonconformity to the standard governing the scope of disclosure, a causal connection must be demonstrated between the injury incurred and the professional's failure to obtain informed consent. Causation must be distinguished from materiality. What information is material is determined by the standard governing the scope of disclosure—for instance, the professional standard or one of the client materiality standards. Failure to disclose information deemed material by the applicable standard violates the duty of informed consent; yet only if the injury resulted because of the nondisclosure is there a causal connection between the breach of duty and the injury. An example here illustrates the difficulties that may be encountered in proving causation in the context of psychotherapy.

A client complains that excessive passivity and inability to direct subordinates are preventing advancement in employment to the full extent permitted by the client's intellectual skills. The therapist employs assertiveness training. The training is successful, and the client becomes more assertive; however, the change in personality precipitates difficulties with the client's spouse: The spouse is unable to adjust to the client's new and more assertive style. The client now contends that assertiveness training would have been refused had information about this potential risk been provided. In this situation, the client faces significant diffi-

[63]*Id.* at 188.

culty in proving both that the psychotherapy in fact led to the personality change (factual causation) and the change in personality is so closely connected to the marriage's dissolution that it may be considered the legal (proximate) cause.[64]

The distinction between materiality and causation is especially clear in jurisdictions that determine materiality by the professional standard because causation will always be determined by a client-oriented standard—for example, see *infra* New York Statute. Causation has three dimensions. First, the plaintiff must show that the risk which should have been disclosed actually materialized.[65] Second, the plaintiff must show factual causation by showing that "but for" the treatment the injury would not have occurred. Finally, to satisfy legal (proximate) causation, the plaintiff must show that a "prudent person in the client's position"[66], or in some jurisdictions the client personally,[67] would have declined treatment had disclosure been adequate.

The plaintiff must first demonstrate that the undisclosed material risk (as determined by the applicable standard governing scope of disclosure) actually materialized. If a risk does not materialize, or a risk that was unforeseeable and therefore not within the required scope of disclosure materializes, there is no connection between the duty breached and the actual injury, if any. Mere failure to disclose a risk that does not materialize will not provide a cause of action because there is no injury.

Second, factual causation must be shown, which requires connecting a causal chain between the materialized risk and the treatment. This poses the question "But for" the treatment would the injury complained of arisen? This requires the plaintiff to rule out other possible causes of the injury—such as an event subsequent to and unrelated to the treatment. Here the plaintiff links a factual (or historical) chain of events from the treatment to the undisclosed risk that materialized.

Finally, the plaintiff must demonstrate legal (proximate) causation. Proximate causation requires that the jury find that the plaintiff would have foregone treatment if the plaintiff had been informed of the risk that actually materialized. As with the standard of disclosure, either an objective or subjective approach may be used. Remember, however, that the standard governing the scope of disclosure determines materiality and answers whether or not the information would be significant in the client's decision. In causation, the inquiry is whether or not knowledge of the information would have caused the client to forgo treatment. Jurisdictions having adopted the client-oriented materiality standard will find this inquiry similar, whereas in jurisdictions operating under a professional standard the inquiry will be quite different.

Under the objective approach, the jury determines whether the average, prudent client would have foregone treatment had the client been informed. As

[64]Example drawn from Reisner, *supra* note 3, at 134–135.
[65]*Canterbury,* 464 F.2d at 790.
[66]*Canterbury,* 464 F.2d at 791.
[67]*See Wilkenson v. Versy* 110 R.I. 606, 629 295 A.2d 676, 690 (1972).

stated by the court in *Largey v. Rothman*:[68] "Proof of proximate causation in informed consent cases, under the 'prudent patient' standard, requires objective proof that a prudent person in the patient's position would have decided differently if adequately informed."[69]

This objective measure of legal causation is designed to protect the professional from the possible bitterness and reevaluation of a situation by the client through hindsight, while entrusting the jury to evaluate the client's position.

Legal (proximate) causation may also be determined by a subjective approach, which focuses on whether or not the particular client suing would have foregone treatment had the client been aware of the risk that materialized. Here the plaintiff's credibility as judged by the jury is paramount. Jurisdictions adhering to this approach criticize the objective rule as attenuating the client's right to self-determination by precluding its application beyond its predictable exercise by the hypothetical, average prudent client.[70]

Damages

An informed consent plaintiff must show that the materialized risk resulted in damages. The measure of damages is generally the same as in malpractice cases. The plaintiff is entitled to recover compensation for the loss or injury resulting from the risk that materialized. It has been argued that this rule would be unduly harsh from a psychotherapist's perspective because the recovery is not reduced by an amount attributable to whatever injury or loss would have occurred if no treatment had been undertaken or if an alternative therapy had been adopted.[71] In psychotherapy, this approach of demonstrating the "net" injury from treatment is laden with evidentiary dilemmas; speculation and conjecture replace tangible evidence. It is precisely this problem that has led to the restrictive rules generally requiring physical injury in negligence actions.

Under the current state of the law, violations of psychological integrity do not ordinarily constitute compensable injuries unless accompanied by physical impact.[72] As a result, conventional psychotherapists who do not use treatment modalities with the potential of inflicting physical harm have been unscathed by the growing body of informed consent litigation. The trend in the law, however, is clearly toward recognition of psychological harm as a sufficient basis for recovery of monetary damages even when not associated with physical injury. Instead of merely accepting an arbitrary distinction between physical and psychological injury, courts have shifted their focus of recovery for mental distress as merely a question of proving the genuineness of a claim.[73] This is an especially

---

[68]*Largey v. Rothman*, 110 N.J. 204, 540 A.2d 504, 510 (1988).
[69]*Id.*
[70]*See Scott v. Bradford*, 606 P.2d 554 (Okla. 1979).
[71]Reisner, *supra* note 3, at 167.
[72]*Id.*
[73]*Informed Consent in Psychotherapy, supra* note 9, at 1660.

important trend in psychotherapy, where fictitious claims can be somewhat controlled by treatment records that reflect the therapist's perceptions of the client's condition.

Rules governing damages will be different in jurisdictions recognizing informed consent as a variant of battery. In battery, because the unauthorized act is itself the legal violation, the professional may be liable for monetary damages even if actual damages cannot be shown. Also, because battery is an intentional tort, punitive or exemplary damages may be available if the professional behavior was wanton, willful, or in reckless disregard of the client's welfare.

State Statutes

The growing body of informed consent case law has prompted many states to enact statutes governing informed consent requirements and recovery for violations.[74] Generally, these statutes are drafted as medical malpractice statutes, thus doing little to clarify the problems of application to psychotherapy. Other states have adopted statutes specifically directed to mental health. We discuss the California and New York statutes here because these states have a persuasive influence on other jurisdictions.

California has led the way in providing an informed consent statute with clear and direct application to mental health. The California statute applies specifically to the civil rights of persons involuntarily detained. The statute provides:

§ 5326.2. Information for informed consent

To Constitute voluntary informed consent, the following information shall be given to the patient in a clear and explicit manner:
(a) the reason for treatment, that is, the nature and seriousness of the patient's illness, disorder or defect.
(b) The nature of the procedures to be used in the proposed treatment, including its probable frequency and duration.
(c) The probable degree and duration (temporary or permanent) of improvement or remission, expected with or without such treatment.
(d) The nature, degree, duration and the probability of the side effects and significant risks, commonly known by the medical profession, of such treatment, including its adjuvants, especially noting the degree and duration of memory loss (including its irreversibility) and how and to what extent they may be controlled, if at all.
(e) That there exists a division of opinion as the efficacy of the proposed treatment, why and how it works and its commonly known risks and side effects.
(f) The reasonable alternative treatments, and why the physician is recommending this particular treatment.
(g) That the patient has the right to accept or refuse the proposed treatment, and that if he or she consents, has the right to revoke his or her consent for any reason, at any time prior to or between treatments.[75]

---

[74]For a state-by-state summary of informed consent statutes and case law, see A. Rosoff, Informed Consent (1981).
[75]CAL. WELFARE AND INSTITUTIONS CODE § 5326.2. (Deering 1988).

Note that the California statute excludes any reference to the standards governing the scope of disclosure; it simply lists the information to be disclosed.

The New York statute invokes a professional standard to govern the scope of disclosure while basing causation on the prudent client standard. The statute provides:

§ 2805–d. Limitation of medical, dental or podiatric malpractice action based on lack of informed consent

1. Lack of informed consent means the failure of the person providing the professional treatment or diagnosis to disclose to the patient such alternatives thereto and the reasonably foreseeable risks and benefits involved as a reasonable medical, dental or podiatric practitioner under similar circumstances would have disclosed, in a manner permitting the patient to make a knowledgeable evaluation.

2. The right of action to recover for medical, dental or podiatric malpractice based on a lack of informed consent is limited to those cases involving either (a) non-emergency treatment, procedure or surgery, or (b) a diagnostic procedure which involved invasion or disruption of the integrity of the body.

3. For a cause of action therefore it must also be established that reasonably prudent person in the patient's position would not have undergone the treatment or diagnosis if he had been fully informed and that the lack of informed consent is a proximate cause of the injury or condition for which recovery is sought.[76]

Defenses under the New York statute include situations where (1) the client waived the right to render informed consent, (2) the risk was too common to warrant disclosure, (3) treatment was rendered in an emergency, and (4) the practitioner reasonably believed disclosure would adversely and substantially affect the client's condition.[77]

Where an informed consent statute has been enacted, legislative intent supersedes case law in balancing competing policy interests. Although the statute controls the governing standards and defenses, poststatute case law must be observed to determine how the courts construe and apply the statute.

SUMMARY AND CONCLUSIONS

The doctrine of informed consent is a product of social and judicial devotion to the right of self-determination. The doctrine of informed consent is slowly infiltrating the mental health professions, and legal trends suggest that psychotherapists will be directly subject to informed consent actions in the immediate future. State statutes that apply the informed consent doctrine to mental health treatment have already emerged.

---

[76]N.Y. PUBLIC HEALTH LAW § 2805–d. (McKinney 1985 & 1990 Supp.).
[77]*Id.*

The fundamental requirements of informed consent, disclosure of information, and consent to treatment have been subject to a vast array of interpretations by the courts. As the informed consent doctrine expands to encompass the mental health professions, one should anticipate even greater divisions as to the doctrine's substance and application. Psychotherapists will no doubt experience significant discomfort as the judiciary struggles to apply turbulent legal doctrine to a profession with unsettled standards.

8

Informed Consent: Clinical Duties

I f providers find the ambiguities and paradoxes of practice they encounter in clinical work with self-destructive and dangerous clients perplexing, then they will find similar uncertainties and equally conflicting duties in the doctrine of informed consent. Informed consent is problematic for mental health providers for at least four reasons:

1. It is not clear that therapists can actually explain some of the more important aspects of therapy or the risks and consequences of undergoing therapy for specific clients.

2. It is not clear that clients are interested in explanations of processes (with their uncertainties) at the time they enter treatment.

3. The doctrine of informed consent is based on medical practice in which specific high-risk interventions are common, alternatives and their consequences are known, information is more easily offered, and lawsuits are common (Legal opinions and clinical practice have a long history of interaction because of the physical interventions involved in medicine. This relatively longstanding interaction has provided a more solid basis for practice).

4. Procedures necessary for gaining clients' informed consent (if it can be accomplished with psychotherapeutic interventions) often conflict with what practitioners feel is in the best interest of clients. Thus the ambiguities of therapy, the resistance of clients, the focus of legal opinions on physical interventions, and conflicts about what is really in the best interest of clients combine to make the standards for disclosure in psychotherapeutic practice unclear.

The issues surrounding informed consent in psychotherapy are both more problematic and more subtle than those involving dangerous and self-destructive clients. At the same time, and probably because informed consent issues are less clear and more subtle, they arouse far less anxiety in the practitioner. Informed consent in psychotherapy does not have to do with the loss of life but with the loss of autonomy, so negligence in this area of practice seldom has glaring consequences. Nevertheless, there is every reason to believe that practitioners can improve the manner in which they deal with informed consent and that this improvement will serve the interests of both clients and providers. Failures, on the other hand, can result in legal problems for the provider, with disastrous consequences that parallel those associated with more obviously dangerous situations.

Here we further define informed consent, place it into a historical perspective with regards to its legal and ethical underpinnings, discuss issues generated by the concept, and provide guidelines for practice. In so doing, we recognize that informed consent is a relatively new issue for most mental health practitioners, one typically considered with indifference, if at all. We are confident nonetheless that because of increased legal involvement, it is a concept that will be fully embraced in theory as well as practice by most conscientious psychotherapists during this century. It is a concept that can be easily integrated into treatment techniques, like psychotherapy, which emphasize the importance of the interaction between the participants for a positive therapeutic outcome.

THE INFORMED CONSENT DOCTRINE— LEGAL ISSUES AND THE CLINICAL CONTEXT

What is informed consent? Simply stated, it is the idea that clients making decisions about their health care will do so in collaboration with the health care professional. The obligation to provide clients with the opportunity to give their informed consent to treatment, assessment, and research implies a respect for their dignity as competent, intelligent individuals who have a right to know what their treatment involves. Contrast this respect with the "doctor knows best" standard of care that implies clients are not capable of making intelligent decisions about treatment, thus diminishing their capacity to participate fully in treatment. In fact, most professional relationships, especially the therapeutic relationship, rest on the consent of the client who initiated it. Since the authority to terminate the relationship typically rests with the client and not the practitioner, informed consent is an essential responsibility of the provider. Despite the obligation of informing and encouraging clients to fully participate in treatment planning and implementation, the specifics of doing so (to the extent that it is in any way possible) are complicated and require both good judgment and technical skills. The content, manner, and timing of meeting this obligation have considerable impact on the treatment (professional) relationship and the benefits such procedures will have for clients. The idea of informed consent is put into operation (1) by the legal doctrine of informed consent derived from case law, legislation, and legal theory alluded to in the previous chapter and (2) through the ethical standards and professional guidelines the various mental health professions foster. The doctrine generally requires that the provider declare information to clients and subsequently obtain their consent before administering treatment. The legal requirements and particulars of this process vary substantially across states, even between particular cases within states! No simple set of legal requirements for informed consent exists, but the comprehensive following guidelines (although most appropriate for medical interventions) embody the doctrine as it has evolved to the present.

To give a valid consent, clients must have sufficient information about a particular procedure and its possible consequences to make a rational decision for or against it. Clients must also be informed that they can withhold consent or later withdraw consent at any time. A fair and reasonable description must be provided in a language that clients can understand and at the level of complexity they request. It therefore should be individualized. It might include a diagnosis, a description of the recommended approach, resulting benefits and probability of occurrence, possible adverse effects that typically follow and their likelihood, and alternative treatment approaches and their incumbent risks and benefits. If the approach is novel or experimental, clients should be so advised.

Most providers would probably agree that the doctrine, as it has evolved, is rarely put into practice in a systematic way in psychotherapy. Although the legal consent doctrine is most clearly grounded in medical practice, with its many intrusive and risk-laden treatments, it is also relevant to psychological interventions because they also carry risks and negative effects (Lambert, Bergin, & Collins, 1977). Quite apart from outright harm, ethical practice supports the importance of client autonomy. And to some extent professionals must provide informed consent not only as a matter of providing needed information but as a matter of interacting respectfully with clients. There are also important constitutional underpinnings to this right: Individual autonomy, or the right to choose or decide, has common-law and constitutional antecedents (Appelbaum, Lidz, & Meisel, 1986, p. 13).

When providers fail in their obligations or are thought to fail, clients can seek redress in the courts (as well as through hospital boards, licensing boards, and ethics committees) through a lawsuit aimed at a monetary recovery. Despite the fact that numerous court cases have been heard, and the courts and legal scholars have written much about the doctrine of informed consent, many issues remain. Still left undefined by the courts and professional associations are a host of practical issues regarding standards of practice. Should every risk, no matter how trivial or rare, be disclosed to the client? What is to be done when predictions about responses to treatment (risks and benefits) cannot be made with any certainty? At what points in the process should information be provided?

As one reviews case law, it becomes apparent that the great variability in judgments and decisions about client welfare and rights provide insights into the legal system but few specific guidelines for practice. Since the concern of the courts is not to develop standards for providers but to address grievances, the rulings are generally an inadequate basis for practice. The courtroom is, however, an arena in which various points of view can be heard and weighed. As such, legal opinions are quite helpful to the consumer of mental health services and to the profession. The courts have dealt with standards of practice and the question of how much information to give clients and also the related question "What information must be given?" We now turn to this question.

ELEMENTS AND CONTENT OF DISCLOSURE

The general information considered central for properly informing individuals is based to a large degree on prescriptions suggested in the decision of *Natanson v. Kline* (1960), a case dealing with radiation therapy for cancer, rather than psychotherapy. The court suggested that disclosure include the nature of the illness and treatment, the probability of success and risks, and alternative treatments and risks. All this was to be provided in a language that was as simple as necessary to ensure that a meeting of minds had occurred. Each of these elements of informed consent is controversial, yet certain recommendations are useful to practitioners.

Nature of Procedures

Although giving certain limited information about procedures is common in psychological practice, information may not be as systematic or comprehensive as is ideal. Procedural information should include the following.

Business and Administrative Details.   Of interest to the client in decision making are the cost of treatment and related insurance issues; the handling of missed appointments and related charges, if any; the anticipated length of treatment; frequency of sessions; duration of sessions; limits on the availability of the therapist and extratherapeutic contacts; any expected interruptions in the treatment process, and the like.

Treatment Procedure/Process Issues.   When the therapist is explaining the nature of the therapeutic process, the client may want to learn of particular activities that will be a part of therapy. These activities are often dealt with in role-preparation instructions (compare with Orne & Wender, 1968) to make clear the relative responsibilities of client and therapist. Disadvantages of these interviews are that they are general and not appropriate for all therapies. In addition, they are not primarily aimed at informing clients so that they can choose but at encouraging the client to ideally participate in the client role. Each individual practitioner can make clear something about the way therapy is to proceed, including the use of specific techniques such as suggestion, catharsis, biofeedback, exposure to feared objects, and hypnosis.

Training Status, Supervision, Credentials.   The client needs complete information about important features of the treatment provider that could have a bearing on the boundaries of the relationship. Clearly, the client needs to know if the provider is a trainee and the meaning of this status (for example, tape recordings will be made, the supervisor and perhaps other students will observe the therapy, the supervisor may enter the therapeutic relationship, others have access to the records). If the provider is going to be under supervision, this fact should be made known to the client. Clients have a right to know about the therapist's professional credentials and orientation.

Confidentiality and Its Limits.   Related to the above issues is information about confidentiality, which includes the release of diagnostic and treatment information to insurance carriers, government agencies, and peer review committees. Especially important are issues of confidentiality, discussed in other chapters, that concern dangerousness and child abuse. The obligations of health service providers vary from state to state. Providers must be aware of, and clients need to be fully informed about, these limits to their rights. We return to this issue later as it is closely tied to issues of voluntary participation in treatment by the client.

Diagnostic and Prognostic Information. Providing clients with diagnostic and prognostic information is one of the more controversial areas of practice. While strong arguments can be raised about the limited value and necessity of formal diagnosis in DSM terminology, the fact is that the practice of most mental health professionals depends on the diagnostic enterprise. Agreements can be reached to focus therapy on specific client issues and needs without drawing attention to symptom clusters that are consistent with various diagnostic classifications. Even so, when a formal diagnosis is made and is the focus of treatment, the client has a right to that information and a discussion of its meaning. Such a discussion has more meaning with strictly medical disorders because physical disease often involves more certainty about alternative treatments and prognosis. Given the instability and unreliability of mental disorder diagnoses, their lack of clear implications for treatment, and often vague prognostic indications, the meaning and value of discussions about diagnostic and prognostic information may be less important and critical in client decision making with regard to undergoing psychological treatment or entering alternative treatments.

Alternative Treatments. The issue of diagnostic and prognostic information is closely tied to the possibility of entering into or offering alternative treatments for the problems that the client has agreed to work on. To a large extent, the clinician is dependent on research into the effects of competing psychotherapies on clients. Numerous authors, such as Lambert, Shapiro, and Bergin (1986), Rachman and Wilson (1980), and Smith, Glass, and Miller (1980), reviewed this research and reached a variety of conclusions. Six relevant conclusions are relatively certain at this point: (1) few of the hundreds of available therapies have been empirically tested; (2) those that have been tested in studies attempting to show differential effects on homogeneous client samples have not provided evidence that clearly favors one treatment approach over another; (3) treatment effects for most clients are achieved in the first 6 months of treatment; (4) many alternative therapies are equally effective with a variety of disorders; (5) client variables are better predictors of outcome than therapy techniques; and (6) the specific therapist may be more predictive of outcome than the therapeutic technique itself (Lambert, Shapiro, & Bergin, 1986).

Given the state of psychotherapy research, on the basis of empirical findings it is difficult to discuss the advantages of alternative treatments and make recommendations. Certainly research results suggest modest claims of superiority of one method over another and equally modest negative statements about alternate treatments. Because these issues are too complex to fully discuss in this context, the interested reader is encouraged to consult the *Handbook of Psychotherapy and Behavior Change: An Empirical Analysis,* edited by Garfield and Bergin (1986), for a more complete analysis. The intelligent recommendation of alternative treatments is related to the last two issues to be addressed here: informing the client about the benefits and risks of treatment.

Benefits from Treatment.   Psychotherapy research (Lambert, Shapiro, & Bergin, 1986; Smith, Glass, & Miller, 1980) clearly demonstrates that many of the treatments that have been tested have shown positive effects. Anticipated benefits include the remission of a variety of symptoms, reduction and elimination of maladaptive behaviors, crisis resolution, conflict resolution, increased self-esteem, and improvement of interpersonal relations and social role performance. Given that the client is largely responsible for the outcome of therapy, it should be made clear that no promise of benefits or "cure" can be offered and that the outcome of treatment remains, both fortunately and unfortunately, largely the responsibility of the client.

Risks.   To a great extent, the elements of disclosure that have received the most attention in jurisprudence and legislation are the so-called risks, dangers, and side effects of treatments. Katz (1977) suggested that informed consent, as envisioned by courts, has been reduced to little more than the "duty to warn" about risks. This aspect of informed consent also appears to be the one of most concern to health service providers. Both trends suggest that the important and more subtle values of respect and autonomy may be overlooked in attempts to satisfy only the most obvious and egregious problems associated with medical practice. Psychotherapists, whose practice is often focused on increasing client autonomy (restoring a sense of self-confidence and self-respect), must be concerned not only with obvious harm to the client but with these more subtle ways of injuring the client's sense of self-worth and importance. Despite the overemphasis on risks of *bodily damage* in case law (legislation and clinical practice), the risks associated with treatment and diagnostic procedures are highly important elements of the consent process in psychotherapy.

The risks of undergoing certain psychological procedures have been documented in psychotherapy outcome studies, clinical case reports, and surveys of clients who have had negative therapeutic experiences. This evidence has been summarized in several sources (for example, Lambert, Bergin, & Collins, 1977; Mays & Franks, 1985; Strupp, Hadley, & Gomes-Schwartz, 1977), and contrary opinions have also been expressed (Franks & Mays, 1980; Rachman & Wilson, 1980). Several important variables have been implicated as possible causes of negative outcome in therapy: (1) client diagnosis—mainly borderline and psychotic disorders (degree of disturbance)—especially in combination with certain therapeutic procedures that encourage regression through breaking down defenses; (2) a host of client variables, including unrealistically high expectations, expectations of being harmed, poor history of intimate relationships, and poor interpersonal skills; (3) a variety of therapist factors, including negative attitudes toward clients (disrespect, lack of warmth, exploitiveness) and low levels of empathy; (4) client deterioration and negative effects found across a wide range of therapeutic schools (dynamic, cognitive, humanistic, and behavioral approaches) and therapeutic modalities (individual, group, marital, and family therapies).

Legislation and case law seldom address the negative effects of verbal interventions, but charges of assault or battery arise without the body actually being invaded by the treating person. Psychological interventions can have powerful effects on people, for better or worse, and recognition that these powerful effects can be negative even when offered with the best of intentions is an important fact that clients may want to know. It behooves all practicing clinicians to carefully consider the evidence and to be sensitive to the possibility of negative effects with particular clients, with the aim of reducing the likelihood of their occurrence and indicating the dangers in therapy for some people. At the very least, therapy for some clients reawakens painful experiences and memories as well as frustration, anger, and anxiety. For others, acting out, divorce, loss of custody of a child, or hospitalization are possible outcomes that deserve mention to help the client make choices about entering and continuing therapy. Discussion of these and related issues seems morally, if not legally, required.

Judgments about the nature of particular risks for particular clients, the magnitude or intensity of their response, and the likelihood of occurrence are all factors that the clinician can weigh in deciding what (and when) information to disclose to clients. Some states have adopted a checklist approach to the problems encountered (in specific common medical interventions) and are specific about certain medical risks that must be mentioned: death, brain damage, paralysis, loss of limb or function of organ, disfiguring scars, and so forth—even if the probability of their occurring is low (Meisel & Kabnick, 1980). Texas embodied a panel of physicians and lawyers to establish a list of specific procedures and risks that must be disclosed as well as a list of procedures for which no disclosure need be made (Vernon, 1985). Hawaii similarly relies on an administrative agency to establish the scope of required disclosure for specific treatment and surgical procedures (*Hawaii Rev. Stat.*, 1984). No such guidelines exist for psychological practice, although we later show the feasibility of a more general procedure that has been proposed.

Courts and legislatures have also defined the scope of required disclosure by defining, in general, *what risks need not be disclosed.* Usually these risks include (1) "commonly known risks"; (2) risks that are relatively unforeseeable or remote; and (3) those risks deemed minor because they do not cause substantial harm, discomfort, or pain. The types of treatment and diagnostic factors that fall into this category have not been spelled out. Certainly the risks inherent in typical psychological interventions may be among those that require little disclosure, but until suits are filed and opinions written, case law cannot provide guidance on the issue of risk disclosure in psychotherapy. But it would behoove the various professions to attempt to formulate a list of procedures and risks as a starting point for discussion about the disclosure of risks to clients. Until more is known about risks, the wise clinician should make every attempt to note negative reactions and begin to develop ways of helping clients make more informed choices about treatment in their own particular cases.

Other Questions.   Although it is customary in many therapies to treat questions about the therapist as "grist for the therapeutic mill" and as evidence of client problems, issues, and "transference reactions" to the therapist, many of the questions raised may indeed require a forthright response from the therapist. Even those that go beyond the training, credentials, orientation of the therapist, and the like may be viewed as information that could bear on the client's decision to undergo treatment or continue in treatment, even if asking the questions is also a manifestation of the client's psychopathology.

THE TWO REQUIREMENTS OF CONSENT

In addition to proper *disclosures* that are aimed at helping the client decide the effects of treatment on life plans and goals, valid consent also requires that the person be free from coercion and able to comprehend the information offered. Valid consent must be given with *understanding* and be *voluntary*.

Understanding

Understanding the nature of procedures, and other information the provider discloses, is not always simple. Numerous empirical studies have produced data that cast doubt on the degree to which clients actually understand or care to understand the information presented. Schultz, Pardee, and Ensinck (1975) provided a typical example. They studied 50 clients in an actual clinical setting within an hour of their admission (which included a consent interview and reading and signing a consent form). All subjects consented to be in a clinical research project, and their understanding of the clinical procedures were tested via a 19-item questionnaire. The results showed that 22% of the clients failed to read the form in its entirety. In all, only 52% of the subjects were viewed as adequately knowledgeable. Only a minority of clients had sufficient knowledge of the procedures (34%), purpose (22%), and risks (20%) of the procedures. In assessing the weaknesses of their attempts to attain proper informed consent, the authors found several inadequacies in their procedures. Nevertheless, this study is typical of findings in this area, and similar results have been regularly demonstrated in one form or another.

Considerable evidence proves that many people actually make decisions to participate in research and treatment (even to treatment that includes intrusive medical intervention) without referring to the information provided. For example, Fellner and Marshall (1970) studied the decisions of kidney donors and found that the decision to donate or not to donate was made before information was provided. Similarly, Kaplan, Greenwald, and Rogers (1977) reported the same trend for contraception. Similar trends can be seen, in general, in many clients who seem so passive that they place the decision to be treated in the provider's hands without considering any information.

In addition to these problems, which are indeed serious, there is also the issue of medication effects. Where it has been established that clients who received medication prior to consent and who thereby did not understand (or claimed not to understand) the information given them, clients could not be bound by their consent. This of course is a matter of great concern to the mental health practitioner, who is frequently working with clients under the influence of sedatives.

It is not clear whose responsibility it is to demonstrate an ability to understand, but it is likely that the provider will have a primary responsibility for assessing the client's level of understanding. While courts have not yet required the administration of tests to verify whether in fact understanding has occurred, this could become a future trend and may be a partial solution to this difficult problem. Issues arising with persons who cannot understand disclosure by virtue of their lack of mental capacity (including children) is discussed later in the "Exemptions to the Informed Consent Doctrine" section.

Voluntary

Related to the concept of understanding is the concept of consent that is voluntary, in many ways an even more complex problem than that of understanding. As Lynn (1983) pointed out, communication is not simple but highly complex and often aimed at social influence rather than the mere provision of information. However, since people's considerations of an issue are always shaped by social and interpersonal roles and expectations, their decisions are always somewhat subject to subtle control by others. Physicians and other mental health providers can probably gain consent to virtually any treatment plan without overt force or fraud largely because of their power as authority figures, behavioral manipulation through information control such as framing effects (Tversky & Kahneman, 1981), and social pressures to conform (Lynn, 1983, p. 31). These effects are of course unavoidable, and so the question becomes one of judging when the influence is unacceptably coercive and what procedures are likely to enhance rather than restrict choice. It is here then that the conflict between encouraging clients to enter into needed treatments to attain their inherent benefits and the desire to respect client autonomy comes clearly into focus.

Providers are frequently in a position to judge the degree of coercion present in a given case, if they are interested and sensitive to the issue. They are also in a position to actively reduce the coercion and manipulation present in a given case (President's Commission, 1982; Rennie, 1980). Above all, the provider needs to be careful to not place a new coercive force on the client. Many examples can be given of subtle and obvious situations in which coercion is present: A wife threatens divorce unless her husband attends individual or marital therapy, an employee is given a choice of attending therapy or being fired, an inpatient is told to attend this group or face restrictions on visitors and privileges. In all these situations, efforts can and should be made to help clients gain more control over their free choice rather than further restricting their choice. This action may include working with the "silent" member of the therapeutic or diagnostic encounter, delaying treatment, or foregoing treatment altogether.

EXCEPTIONS TO THE
INFORMED CONSENT DOCTRINE

Societal interests in the health and well-being of clients sometimes must override concern for their autonomy and individual choice. At other times, the health of society at large must take an overriding precedence over the individual's rights (such as in the case of the dangerous client). Thus there are a number of exceptions to the doctrine of informed consent that when applied judiciously may be justified. These exceptions—emergency, waiver (refusal of involvement), therapeutic privilege, and incompetence—were defined and discussed in the previous legal chapter.

Emergencies

In general, a provider in an emergency may administer treatment without the client's consent since the consent can be considered implied. The reasoning behind such a decision is obvious: The assumption is that if the person were able to do so, he or she would consent. Just what constitutes an "emergency" is unclear and has ranged from "an immediate, serious, and definite threat to life and limb" to as lenient as "suffering or pain would be alleviated by treatment" (Appelbaum, Lidz, & Meisel, 1986).

The urgency of a situation is the usual standard applied to judge the presence of an emergency. The urgency of a situation depends on the immediate consequences of foregoing treatment, especially when those consequences are permanent and extensive. Rarely do the situations faced in mental health practice contain the same degree of urgency often faced in medical practice. Nevertheless, the dangerous client (psychotic or suicidal clients discussed elsewhere in this volume) can constitute an emergency in which the harm that could result from delays in treatment is substantial enough to warrant treatment without informed consent (or simple consent for that matter). Obviously, when the urgency of a situation has passed, informed consent should immediately be obtained.

Refusal of Involvement

Another exception to the requirements of informed consent is when the client refuses or gives up the right to give informed consent. To exercise this right, once clients have indicated their wish not to participate in making an informed decision, the provider should be certain clients know they are giving up a right that is theirs by law and that they are not simply responding to subtle cues from the provider that she or he does not want them to make the decision for themselves. The decision to refuse involvement rarely occurs in psychological treatment, although it is common for clients to try to escape responsibility for their treatment or give therapists a high degree of responsibility for their care. Depending on the situation, the provider may honor or refuse the request. In most instances, it seems reasonable to delay treatments that have the greatest risks until the client is prepared to take responsibility for the decisions. Since the client's reasons for refusing to decide can vary from fear of knowing information (such as a diagnosis), fear of deciding, indifference (due to depression and so on), or not feeling competent, a careful appraisal is necessary.

On occasion, the client will attempt to displace responsibility for the decision onto a family member, clergy, or physician. Such a situation raises many of the same issues and requires careful consideration rather than rapid assent. Obviously, it is especially important in psychotherapy that the client accept responsibility for participation and for the risks that participation implies in the particular circumstance.

Therapeutic Privilege

In some situations, providers may withhold information that they ordinarily would be required to give if disclosure would be harmful to the client (such as cause suicide or result in loss of self-esteem). Thus the provider is freed to uphold a primary obligation: "Above all, do no harm." There is a fear among some (Appelbaum, Lidz, & Meisel, 1986; Katz, 1977) that this exception provides an all-too-large loophole for clinicians to exercise their aversion to disclosing information to clients. This position is typified in the following quote from Appelbaum, Lidz, and Meisel (1986): "If the harm to the patients from disclosure is viewed broadly . . . to include the risk that patients may choose to refuse medical care if informed, the privilege would in effect permit physicians to substitute their judgment for patient's in every instance of medical decision-making" (p. 73). Thus the client should be "protected" from the paternalistic notion that silence will result in conformance with what the psychotherapist thinks is best.

Appelbaum, Lidz, and Meisel (1986) suggested that withholding information from the client is seldom justified and that when therapeutic privilege is exercised, good medical practice might include discussion with a family member about the undisclosed information—especially risks. They suggest that such a dialogue could proceed along the following lines, with the goal of keeping clients in the role of self-determination: "There is some information about your treatment that you may wish to know, and I will tell you about it if you like. There's a chance that this information may upset you, and if you'd like, I'll discuss it with your spouse [or other family member] instead" (p. 77).

In most cases, such a discussion may be impractical for psychotherapists since the information disclosed could be just as disturbing for relatives and much less appropriate for their ears than strictly medical information. But the general principle holds: When the therapeutic privilege is exercised, the clinician may be wise to give the client a choice in the matter, even suggesting that disclosure could be later forthcoming. Court cases have not held that disclosure to a relative is legally necessary, but that it may be of benefit.

Court cases have also varied widely on the circumstances and justifications for withholding information. A frequently quoted case, *Canterbury v. Spence*

(1972), held that withholding information was justified on the basis of anticipated client response which renders the client unable to make a rational decision or engage in decision making. In contrast, *Nishi v. Hartwell* (1970) was so formulated that it permitted nondisclosure of risk information which would be "detrimental to the patient's total care and best interest." There are even cases in medical practice in which the exercise of therapeutic privilege has been mandated by the court (such as *Williams v. Menehan,* 1963).

Given the diversity of opinion, providers could choose to conform their practice to either a very restrictive or a liberal standard. The position clinicians take will depend perhaps more on their principles, education, and values than on a recognized standard of practice in the professions. In our view, clients are best served by providers who have a hopeful and determined attitude about clients' strengths, capabilities, and future possibilities. Exercise of the therapeutic privilege is of special concern because refusal to disclose a diagnosis or reason behind the recommendation of one treatment over another could itself seriously undermine a client's confidence and inadvertently do more harm than frank disclosure itself. The refusal is often a vote of "no-confidence" in the client.

Incompetence

Obviously, certain individuals (infants, the mentally retarded, unconscious persons, some mentally ill, and so on) are unable to consent to treatment, and just as obviously, treatment cannot ethically be denied to these individuals because of their incapacity. As straightforward as this proposition is, the practical matter of defining incompetence, establishing criteria of incompetence, and identifying the incompetent person is a challenging and demanding task, a task that is sure to be the subject of claims of professional liability for damage. Since the legal definition of competence and the client's right to refuse treatment are rapidly undergoing change in the courts and within the policy of hospitals and professions, the evaluation of competence promises to be ambiguous for years to come—a high-risk situation for the provider, who is usually in a position of having to make competency judgments.

Toward a Definition of Incompetence.   The law provides no generally accepted definition of incompetence. Broadly and historically speaking, people are determined to be incompetent if they are minors or if they have been ruled in court to be incompetent. As a result, they lose certain legal rights and have a guardian appointed to make decisions in their behalf. More recently, it has been recognized that just because a person is incompetent in some respects does not mean he or she is incompetent in all respects. Jensen, Siegler, and Winslade (1982) suggested substituting the term "decision-making capacity" for the broader term "competence" to suggest that it is this capacity that is at issue with regards to making treatment decisions. Thus the person who cannot adequately manage financial affairs may well be able to understand treatment options and their implications for health and life goals. Competence is not something that is present or absent; it is a decision-making ability that varies across situations and fluctuates over time in relation to emotional and physical states. This is an important aspect of the legal definition of competence; it is a specific capacity to consent to treatment. One may be competent to consent to a specific treatment while at the same time mentally disabled, legally incompetent for other purposes, and even incompetent to consent to other treatments (Schwitzgebel & Schwitzgebel, 1980).

Both judicial opinions and legislation have dealt with the specificity of lapses in the decision-making capacity by drafting court orders that give decision-making rights with a limited range—for example, for the purpose of managing a person's finances, consenting to specific operations, taking psychotropic medication, or deciding place of residence. Even in the case of minors, the age at which people can make decisions for themselves can vary depending on the type of decision. For example, Grisso and Vierling (1978) suggested there are three types of consent that courts would view differently in their determination of incompetency in minors: (1) the right to consent to treatment independent of their parents' consent or knowledge; (2) the right to refuse treatment that their parents have consented to; or (3) the right to participate in or know about treatment that is being decided. In many states, statutes give minors of various ages the right to make choices about limited types of medical care such as abortions, drug abuse counseling, and contraception.

The notion that competence should be defined specifically, within the legal context, is further strengthened by recent lawsuits dealing with the right of involuntarily committed clients to refuse treatments, particularly psychotropic medications. Clients who have been civilly committed to a hospital or related facility often have been considered incapable of making competent treatment decisions. They have been routinely treated without their informed consent, and often without any consent. The treatment that routinely involves various psychotherapeutic interventions (some of which are quite coercive), behavior therapy, and psychoactive medications are the standard practice of hospitals that see their goal as the restoration of mental health. Mental health professionals' assumption that involuntary treatment was generally permissible following commitment was possibly strengthened by the "patients' rights movement" of the 1970s, which lobbied for the right of civilly committed clients to receive adequate treatment for their condition in the hospitals they were confined in. As Meisel (1983) pointed out, several court opinions dealing with this topic aided in the impression that committed clients *must* undergo treatment. The assumption is heightened by civil commitment laws themselves, which may specifically mention clients' lack of insight into the fact they have an illness and need treatment as one criterion for committing them (Utah Code, 1988). The line of reasoning may be something like this: Hospitalization is for involuntary treatment—if psychiatric hospitals have an obligation to provide treatment, then involuntary clients have an obligation to accept it. A client's right to treatment and a hospital's obligation to provide treatment become confused and come to mean that a client is compelled to undergo treatment without consenting.

Beginning in the 1970s, serious questions were raised about particular treatments and the need to seek informed consent from the clients who were to undergo them. Electroconvulsive therapy was the clearest example of a treatment with serious side effects that clients won a right to forgo. Given this concession to client competency (in hindsight), it is perhaps surprising that the psychiatric community reacted with ". . . incredulity, astonishment, and hostility . . . " at the cases brought to the courts by clients who wanted the right to refuse treatment.

Foremost among these cases was *Rogers v. Okin* (1979), in which a group of involuntarily committed clients at Boston State Hospital sued the Massachusetts officials responsible for the hospital. They claimed that they had a constitutional right to forgo treatment imposed on them without their informed consent. They also argued that this right had been violated. Rogers was substantially upheld by the federal appellate court in Massachusetts, which ruled that involuntary clients could not, just because of their status, be compelled to undergo treatment. This case is still under review, so a final decision and its implications are not settled. To a degree, the decision will rest partially on the extent of incompetence that is assumed to be known from hospitalization. Is the person only unable to make a decision about the need for hospitalization or more broadly incompetent and unable to judge the dangers and benefits of noreleptic medications and the like?

Another case of importance is *Clites v. State* (1982). In this suit, the father of Tim Clites, a retarded resident of an Iowa hospital/school for the retarded, sued the hospital because he was not informed of the risks of medication. Seven years after Tim's admission to the hospital, major tranquilizers were prescribed to curb his aggressive behavior. Five years after the use of a variety of tranquilizers administered by various physicians, Tim was diagnosed as suffering from tardive dyskinesia. The eventual award of $700,000 was based on the fact that the hospital failed to both inform the client's father about the risks of the medications and show that Tim's behavior was a serious risk to other residents. Both *Rogers v. Okin* and *Clites v. State* emphasize the changing definition of competence and the serious implications of this changing definition.

Several legal analysts and social scientists have made recommendations concerning the specific cognitive abilities and characteristics of clients that define competence within the legal framework of competence as specific abilities (Appelbaum & Roth, 1982; Grisso, 1986; Grisso & Vierling, 1978; Presidents' Commission, 1982; Shinn & Sales, 1985; Tepper & Elwork, 1984). Two aspects of competence—*reasoning* and *understanding*—are common across these analyses and provide a basis for defining competence for the purpose of evaluating clients in the context of their informed consent to treatment. A competent person is one who understands treatment-related information and who can integrate, analyze, and process this information to formulate a plan of action.

Given these broad definitions of competence, the practitioner is still left with the task of translating these definitions into adequate assessment activities that should have the dual purpose of rendering accurate judgments in regard to the client and standing up to judicial review.

As the therapist attempts to evaluate the client's competence, a perplexing paradox emerges. Legal definitions of competence assessment emphasize the importance of competence in specific tasks such as treatment choice, but many of the most vocal advocates of the informed consent doctrine argue that the *particular decision* a person makes should not be used to assess the person's competence. This latter position is based on the following logic:

The more that decisions of incompetence are based on the nature of the decision itself, the greater the risk that clients' autonomy will be neglected. In this view, incompetence cannot be equated with irrational or unreasonable thinking. The client should have a right to refuse treatment even if the refusal is based on whim, caprice, or fear. The fact that a client does not agree to a procedure which is useful does not mean that a client failed to understand the alternative and its risks and benefits. To make judgments of competence based on a client's particular choice is an unnecessary paternalistic standard that also has the effect of biasing clients' decisions to accept treatment recommendations made by clinicians who are often caught in a conflict of interest since they may well profit from such decisions financially.

A partial solution to this dilemma is found in the distinction between the *capacity* to reason and choose and the fact of choosing. In reality, the capacity to decide can be assessed independent of a particular treatment decision and integrated into a final decision about the client's competence.

Toward the Assessment of Competence.   Although treating professionals have been more likely to base judgments about competence to consent on global evaluations of mental status or merely psychiatric diagnosis, this is an inadequate practice given the specific definition of competence many courts recognize. In many contexts in which other legal competencies are assessed—such as competency to stand trial—well-developed assessment procedures have evolved. Most evaluations for competence to consent are less formal and less well developed, possibly because competence to consent is subjected to judicial review with much less frequency. As a consequence, no specific standardized instruments are available for the evaluation of competence to consent. Several experimental procedures exist and provide reasonable guidelines for practice in both specific and more general situations; they are now briefly reviewed.

The most obvious way competence is assessed is in response to a specific treatment decision. Since the highest-risk treatments have involved psychotropic medications, electroconvulsive therapy, and psychosurgery, competence has most often been assessed with regards to participation in these treatments.

Binney and Veliz (1984) prepared a list of 32 points that they felt required attention by examiners in Massachusetts in the wake of *Rogers v. Okin* (1979). The 32 points fell under three major headings: "Insight into Illness," "Judgment Regarding Treatment," and "Understanding of Information about the Nature of One's Illness and Risks and Benefits of Treatment." The assessment of these points is based on interview and case history data.

Culver, Ferrell, and Green (1980) set minimal competency standards in relation to the use of electroconvulsive therapy. They suggested that a client be judged competent to choose or dissent from a specific treatment intervention when the following criteria are satisfied:

(1) The patient knows that the physician believes the patient is ill and in need of treatment (although the patient may not agree).

(2) The patient knows that the physician believes this particular treatment may help the patient's illness.

(3) The patient knows he or she is being called upon to make a decision regarding this treatment. (p. 587)

These are minimal standards that require freedom from relatively gross distortions of reality but could provide a starting point or first level of screening. They do imply a minimal understanding of the decisional situation. If understanding is one critical element of decision making, failing to grasp this essential information does render one incompetent and alleviate the need to go further in the assessment. However, these guidelines do not deal with more than minimal aspects of competence.

Three assessment instruments have been developed for assessing individuals' functional abilities to participate in decisions about their treatment. All three instruments were developed for clinical and policy-oriented research rather than clinical practice. Consequently, all three have implications for practice but cannot be directly applied in clinical settings as standardized tests. These three instruments have distinctly different formats and contents.

The Two-Part Consent Form for Electroconvulsive Therapy (TCF-ECT) was developed by Roth et al. (1982) to assess clients' understanding of information disclosed to them about ECT. Part I is a two-page description of the procedure, nature, physiological effects, risks (such as fractures and dislocations), the things the client must do to prepare for ECT, preparation with atropine sulfate and its effects, preparation with anesthesia and muscle relaxant and their effects, as well as what the client may experience afterward (for example, confusion; slight, temporary memory loss). Part I also indicates that treatment is voluntary and that the client can withdraw from treatment at any time.

Part II asks 15 questions that call for a written response and addresses the information provided in part I: name of the treatment, illness for which it is prescribed, why the treatment was recommended, risks, nature and reason for probable side effects, and so forth. The authors suggest the questions asked are aimed to test recall of information, understanding of language (such as anesthesia), and reasoning from the information on the form (for example, "The form explains that you will not remember the treatment itself. Can you explain why?"). Each question is scored 0, 1, or 2, with a total score of 30. No cutoff scores have been developed for clinical use. The TCF-ECT is administered after a doctor explains ECT, so that the form itself is not the sole basis for information on ECT. When this instrument was applied to a group of 57 clients (44 of whom consented to ECT), several clients required assistance in completing the form. The mean score was 19.5 (SD = 7.9), even though the clients were invited to consult part I while they filled out part II. Scores on the form were strongly correlated with the need for assistance in completing it and the presence of psychosis. Lower but statistically significant correlations were found with educational/occupational levels.

Weithorn (1980) developed a means of assessing competence based on analogue treatment dilemmas presented to nonclients. By using various panels of experts, she created two medically based and two psychologically based scenarios. These dilemmas are followed by a series of questions presented in a 1-hour structured interview. The Measure of Competency to Render Informed Treatment Decisions (MOC) has both a child and an adult form that vary as to the age of the subject and the amount of explanation of technical words. Each written dilemma (diabetes, epilepsy, depression, enuresis) presents information about the symptoms and problems of a hypothetical person consulting a physician or psychologist who provides a diagnosis, description of two to four treatment alternatives (including the alternative of no treatment), side effects, risks, and probable benefits of each alternative. After this material is described, it is summarized, and the subject is asked the first question (such as, "If you were in Kate's position and had to decide between these two choices, what do you think you might decide to do?"). Further standard questions are pursued, and all responses are rated in relation to four scales based on the Roth et al. (1982) criteria for competence. Table 8-1 presents the criteria (scales), scoring procedures, and sample questions.

Table 8-1   The Measure of Competency to Render Informed Treatment Decisions*

Scale	Scoring	Sample Questions
Evidence of choice	0–1, depending on the expression of any choice	If you were in Kate's position, and had to decide between two choices, what do you think you might do?
Reasonable outcome	1–5, based on expert judgments of choice being rational	(see above)
Rational reasons	1 point for each bit of information dealing with risk, benefit, discomforts during explanation of reasons for rejecting alternatives	Why did you choose (blank) instead of (blank) treatment?
Actual understanding	1 or 2, scored separately for either Rote Recall and Inference	*Rote Recall:* What are the disadvantages about the medication Tofranil? *Integration:* What do you think might be some disadvantages about using the bell and pad? (No information given in story.)

*Based on Weithorn, L. (1984).

Besides lending itself to research uses, the MOC could be used clinically in one of two forms. It may be used as a preliminary assessment of decision-making *capacity,* thus identifying clients who may have diminished decision-making capacity and for whom extra efforts will need to be expended if informed consent is to be obtained. It could also serve as a limited measure of competence because performance on it taps at least two relevant dimensions: the general capacities to understand and to reason. Unfortunately, the legal definition of competence focuses more on actual understanding and reasoning in the real-life treatment decision than the general capacity manifest in similar decisions. Thus the MOC may not be directly useful as a clinical tool but more useful for demonstrating the application of a procedure that applies the major definition of competence with clinical phenomena. It therefore is a model that can be adapted to a wide variety of treatment decision situations and demonstrates numerous procedures for assessing competence.

Summary and Conclusions Regarding Competence.   Treatment may proceed without informed consent if the client is not competent to consent. Competence, in the legal context, is usually narrowly defined in terms of the specific treatment decision that the client is called on to make. The provider, rather than the court, usually is responsible for making this decision in actual everyday practice. Competence is usually assessed by reference to two major factors: understanding and the ability to reason. These factors can be viewed as either *capacities* or as actual activities in the particular decision-making context. Typically, standardized tests of cognitive ability (intelligence tests, psychoneurological batteries) can contribute something to this assessment. However, the ideal assessment includes evidence of failures to reason and understand in the context of a specific decision. No standard tests for this purpose have been developed. Good models for assessments of competence exist and can be used by individual clinicians to develop tests of understanding and reasoning ability in their own practice.

Competence and Age.   An exception to informed consent that is especially difficult for mental health providers is related to the age and developmental capacities of both younger and older persons. The law deals differently with the issue of minors' competence to consent to treatment than with adults'. Most statutes recognize the right of consent for a "mature" minor—one who is in the latter years of minority and living independently of parents or other caretakers. But as already noted, statutes generally deny minors the right to an independent consent or refusal regarding their treatment because of their presumed incompetence to consent. This limitation has been based on both the presumed immaturity of minors and social values concerning the rights of parents to control the activities of dependent children for whom they are legally responsible (Grisso, 1981). Several exceptions have already been noted: the right to decide about birth control, abortion, drug counseling, and some other procedures. At least one state (Virginia) recognizes a minor's right to consent to or refuse any treatment, including parents' requests for the child's mental hospitalization (Melton, 1981). In these exceptional instances, a child's competence to consent would be evaluated by the same procedures used with adults. Although there is a trend to grant greater rights to minors, the Supreme Court has maintained that minors have fewer rights than adults. For example, in *Bellotti v. Baird* (1979), Chief Justice Burger wrote ". . . most children, even in adolescence, simply are not able to make sound judgments concerning many decisions, including their need for medical care and treatment . . ." (p. 603).

Despite present practices and assertions one way or another, empirical findings can and should be considered with regard to this question. Empirical research on this specific topic has only begun to accumulate. While there has been considerable research on the development of cognitive abilities in children and adolescents, far less research has been aimed at court-related issues (that is, the child's ability to understand treatment alternatives, risks, and benefits; research on certain aspects of understanding, including appreciation of the personal consequences of choices and long-term consequences of the alternatives). If there were a clear standard of competence, the adolescent's competence could be compared with the minimum standard. However, the criteria are not clear. Therefore, the usual research approach is to compare the minor's decision making with adults (who are not ideal decision makers but are granted the right to make decisions for themselves).

Recently, briefs presented by the APA to the Supreme Court (Bersoff, 1987; Grisso, 1987; Melton, 1987a, b) indicated that there is a

> . . . growing body of methodologically sound and generally accepted psychological research which concludes that minors fourteen years of age and older generally possess the ability to understand treatment alternatives and their attendant risks and benefits, as well as the demonstrated capacity for rational decision-making, to a degree that is not measurably different from that of adults. (Bersoff, Malson, and Ennis, 1985, p. 4)

Gardener, Scherer, and Tester (1989) challenged these findings. They suggested that the briefs went beyond these data in asserting adolescent abilities. Their most powerful argument was that the available data on adolescent treatment decisions are limited. The APA briefs were forced to relay on only two studies that actually compared adult and adolescent decision-making capacity (Lewis, 1981; Weithorn & Campbell, 1982). Another criticism of considerable merit is that the brief inappropriately interpreted the failure to find significant differences between children and adults as evidence that no differences actually exist (that is, the problem of interpreting null findings).

Despite the well-taken arguments of Gardner, Scherer, and Tester (1989), there is support for questioning the offhand assumption that adolescents cannot be trusted to effectively reason about decisions regarding their need for mental health interventions. Adolescents can understand some of the risks and benefits associated with psychotherapeutic interventions (Adelman, Lusk, Alvarez, & Acosta, 1985; Bastian & Adelman, 1984; Kaser-Boyd, Adelman, & Taylor, 1985). Even children as young as 9 appear to understand, reason, and make competent decisions about their rights, once the rights have been explained (Belter & Grisso,

1984). Much of this research (such as Weithorn & Campbell, 1982) unfortunately deals with hypothetical situations in which the subject is not a client, not emotionally invested in, or stressed by having to make a personal decision. We do not know the effects of emotional arousal on adolescent decision-making capacity. It seems likely, however, that many adolescents have capacities that equal or surpass adult capacities. Based on the current status of empirical research, it is wise to keep an open mind about the issue and to be sensitive to the capacities of minors and, where possible, accord them the same respect and dignity accorded adults.

Additional problems and issues have been raised in the treatment of aged persons, especially those who demonstrate evidence of organic impairment. Stanley (1983) addressed some of these issues in an article on informed consent and senile dementia. Of central importance, in competence determinations with organically impaired clients, is the effect of memory impairments. Understanding the information presented involves both comprehension and memory. Memory of decisional information is a special burden for the organically impaired. Thus if memory is emphasized in the evaluation of competence, many clients who were originally able to comprehend and process information as well as its implications would later be unable to do so. They may even forget having made a decision to enter into treatment or of having the right to withdraw.

There are no studies that examine the effects of senile dementia on competency to consent to treatment (Stanley, 1983). Research does show that moderately to severely cognitively impaired adults are less able to consent to research than normal elderly adults (Stanley, Stanley, & Pomara, 1983). In addition, the normal elderly were less able by some criteria and equal on other criteria than younger physically ill clients (Stanley, Guido, Stanley, & Shortell, 1984). This research suggests the elderly may need more extensive help than their younger counterparts in making autonomous decisions.

Incompetence and Surrogate Decision Makers.   Incompetence, when it has been determined, requires that informed consent be obtained from a surrogate who will act in the client's stead. In formal arrangements this person is appointed by the court as a guardian, but in practice this arrangement is seldom used. Court proceedings are costly and time consuming. The cost of care during such proceedings and the possible risks to the client's well-being caused by delays are also factors. The adversarial forum and its negative effects on all parties as well as the public exposure of the client's private life are additional reasons for formal court hearings being rarely used. Typically, family members are asked to make decisions about the treatment of persons who have been determined to be incompetent. Some states have identified persons who might naturally assume this status, such as a spouse. When family members disagree, more formal legal procedures may be necessary. When no family is available, a close friend or person who knows the client well may be called on. A hospital (in the form of an ethics committee) or professional staff often may have to assume the role of surrogate or be involved in the selection of a surrogate.

Decision making by a surrogate can proceed much the same as it might if the client were being informed. Ideally, the person acting for the client will (or will be encouraged to) consider the client's wishes, values, goals, interests, and beliefs when making a decision about treatment. In this regard, clients can express their wishes beforehand, although in mental health care this would be highly unusual. The typical practice is for the surrogate to render a judgment that is in the best interest of the client. The better the client's wishes are known, and the better the surrogate knows the mind of the client, the more possible it is to strive to render the same judgment the client would have rendered. Thus, the "substituted" judgment of the client could be strived for, and has been recommended by some (President's Commission, 1982).

Ambiguities in surrogates' legal status and the validity of their judgments abound. Nevertheless, their involvement is worthwhile for various reasons. Rozovsky (1974) suggested that in the absence of a legal guardian, it is always advisable to obtain consent from a spouse or relatives, not because they represent the client but to prevent them from taking any action to which they might conceivably have a right. It will also weaken any case brought by the client since it demonstrates the good intentions of the provider, which could lessen or remove any punitive damages that the court might award.

Although these reasons for seeking consent are stated in financial terms, it is probably true that the greater the communication and collaboration in the decision process, the better the outcome.

INFORMED CONSENT AND THE USE OF STANDARD FORMS

To the extent that providers view "consent" as a single event and obtaining signed consent as a protection against liability, the use of forms is a highly practical and necessary part of providing services. In fact, forms are only one of several methods that can be used to meet the duty to obtain the client's informed consent. The frequent use of forms in hospitals and research projects adds to the notion that a form and signature are necessary parts of the process of informing clients about proposed treatments. However, other procedures will suffice. Some surgeons, for example, have adopted videotape or audiotape consent interviews, and in psychotherapy it is common to merely record notes into the process records.

Common law and courts do not require signed forms; in fact, their value has been questioned in a number of cases (Appelbaum, Lidz, & Meisel, 1986). Foster (1978) suggested that lawyers look at the forms with disdain and as only a minor irritation. They will not be much of a hurdle to an aggressive attorney who will have little difficulty finding their limitations or weaknesses or even turn them as evidence against the provider since the form could be viewed as representing the extent of information provided (which is often far from true). Nevertheless, signed forms are a part of the evidence that can be entered into a court record. And tort law places a high value on being able to *prove assertions of compliance* with informed consent requirements rather than compliance itself. Meisel and Kapnick (1980) reported that 11 states had statutes which encouraged consent forms by according their use "as having the presumption of validity" that the requirements of proper consent had occurred. Although the validity of these statutes can be questioned (and at least one has been found to be unconstitutional), they suggest the possible importance a signed form could have in legal proceedings. At the same time, it is ironic that although these statutes were initiated to protect physicians, they shift the burden of proving consent from the client (who normally has to prove it did not occur) to the physician, who must now assume the burden of proving the adequacy of disclosure (Meisel, 1982).

Regardless of the forms' value or irrelevance in legal proceedings, remember that the duty to inform can never be filled by the form itself, and as suggested above, forms have the possible disadvantage of falsely reassuring providers that they have exercised their duty and that their duty is limited to obtaining the signed forms. If one looks beyond the use of forms as a "protection" for the provider and focuses on their value in the process of informing the client, then several advantages of forms can be identified.

One advantage of a form is that it allows the summary of core issues in frequently used treatments and diagnostic procedures. It is a convenient way of organizing and listing the general benefits, risks, and limitations of often applied procedures (which are also communicated orally). The form can be presented prior to the discussion of whether to undergo treatment so that the client can formulate questions and concerns. It can also be presented following oral disclosure, in which case it would facilitate reflection, memory, integration, and the formation of additional questions and be an opportunity to efffectively discuss the treatment contract with other concerned persons, such as family members, other professionals, or friends, should that be desired. Used in either way, the form can enhance understanding and communication, both of which should have a positive effect on the individual's decision-making capacity as well as the provider's knowledge of which parts of the form and procedures are confusing, troubling, or misunderstood.

Stromberg et al. (1988) suggested the use of a two-step process that is attractive and feasible. Following reading and oral discussion of the consent form, the client is asked to write out a statement demonstrating understanding of the information presented (such as "I understand that this data can be used by my employer"). This procedure lets the provider correct misconceptions as well as monitor understanding. This practice is similar to procedures that call for a brief structured "examination" following disclosure of medical procedures and, as discussed in our earlier presentation, assessment techniques. These examinations provide both provider and client with immediate feedback, allowing for further discussion. Following this, additional notes that document the procedure, the client's understanding, and the provider's conscientious efforts to obtain informed consent can be entered into the client's record.

Strong arguments can be raised against the use of formal consent forms in mental health practice, especially when intrusive procedures such as electroconvulsive therapy or psychotropic medications are not used. Clients who enter psychotherapy often visit in an agitated, alienated, anxious, or fragile state. They often come to therapy as a last resort (Christensen & Magoon, 1974), and with considerable ambivalence. Effective treatment is based on the development of trust, which is not likely to be enhanced by the therapist rapidly presenting a comprehensive consent form. It is this practical reality—that the procedural requirements (and especially an impersonal form) may damage the therapeutic relationship and thwart the development of the therapeutic enterprise—which may be at the root of mental health providers' noncompliance with the requirements of informed consent.

In many, if not most, cases, the immediate presentation of a form (part of whose purpose is to protect the provider) with an adversarial or even neutral tone is not feasible or desirable. It is hard to envision a competent and successful provider detailing risks and dangers to a client who is already filled with apprehension and misgiving but who at the same time is badly in need of professional help. Yet at some point the details of treatment must be discussed, including confidentiality and its limits, meeting times, and the like. Informed consent can be obtained as soon as it is at all feasible and clinically acceptable, followed by adequate record keeping of discussions. *Adequate clinical practice demands the disclosure of information and record-keeping efforts that document the fact that full disclosure took place.* Important also are notes dealing with the important question of the client's comprehension and *appreciation* of those treatment or diagnostic procedures necessary for meaningful decision making. This goal is slightly facilitated by use of a form, but use of a form is best viewed as a process that takes considerable time and is really part of the therapeutic process, regularly noted in client records.

Content of Informed Consent Forms

The application of particular forms developed for use in clinical practice depends on the treatment and diagnostic procedures specific practitioners use and their purposes. These forms should meet the general requirements of informed consent and be tailored to the practitioner's specific requirements. It is necessary to carefully consider length and language. Appelbaum, Lidz, and Meisel (1986) suggested that when forms are created mainly for dealing with liability problems, they tend to be lengthy, detailed, and technical. All three qualities diminish the communicative capacity of forms and, therefore, the likelihood that the clients they are intended to inform will understand them. A balance needs to be struck between the tendency to be overly inclusive and the need to provide a useful, informative document that includes the information necessary for decision making.

The burden of achieving this balance is easier to obtain when, as recommended, the form is viewed as an adjunct to disclosure rather than the extent of disclosure. The form should emphasize several factors:

1. The client is being asked to make a choice about treatment.
2. Information is being presented to help the client make a choice.

3. Nature of the procedure.

4. Administrative details: appointments, fees, missed appointments, use of collection agency, insurance, emergencies, and vacations.

5. Likely benefits.

6. Inherent risks.

7. Possible alternative treatments.

8. Issues of confidentiality, privilege, and their limits.

9. The form does not cover everything that may be of interest to this particular client; any questions are welcomed and will be answered.

10. Signing forms does not bind the client to completing therapy, which they can withdraw from at any time.

While these guidelines are general procedures, lengthier, more specific, or shorter forms may be developed for any particular purpose. Two sample forms—Figures 8-1 and 8-2—are presented on pages 180–182. The forms are considered suitable for the general purpose of informing clients about the procedures they are contemplating entering into and generating further discussion about the decision to participate in the professional relationship. Upon examination, one can immediately see the difficulties and shortcomings of standard forms. The need to tailor them to the procedures specific providers use and the needs, sophistication, and educational level of particular clients is also apparent. At the same time, the forms do provide information that the typical client is unlikely to have and, in this regard, at the very least will supplement the client/therapist dialogue about the choice to undergo treatment.

CASE PRESENTATION AND DISCUSSION

The following fictional case, created for the purposes of this book, is presented with the intention of stimulating thinking about application of the informed consent doctrine to a clinical situation. The case has several challenging aspects that have no single solution.

Ms. Smith, a middle-aged employed mother of three, called a private practitioner for help regarding Ann, her 15-year-old daughter. She thought having an appointment was urgent because she felt her daughter was "depressed" and "suicidal." She described her daughter as performing poorly in school and refusing to go to school. Smith was a divorced woman who had a clerical job during the daytime. She felt her daughter was out of control and expressed concern about her ability to help and control Ann. Smith wondered if Ann should be hospitalized. An appointment for later in the day was scheduled for both mother and daughter.

The somewhat relieved and anxious mother indicated that she was divorced and had custody of her and her former husband's three daughters. She indicated that her former husband was a rather passive man who went along with most of the decisions she made but who occasionally tried to take over the parent role.

The following information is being offered to help you decide if you want to participate in psychotherapy with me. I will be happy to help you understand any information that is not clear or answer any questions that might help you in your decision.

1. Psychotherapy is aimed at helping you clarify your problems, goals, feelings, and thoughts so that you can resolve conflicts and free yourself of disturbing symptoms and improve your relationships with other people. It involves talking about and working through concerns and problems.

2. Psychotherapy sometimes involves tolerating uncomfortable feelings, recalling unpleasant and painful memories, facing fears, anxiety, anger, and helplessness. Generally, psychotherapy does not have more serious risks for most people; we can discuss your reactions as we go along.

3. You have the right to have the things we discuss kept in confidence. Information revealed by you will be kept in strict confidence and will not be revealed to any person or agency without your written permission.

4. However, you should also know that there is certain information that I am required by law to reveal to appropriate authorities—with or without your permission. The situations where I am required not to maintain confidence are:

a. Where children are neglected, physically or sexually abused, the proper authorities must be contacted (Division of Family Services, Police).

b. In emergency situations where there may be danger to you or others (suicide, homicide, or where grave bodily harm may occur).

c. If you are here by court order, the results of our work together must be reported.

5. Fees and Payment. The fee for a 50-minute session is _____ . Payment is expected at the time of service.

6. Signing this form is an acknowledgement of having read and discussed the information, not an agreement of continuing in therapy to its mutually agreed on conclusion.

_____   _____
Client Signature   Date

Figure 8-1 Informed consent to treatment.

The statement begins with the therapist's professional qualifications, including (at a minimum) name, office address, telephone number, highest relevant degree, and certification or license number. The sentences that follow suggest what a client's basic rights in psychotherapy ought to include:

1. "You have the right to decide not to receive psychotherapy from me; if you wish, I shall provide you with the names of other qualified psychotherapists."

2. "You have the right to end therapy at any time without any moral, legal, or financial obligation."

3. "You have the right to ask any questions about the procedures used during therapy; if you wish, I shall explain my usual methods to you."

4. "You have the right to prevent the use of certain therapeutic techniques; I shall inform you of my intention to use any unusual procedures and shall describe any risks involved."

5. "You have the right to prevent electronic recording of any part of the therapy sessions; permission to record must be granted by you in writing on a form that explains exactly what is to be done and for what period of time. I shall explain my intended use of the recordings and provide a written statement to the effect that they will not be used for any other purpose; you have the right to withdraw your permisison to record at any time."

6. "You have the right to review your records in the files at any time."

7. "One of your most important rights involves confidentiality: Within certain limits, information revealed by you during therapy will be kept strictly confidential and will not be revealed to any other person or agency without your written permission."

8. "If you request it, any part of your record in the files can be released to any person or agencies you designate. I shall tell you, at the time, whether or not I think making the record public will be harmful to you."

(continued)

Figure 8-2 Client's Rights Statement—An example of a generic statement of clients' rights, treatment contract, and informed consent statement, drawn up by a committee of the California State Psychological Association. (From "Privacy and Confidentiality in Psychotherapy" by L. Everstine, D. Everstine, G. Heymann, R. True, D. H. Frey, H. Johnson, and R. Seiden, 1980, *American Psychologist, 35,* 832–833. Copyright 1980 by American Psychological Association. Reprinted by permission.)

9. "You should also know that there are certain situations in which, as a psychotherapist, I am required by law to reveal information obtained during therapy to other persons or agencies without your permission. Also, I am not required to inform you of my actions in this regard. These situations are as follows: (a) If you threaten grave bodily harm or death to another person, I am required by law to inform the intended victim and appropriate law enforcement agencies; (b) if a court of law issues a legitimate subpoena, I am required by law to provide the information specifically described in the subpoena; (c) if you are in therapy or being tested by order of a court of law, the results of the treatment or tests ordered must be revealed to the court."

Initial Contract Form

1. "I agree to enter into psychotherapy with [name of therapist] for [number negotiated] 1-hour sessions during the next [number negotiated] weeks.

2. "I agree to pay [amount negotiated] for each completed 1-hour therapy session. Payment will be made by me or by a third party when billed.

3. "I understand that I can leave therapy at any time and that I have no moral, legal, or financial obligation to complete the maximum number of sessions listed in this contract; I am contracting to pay only for completed therapy sessions."

Both client and therapist should sign and date this form.

Figure 8-2   (continued).

Ann had failed all her ninth grade classes the first school term and had complained about having no friends at her high school. She refused school, but she agreed to return if allowed to transfer to a different school. The transfer did not prove helpful, and Ann again failed her classes and was adamant that she would not return to school. Smith had allowed her daughter to live for a few weeks with another family in the area. This was temporarily helpful, but the family asked Ann to leave because they were having serious problems of their own (to which they felt Ann was contributing). Smith did not want Ann to live with her father because he was "incapable" of raising Ann.

They had sought treatment before, but Ann refused to return after the social worker told her she would have to be "put away" because she was unmanageable. Ann thought that her mother had brought her for treatment, but Smith felt she could do nothing with Ann, that she was having a negative effect on her sisters, and that she should be in a foster home or in a residential school. She wanted a psychologist to evaluate her daughter and make suggestions for placement or help Ann cope with school and her fears of school. She told Ann that if she did not see the psychologist, she would be sent away.

Before the interview and the assessment of Ann, the psychologist had indicated that she would be giving Ann a series of tests in order to "better understand your problems." No mention was made of the possible consequences of the interviews and tests in relation to hospitalization or a residential school. Ann hoped to be removed from her home and placed in a family of her choice or be allowed to forgo school and stay at home by herself.

In determining the wisdom of obtaining informed consent, the psychologist was concerned about the degree to which Ann was to be informed of the full purpose for the evaluation. The need to obtain consent from Ann was complicated by her age, her emotional and mental maturity, her past experience with a therapist, her mother's fear of her running away (which she had threatened to do on several occasions), her suicidal threats (which were nonspecific and manipulative), and the fact that she had already been misled by her mother about the purposes of coming in to see the psychologist. Ann had not thought about the possibility of her test and interview data being shared with school and hospital personnel.

The psychologist had two general Informed Consent forms that she used in her practice. The first was aimed at her usual caseload, which typically involved voluntary clients undergoing psychotherapy. The second was a consent used in court work with clients who were forced by the court to undergo an evaluation. Neither form seemed appropriate for the present situation.

This case raises several difficult dilemmas for the practitioner. Foremost is the importance of informing Ann about the nature and purpose of the procedures she is undergoing. The limits to confidentiality between Ann and the psychologist should have been addressed more explicitly. In particular, Ann needs to be advised that her communications will not be held in confidence in relation to her mother, father, and possibly hospital personnel. The evaluation is vaguely for the purpose of "better understanding your problems," but more honestly to evaluate the feasibility of various treatment options, including hospitalization. The risks and benefits must be spelled out. The psychologist needs to be clear about what could go back to Ann's mom or dad and what will not go back so that Ann does not later feel betrayed.

A second dilemma concerns the rights of the father to be apprised that a psychological evaluation is being undertaken, its purposes, and so forth. Who has legal custody? What role should the father play? How can he be involved in the evaluation? What information will be revealed to him and by whom? What are Ms. Smith's expectations regarding her husband's involvement in this case? How does this impact confidentiality and decision making? If some kind of custody battle is initiated, will the psychological report, including information from Ann and Ms. Smith, be exposed?

To the extent possible, the psychologist needs to foresee the ramifications of undertaking the evaluation and inform all parties of the risks they may consider important.

SUMMARY, CONCLUSIONS, AND RECOMMENDATIONS

Informed consent is a legal right of clients who undergo assessment, therapy, and other psychological interventions. It is also a process that can promote the general purposes of psychological interventions by enhancing the client's full productive participation in the treatment. Despite ignorance, considerable resistance, and skepticism therapists manifest about the benefits that can be derived from making efforts to inform clients about the risks (if not benefits) of treatment, it is clear that in almost all instances it can be done in such a way that it will decrease client dependence and increase client knowledge and informed choice.

To be most effective, each individual therapist should carefully consider the risks and benefits that may be an outcome of the procedures they employ as well as the growing body of research on alternative treatment methods that could be made available to the client. This information can be provided to clients at the earliest opportunity and at subsequent times when clinically meaningful and relevant. Each therapist must also consider client rights, ethical principles, and state laws in deciding what general information must be made available to every client. Especially important are the limitations on confidentiality that the client cannot reasonably be expected to know.

Given the absence of lawsuits and complaints that directly correspond with therapists' failure to obtain informed consent to therapeutic interventions that rely on verbal techniques, the dangers of litigation are not a sound reason for obtaining informed consent. The basis for obtaining informed consent rests on the values most health care providers share and the ethical codes of the helping professions: respect for the individual's right to autonomous choice or the value of fostering client autonomy. As guiding values, these are sufficient to make *systematic* efforts to promote informed choice in the client's health interests.

The clinical realities of everyday practice, especially the realities of the client's emotional state when initiating treatment, argue against mere reliance on a standard form. Obtaining informed consent is not equivalent to obtaining a signature on a consent form. The sensitive use of a consent form may facilitate the purpose of disclosing important information to the client. It is not, however, in most cases, a required part of the process, and it is certainly not a satisfactory procedure for helping the client appreciate the meaning of the information provided. Consent forms are best viewed as *part* of the ongoing dialogue between therapist and client about the therapeutic/assessment endeavor and its consequences.

REFERENCES

Adelman, H., Lusk, R., Alvarez, V., & Acosta N. (1985). Competence of minors to understand, evaluate, and communicate about their psychoeducational problems. *Professional Psychology, 16,* 426–434.

Appelbaum, P. S., Lidz, C. W., & Meisel, A. (1986). *Informed consent: Legal theory and clinical practice.* New York: Oxford University Press.

Appelbaum, P., & Roth, L. (1982). Competency to consent to research: A psychiatric overview. *Archives of General Psychiatry, 39,* 951–958.

Bastian, R., & Adelman, H. (1984). Noncompulsory versus legally mandated placement, perceived choice, and response to treatment among adolescents. *Journal of Consulting and Clinical Psychology, 52,* 171–179.

Bellotti v. Baird, 443 U.S. 662 (1979).

Belter, R., & Grisso, T. (1984). Children's recognition of rights violations in counseling. *Professional Psychology, 15,* 899–910.

Bersoff, D. (1987). Social science data and the Supreme Court: Lockhart as a case in point. *American Psychologist, 42,* 52–58.

Bersoff, D., Malson, L., & Ennis, D. (1985). In the Supreme Court of the United States: Thornburgh v. American College of Obstetricians and Gynecologists. Briefs of the American Psychological Association in support of appellees (no. 85-673).

Binney, D., & Veliz, J. (1984). Evaluating competence and the decision to refuse treatment. *New England Journal of Medicine, 68,* 114–120.

Canterbury v. Spence, 464 F. 2d 772 (D.C. Cir. 1972).

Christensen, K. C., & Magoon, T. M. (1974). Perceived hierarchy of help-giving sources for two categories of student problems. *Journal of Counseling Psychology, 21,* 311–314.

Clites v. State, 322 N.W. 2d. 917 (1982).

Culver, C. M., Ferrell, R. B., & Green, R. M. (1980). ECT and special problems of informed consent. *American Journal of Psychiatry, 137,* 587.

Everstine, L., Everstine, G., Heymann, G., True, R., Frey, D. H., Johnson, H., & Seiden, R. (1980). Privacy and confidentiality in psychotherapy. *American Psychologist, 35,* 828–840.

Fellner, C. H., & Marshall, J. R. (1970). Kidney donors—the myth of informed consent. *American Journal of Psychiatry, 126,* 1245–1251.

Foster, H. (1978). Informed consent of mental patients. In W. Barton & C. Samborn (Eds.), *Law and the mental health professions* (pp. 71–95). New York: International Universities Press.

Franks, C. M., & Mays, D. T. (1980). Negative effects revisited: A rejoinder. *Professional Psychology, 11,* 101–105.

Gardner, W., Scherer, D., & Tester, M. (1989). Asserting scientific authority: Cognitive development and adolescent legal rights. *American Psychologist, 44,* 895–902.

Garfield, S. L., & Bergin, A. E. (Eds.). (1986). *Handbook of psychotherapy and behavior change: An empirical analysis.* New York: Wiley.

Grisso, T. (1981). *Juvenile's waiver of rights: Legal and psychological competence.* New York: Plenum Press.

Grisso, T. (1986). *Evaluating competencies: Forensic assessments and instruments.* New York: Plenum Press.

Grisso, T. (1987). The economic and scientific future of forensic psychological assessment. *American Psychologist, 42,* 831–839.

Grisso, T., & Vierling, L. (1978). Minor's consent to treatment: A developmental perspective. *Professional Psychology, 9,* 415.

Hawaii Rev. Stat. (1984). 671–673 (b) (supp.)

Jensen, A. R., Siegler, M., & Winslade, W. J. (1982). *Clinical ethics: A practical approach to ethical decisions in clinical medicine.* New York: Macmillan.

Kaplan, S. R., Greenwald, R. A., & Rogers, A. J. (1977). Neglected aspects of informed consent. *New England Journal of Medicine, 296,* 1127.

Kaser-Boyd, N., Adelman, H., & Taylor, L. (1985). Minors' ability to identify risks and benefits of therapy. *Professional Psychology, 16,* 411–417.

Katz, J. (1977). Informed consent—a fairy tale? Law's vision. *University of Pittsburgh Law Review, 39,* 137–174.

Lambert, M. J., Bergin, A. E., & Collins, J. L. (1977). Therapist induced deterioration in psychotherapy. In A. S. Gurman & A. M. Razin (Eds.), *Effective psychotherapy: A handbook of research* (pp. 452–481). New York: Pergamon Press.

Lambert, M. J., Shapiro, D. A., & Bergin, A. E. (1986). The effectiveness of psychotherapy. In S. L. Garfield & A. E. Bergin (Eds.), *Handbook of psychotherapy and behavior change.* New York: Wiley.

Lewis, C. (1981). How adolescents approach decisions: Changes over grades seven to twelve and policy implications. *Child Development, 52,* 538–544.

Lynn, J. (1983). Informed consent: An overview. *Behavioral Sciences and the Law, 1,* 29–45.

Mays, D. T., & Franks, C. M. (1985). *Negative outcome in psychotherapy and what to do about it.* New York: Springer.

Meisel, A. (1982). More on making consent forms more readable. *IRM, 4,* 9.

Meisel, A. (1983). Informed consent and involuntary civil commitment. *Behavioral Sciences and the Law, 1,* 73–88.

Meisel, A., & Kapnick, L. D. (1980). Informed consent to medical treatment: An analysis of recent legislation. *University of Pittsburgh Law Review, 41,* 407–564.

Melton, G. (1981). Effects of a state law permitting minors to consent to psychotherapy. *Professional Psychology, 12,* 647–654.

Melton, G. (1987a). Bringing psychology to the legal system: Opportunities, obstacles, and efficacy. *American Psychologist, 42,* 488–495.

Melton, G. (1987b). *Reforming the law: Impact of child development research.* New York: Guilford Press.

Natanson v. Kline, 350 P.2d 1093 (Kan. 1960).

Nishi v. Hartwell, 473 P.2d 116 (Haw. 1970).

Orne, M., & Wender, P. (1968). Anticipatory socializations for psychotherapy: Methods and rationale. *American Journal of Psychiatry, 124,* 88–98.

President's Commission for the study of ethical problems in medicine and biomedical and behavioral research. (1982). *Making health care decisions.* Washington, D.C.: Government Printing Office.

Rachman, S. J., & Wilson, G. T. (1980). *The effects of psychotherapy: Second enlarged edition.* New York: Pergamon Press.

Rennie, D. (1980). Informed consent by "well-nigh abject adults." *The New England Journal of Medicine, 302,* 917–918.

Rogers v. Okin, 478 F. Supp 1342 (D. Mass. 1979).

Roth, L., Lidz, C., Meisel, A., Soloff, P., Kaufman, K., Spiker, D., & Foster, F. (1982). Competency to decide about treatment or research: An overview of some empirical data. *International Journal of Law and Psychiatry, 5,* 29–50.

Rozovsky, L. E. (1974). *Canadian hospital law: A practical guide.* Ottawa: Canadian Hospital Association.

Schultz, A. L., Pardee, G. P., & Ensinck, J. W. (1975). Are research subjects really informed? *West Journal of Medicine, 123,* 76–80.

Schwitzgebel, R. L., & Schwitzgebel, R. K. (1980). *Law and psychological practice.* New York: Wiley.

Shinn, M. J., & Sales, B. D. (1985). *Empirical research on consent to treatment.* Unpublished manuscript, University of Arizona, Department of Psychology.

Smith, M. L., Glass, G. V., & Miller, T. I. (1980). *The benefits of psychotherapy.* Baltimore: Johns Hopkins University Press.

Stanley, B. (1983). Senile dementia and informed consent. *Behavioral Sciences and the Law, 1,* 57–71.

Stanley, B., Guido, J., Stanley, M., & Shortell, D. (1984). The elderly patient and informed consent: Empirical findings. *Journal of the American Medical Association, 252,* 1302–1306.

Stanley, B., Stanley, M., & Pomara, N. (1983). *Informed consent with the dementia patient: Issues and empirical findings.* Paper presented at the annual meeting of the American Psychological Association, Anaheim, Calif.

Stromberg, C. D., Haggarty, D. J., Leibenluft, R. F., McMillian, M. H., Mishkin, B., Rubin, B. L., & Trilling, H. R. (1988). *The psychologist's legal handbook.* Washington, D.C.: The Council for the National Register of Health Service Providers in Psychology.

Strupp, H. H., Hadley, S. W., & Gomes-Schwartz, B. (1977). *Psychotherapy for better or worse.* New York: Jason Aronson.

Tepper, A., & Elwork, A. (1984). Competence to consent to treatment as a psycholegal construct. *Law and Human Behavior, 8,* 205–223.

Tversky, A., & Kahneman, D. (1981). The framing of decision and the psychology of choice. *Science, 211,* 453–458.

Utah Code. (1988). Vol. 3, chap. 7, 64–7–36.

Vernon, Cum. Sup., *Texas Rev. Civil Statutes Ann. Art.* 4590i, 6.03(a), 6.04(a), (d) (1985).

Weithorn, L. (1980). *Competency to render informed treatment decisions: A comparison of certain minors and adults.* Unpublished doctoral dissertation, University of Pittsburgh.

Weithorn, L. (1984). *Measures of competency to consent to mental hospitalization.* Unpublished manual, University of Virginia, Department of Psychology.

Weithorn, L., & Campbell, S. (1982). The competency of children and adolescents to make informed treatment decisions. *Child Development, 53,* 1589–1599.

Williams v. Menehen, 379 P.2d 292, 294 (Kan. 1963).

9

Involuntary Civil Commitment: Legal Duties

T he involuntary commitment and treatment of severely disturbed individuals is an issue both passionately advocated and criticized. Some argue that, absent a criminal conviction, restricting one's freedom is immoral and violates rights guaranteed by the U.S. Constitution. Conversely, others argue that society has a duty to commit and treat individuals who pose a threat of danger to themselves or others. These conflicts between the values of freedom, compassion, and safety are powerful.

This chapter first briefly details the development of involuntary commitment and the relevant constitutional issues. The remainder of the chapter explores the different bases of liability professionals are exposed to as a result of the civil commitment process.

HISTORY, DEVELOPMENT, AND CONSTITUTIONAL ISSUES

History and Development of Involuntary Commitment

Throughout history, the mentally ill have been treated in a variety of ways. In ancient times, some groups treated the "insane" with reverence, viewing the mentally infirm as individuals who had been touched by God. Other groups, however, persecuted the same group, viewing them as demonic. By the Middle Ages, nearly all of Europe developed an intolerance for the mentally disabled.[1]

In colonial America, the deviant were detained in cages, fences, or pens that were erected on the deviant's own property, to prevent the deranged individual from being a nuisance to neighbors. This treatment reflected the contemporary viewpoint that a person who had been deprived of reason was more an animal than a human being.[2]

As late as the 1830s, admissions to mental hospitals were almost entirely devoid of regulation—that is, private institutions were free to develop their own

---

[1]*See generally,* S. Smith & R. Meyer, Law, Behavior, and Mental Health 588 (1987).
[2]P. Schwartz, *Liberty and Autonomy Versus Confinement and Commitment: The History of Legal Intervention in Colonial Connecticut,* 11 J. PSYCHIATRY & LAW 461, 462 (1983).

involuntary commitment rules.[3] Even when the states began to regulate the commitment of the mentally disabled, most statutes were deficiently vague. Often these statutes would allow a husband to commit his wife or children by merely obtaining the acquiescence of a single doctor who would sign the commitment forms.[4]

In this century, numerous efforts have been undertaken to improve the plight of the involuntarily committed. Serious debate over the constitutional rights and liberties of the mentally ill has brought renewed attention to the involuntary commitment process.[5]

Constitutional Issues

The Fourteenth Amendment to the U.S. Constitution provides that a state cannot deprive any person of his or her liberty without due process of law.[6] While many controversies have raged over the due process clause, it is fundamental that *before* a state can deprive a person of her or his liberty, the state must give that person an opportunity to be heard.[7] Such is every adult person's right to due process under the federal constitution.

However, even though the right to a hearing prior to restraint is paramount, the Supreme Court has recognized that "extraordinary situations" may justify postponing the hearing until after the deprivation has taken place.[8] To pass constitutional muster, however, the state must further a "compelling state interest."[9] In other words, the U.S. Constitution, as interpreted by the Supreme Court, allows a person's liberty to be deprived without a hearing if the state can demonstrate that compelling governmental purposes are furthered by the deprivation.

Police Power Commitments. Two fundamental common law principles have been recognized as compelling interests that justify depriving an individual of liberty without a prior hearing. "The first relates to the right of the government . . . to take whatever actions are necessary to ensure the safety of society."[10] This authority is commonly referred to as the state's *police power,* and through this power the legislature has wide discretion to enact laws designed to protect the public health, safety, and welfare.[11] It is through the exercise of the state's police

[3]J. Smith, Medical Malpractice: Psychiatric Care 485 (1986).

[4]S. Smith & R. Meyer, *supra* note 1, at 588.

[5]*Id.* at 588–589.

[6]The entire text of the fourteenth amendment's first section is as follows: "All persons born or naturalized in the United States, and subject to the jurisdiction thereof, are citizens of the United States and of the State wherein they reside. No State shall make or enforce any law which shall abridge the privileges or immunities of citizens of the United States; nor shall any State deprive any person of life, liberty, or property, without due process of law; nor deny to any person within its jurisdiction the equal protection of the laws."

[7]*Board of Regents v. Roth,* 408 U.S. 564, 570 (1972); *Bell v. Burson,* 402 U.S. 535, 542 (1971).

[8]*Boddie v. Connecticut,* 401 U.S. 371, 379 (1971).

[9]*Goldberg v. Kelly,* 397 U.S. 254, 263 n.10 (1970).

[10]J. Smith, *supra,* note 3, at 405.

[11]*Jacobson v. Massachusetts,* 197 U.S. 11 (1905).

powers that mentally ill persons convicted of crimes or found guilty by reason of insanity can be committed instead of sent to prison. The philosophy of such commitments is that it is better to treat rather than punish an individual who is ill, especially when the individual lacks the capacity to appreciate the deterrent purposes of punishment.[12]

Another manner, however, in which the state exercises its police powers is both more relevant for present purposes and much more controversial than criminal commitments. States can authorize the commitment of individuals who have committed no crime but who because of their illness pose a risk of danger to others in society.

The justification for this civil application of police powers is that mentally ill individuals are likely to commit violent or illegal acts and therefore commitment is a necessary preventative measure.[13] The criticism is that the commitment is in response to a contingent future harm which may or may not occur. Further, because predicting dangerousness is extremely inaccurate,[14] the inevitable conclusion is that police power civil commitments authorize the state to deprive some individuals of their personal liberty when they in fact pose no danger of harm to themselves or others.[15]

Parens Patriae **Commitments.** The other rationale used to justify the involuntary commitment of the mentally ill is the doctrine of *parens patriae,* which recognizes the sovereign as the parent of the state and as such is vested with both the authority and responsibility to act for those who have lost the capacity to act for themselves.[16] Commitment under the *parens patriae* doctrine differs from commitment under the state's police powers in that the mentally ill need not be deemed dangerous to be committable. The rationale is that individuals ought to be subject to involuntary civil commitment when they become mentally incapacitated to the extent that they are unable to perceive the impact the illness has on their lives, unable to appreciate the treatment alternatives available, and unable to analyze the relative costs and benefits of such treatment. Further, most rational individuals would not want to live in a society that is powerless to act in their best interest should they become unable to do so themselves because of mental incapacity.[17] Thus individuals who are considered gravely disabled can be involuntarily committed under the *parens patriae* doctrine.

---

[12]J. Smith, *supra* note 3, at 485; J. LaFond, *An Examination of the Purposes of Involuntary Civil Commitment,* 30 BUFFALO L. REV. 499 (1981).

[13]J. Smith, *supra* note 3, at 485.

[14]J. LaFond, *supra* note 12, at 511 (see authorities cited by LaFond at footnote 59).

[15]*Id.*

[16]*See, e.g.,* J. LaFond, *supra* note 12, at 504; J. Smith, *supra* note 3, at 485; *Developments in the Law, Civil Commitment of the Mentally Ill,* 87 HARV. L. REV. 1190 (1974); ROSS, *Commitment of the Mentally Ill: Problems of Law and Policy,* 57 MICH. L. REV. 945 (1959).

[17]J. LaFond, *supra* note 12, at 526–527.

State Action Required. The Fourteenth Amendment forbids deprivations of liberty without due process only by "states." Therefore, if a state actor is not involved in the liberty deprivation, the due process clause cannot be violated. This does not mean, however, that private practitioners can involuntarily commit an individual without consideration to due process; it means that the U.S. Constitution is not implicated, and therefore the plaintiff may be required to bring the action in a state court under a state law tort claim when the actors are merely private.

There are great advantages, however, to plaintiffs who can transform a state common law tort action into a federal constitutional action. For example, states frequently impose damage ceilings on suits against their public officials or grant those officials immunity from suit altogether.[18] And some federal causes of action allow a successful plaintiff to recover attorney's fees.[19] Therefore plaintiffs frequently attempt to characterize the defendant as a state actor in order to take advantage of these benefits.

In fact, the benefits of characterizing the case as a federal cause of action are so great that some plaintiffs will argue that even the clearly private practitioner is a state actor when the practitioner involuntarily commits a client against the client's will. The rationale for such an argument is that even private doctors can involuntarily commit only because a state statute authorizes them to do so. Therefore, the argument continues, the physician has such as close nexus with the state that the physician should be considered a deputy of the state for purposes of satisfying the Fourteenth Amendment.

The courts, however, have generally rejected this argument, distinguishing between statutes that merely *allow* a thing to be done (such as involuntary commitment) and those that *require* a thing to be done.[20] Because involuntary commitment statutes do not compel the commitment of all mentally disabled but allow for professional discretion, the courts have held that physicians do not become state actors merely by acting pursuant to state statute.[21]

WRONGFUL COMMITMENT

All states have enacted statutes authorizing the involuntary commitment of mentally ill persons who either are unable to care for their most basic needs or pose a threat of danger to themselves or others. The need for such procedures is obvious and serves at least two purposes. First, commitment procedures temporarily remove from society individuals who may be dangerous. Second,

---

[18]*See, e.g., Spencer v. Lee,* 864 F.2d 1376, 1382 (7th Cir. 1989), *cert. denied,* 110 S. Ct. 1319.
[19]*See* 42 U.S.C. § 1988 (1982).
[20]*See, e.g., Blum v. Yaretsky,* 457 U.S. 991, 1004 (1982); *Spencer,* 864 F.2d at 1378; *United States v. Koenig,* 856 F.2d 843, 847–851 (7th Cir. 1988).
[21]*Id.*

commitment places the mentally disturbed person in an environment where the person can receive rehabilitative treatment for the disabling illness.[22]

As with any evaluation that involves a certain amount of subjective judgment, errors will be made and individuals who should not be committed will be committed. Even a brief wrongful commitment, however, is perceived as a serious deprivation of a person's constitutional right to liberty and is therefore actionable. Increasingly, clients who feel they were wrongfully committed have successfully brought tort actions against the certifying professional. The legal theories that have proved most successful in attaining a judgment against the certifying clinician are false imprisonment, malicious prosecution, battery, unlawful detention, and failure to treat in the least restrictive manner.[23]

False Imprisonment

The very essence of individual liberty is the right and the freedom to come and go when and where one desires. This is a fundamental right of all citizens, and the courts have long recognized a cause of action in tort for false imprisonment as the remedy for an invasion of this right.[24] In fact, false imprisonment is the tort theory most frequently advocated in a wrongful commitment action.[25]

Simply stated, "false imprisonment is the unlawful restraint of an individual's liberty."[26] The term "false," as used in connection with this tort, implies the absence of authority and is therefore synonymous with "unlawful."[27] The test for the tort of false imprisonment, although variously stated,[28] can be simplified into a two-pronged test: (1) an individual is intentionally confined, detained, or restrained against his or her will (imprisonment prong); and (2) the imprisonment is unlawful (false prong).

Imprisonment Prong. The clearest case of false imprisonment involves the wrongful physical detention or restraint of the client against her or his will, where the client is literally imprisoned within some fixed boundaries. All courts, however, will find liability for false imprisonment upon a lesser showing of confinement. For example, even when an individual is committed in accordance with a valid court order, false imprisonment has been found when the client was denied the opportunity to communicate with a lawyer or relative to secure his or her own release. In *Stowers v. Wolodzko*,[29] the court declared:

[22]*See, e.g.,* 2 D. Louisell & H. Williams, Medical Malpractice para. 17A.43 (1988); *In re Medlin,* 295 S.E.2d 604 (N.C. Ct. App. 1982).
[23]D. Louisell & H. Williams, *supra* note 22.
[24]Annotation, *False Imprisonment in Connection With Confinement in Nursing Home or Hospital,* 40 P.O.F.2d 81, 91 (1984).
[25]*See, e.g.,* J. Smith, *supra* note 3, at 494.
[26]*Id.*
[27]Annotation, *supra* note 24, at 91.
[28]J. Smith, *supra* note 3, at 251 (three element test); Annotation, *supra* note 24, at 112 (seven element test).
[29]386 Mich. 119, 191 N.W.2d 355 (1971).

Psychiatrists have a great deal of power over their patients. In the case of a person confined to an institution, this power is virtually unlimited. . . . The law must provide protection against the torts committed by these individuals. In the case of mental patients, in order to have this protection, they must be able to communicate with the outside world.[30]

The *Stowers* court then went on to find the defendant psychiatrist liable for false imprisonment because "[h]olding a person incommunicado is clearly a restraint of one's freedom sufficient to allow a jury to find false imprisonment."[31]

According to some authorities, an essential element of false imprisonment is the confinement within fixed boundaries such as to negate the existence of an opportunity to escape.[32] In other words, a mere interference with passage does not amount to false imprisonment if the plaintiff can turn and escape in another direction. However, even those courts that require total confinement as a prerequisite to finding liability have easily found such confinement in civil commitment cases.

In *Geddes v. Daughters of Charity of St. Vincent de Paul, Inc.,*[33] for example, Ms. Geddes, a 59-year-old Mississippi woman, was admitted into a New Orleans mental health center by her brother. Ms. Geddes thought that the center was a general medical hospital and that she was being admitted for treatment of her physical ailments. Upon discovering the center was actually a mental health facility and that she had been admitted for psychiatric evaluations, Geddes repeatedly demanded her release. The hospital staff, however, ignored these requests.

During her period of commitment, Geddes was occasionally allowed to take shopping or entertainment trips to New Orleans. On each such occasion, Geddes was accompanied by a member of the hospital staff and given an amount of money to cover only the day's anticipated expenses.

At trial, the defendant hospital argued that it could not be held liable for false imprisonment because Geddes had numerous opportunities to escape on any of the trips to town. In essence, the hospital contended that the level of restraint was not sufficient to constitute an imprisonment. The trial court accepted this argument and accordingly entered a verdict in favor of the hospital.

On appeal, however, the Court of Appeals for the Fifth Circuit reversed the verdict. The court reasoned that even though Geddes was taken on trips to New Orleans, because she was not given enough money to return to her hometown in Mississippi and because she knew no one in New Orleans who could help her even if she did escape, the practical effect was the same as total confinement. Therefore, the court held that the verdict was in error because reasonable jurors could conclude that such restraint on Geddes' personal liberty was sufficient to establish false imprisonment.

---

[30]*Id.* at 363.
[31]*Id.*
[32]*See, e.g., Pounders v. Trinity Court Nursing Home, Inc.,* 576 S.W.2d 934 (Ark. 1979).
[33]348 F.2d 144 (5th Cir. 1965).

False Prong. A major obstacle for plaintiffs in establishing a *prima facie* case of false imprisonment is the unlawfulness of the detention. Most courts defer to the clinician's judgment and discretion and find the cause of false imprisonment established only when the clinician fails to follow the statutory procedures for involuntary commitment.

For example, courts have not hesitated to find physicians or other examiners liable for false imprisonment when the statute requires an examination before certifying commitment but in fact no examination took place or the examination was so remote in time to the actual commitment that the prior exam was not considered relevant for commitment purposes.[34] On the other hand, when the certifying physician in fact examines the client prior to commitment and follows all other statutory procedures, the courts have been reluctant to impose liability for false imprisonment. That is, even though the physician's examination is later deemed inadequate or the client's sanity misdiagnosed, the courts generally have not imposed liability for a mere error in professional judgment when that error does not amount to malpractice or fraud.[35]

Malicious Prosecution

Without exception, the courts are in agreement that the wrongful institution of insanity proceedings may form the basis of an action for malicious prosecution.[36] The action imposes liability for using the legal system for the mere purpose of harassment or injury.[37]

Malicious prosecution must be distinguished from false imprisonment; these two causes of action are fundamentally distinct. If a person is confined in strict adherence to legal procedure but for malicious reasons, the action is one for malicious prosecution because the imprisonment is not false or unlawful. On the other hand, if a person is detained without adherence to statute, an action lies for false imprisonment even though the confinement was affected without malicious intentions.[38]

Although the elements of an action for malicious prosecution have been stated in varying ways, the courts are in general agreement concerning the essential elements. To successfully maintain the action, the plaintiff must prove (1) the institution or continuation of judicial proceedings; (2) by, or at the instance of

[34]Annotation, *Liability for False Imprisonment Predicated upon Institution of, or Conduct in Connection with, Insanity Proceedings,* 30 A.L.R.3d 523, 549–553 (1970).

[35]For example, in *Carter v. Landy,* 163 Ga. App. 509, 295 S.E.2d 177 (Ga. 1982), the court held: "[W]hile this is a false imprisonment case, the standard to determine whether or not the plaintiff was unlawfully detained, that is, deprived of her personal liberty for any length of time, was a medical standard. Therefore, we look to the cases involving medical malpractice . . . to determine whether or not the [physician] exercised reasonable medical care in diagnosing the plaintiff's mental condition and acted properly based upon that diagnosis." *Id.,* 295 S.E.2d at 179.

[36]Annotation, *Liability for Malicious Prosecution Predicated Upon Institution of, or Conduct in Connection With, Insanity Proceedings,* 30 A.L.R.2d 455, 459 (1953).

[37]52 AM. JUR. 2d *Malicious Prosecution* § 1 (1970).

[38]Annotation, *Malicious Prosecution,* 7 P.O.F.2d 181, 191 (1975).

the defendant(s); (3) malice as a primary purpose for that proceeding; (4) lack of probable cause; (5) termination of the proceedings in plaintiff's favor; and (6) some injury or damage to the plaintiff as a result of the proceeding.[39] To be successful, the plaintiff must prove each and every element.

Commencement of Proceedings. To successfully maintain an action for malicious prosecution, the plaintiff must prove a proceeding was actually commenced against him or her. In other words, no matter how malicious or unfounded, neither a mere threat nor an unsuccessful attempt to initiate commitment proceedings is actionable.[40]

Interestingly, some jurisdictions hold that physicians can be liable not only for the wrongful commencement of commitment proceedings but also for the *continuation* of such.[41] Theoretically, then, a certifying physician can be held liable for malicious prosecution when, even though the commitment proceeding commenced with probable cause and in the absence of malice, the proceeding was continued after the plaintiff was deemed to be of sound mind.[42]

By or at the Insistence of the Defendant. As part of the case, the plaintiff must find and sue the individual who actually set the legal proceedings in motion against the plaintiff, not those individuals whose involvement were mere formalities.[43] That is, a mere passive knowledge of or acquiescence in the wrongful commitment by one is not sufficient to impose liability on another. Rather, to be liable for malicious prosecution, the specific defendant must be shown to have affirmatively instigated or participated in the prosecution.[44] *Pendleton v. Burkhalter*[45] is a case in point.

Doctors Pendleton and Burkhalter joined to build a private hospital, which they operated for several years as the principal stockholders. Numerous disputes arose between them, however, and finally at a special stockholder's meeting, each sought to oust the other from the board of directors. Later that day, at the insistence of Dr. Burkhalter, the medical staff voted to withdraw Dr. Pendleton's privilege to practice at the hospital. Dr. Pendleton countered, however, by obtaining a temporary restraining order that precluded the medical staff from interfering with his access to the clinic.

On the same day the court issued this restraining order, the medical staff's executive secretary filed a lunacy complaint against Dr. Pendleton. Accordingly, Dr. Pendleton was detained for three hours, examined, and released. Dr. Pendleton

[39]*See, e.g., Pellegrini v. Winter,* 476 So. 2d 1363, 1365 (Fla. Dist. Ct. App. 1985); *James v. Brown,* 637 S.W.2d 914, 918 (Tex. 1982); Annotation, *supra* note 38, at 191–192; 52 AM. JUR. 2d, *supra* note 37, at § 6.

[40]52 AM. JUR. 2d, *supra* note 37, at 198; Annotation, *supra* note 38, at 199.

[41]*See, e.g., Pellegrini,* 476 So. 2d at 1365 (Florida); *James,* 637 S.W.2d at 918 (Texas).

[42]AM. JUR. 2d, *supra* note 37, at 203.

[43]Comment, *supra* note 48, at 122.

[44]52 AM. JUR. 2d, *supra* note 47, at § 23.

[45]432 S.W.2d 724 (Tex. Civ. App. 1969).

filed a civil suit against the executive secretary and Dr. Burkhalter as a result of this action.

The trial court found Dr. Burkhalter not liable for malicious prosecution because he was not the individual who set the legal proceedings in motion. Dr. Pendleton appealed the judgment, arguing that even though Dr. Burkhalter did not file the complaint which brought about Dr. Pendleton's detention, Dr. Burkhalter was the instigating cause and as such should be held liable. The appellate court agreed and accordingly reversed the trial court's judgment.[46] Therefore, while a plaintiff must show that the defendant affirmatively instigated the commitment proceeding, a certifying physician who acts with malice cannot expect to be shielded by having someone else swear out the complaint.

Malice.   As its name implies, malice is the heart of an action for malicious prosecution. Proving a person's motives, however, is always a very difficult task— that is, rarely will defendants readily admit to acting on improper, malicious grounds. Therefore, malice generally must be inferred from the circumstances of the commitment. If circumstances reasonably suggest that the committing party was activated by wrongful motives in instigating or continuing the commitment proceedings, malice will be inferred.[47]

Malice, however, does not necessarily imply anger or vindictiveness. Showing that the physician had a reckless disregard for the client's rights is sufficient to establish malice.[48] For example, in *Walder v. Manahan*,[49] the court found two certifying physicians liable for malicious prosecution because they certified that on the day the plaintiff was committed, each examined the plaintiff and found him insane. The evidence, however, established that the physicians had not examined the plaintiff at any time prior to commitment. Therefore the court found malice not because the physicians acted out of anger or vindictiveness but because they acted with a reckless disregard for the plaintiff's rights.

Lack of Probable Cause.   Lack of probable cause for instituting civil commitment proceedings is an essential element in the plaintiff's case for malicious prosecution. Therefore, if the committing professional has probable cause for commencing the proceeding, such cause constitutes an absolute defense and liability will not be found, not even if the plaintiff acted with malice.[50]

The absence of probable cause can be established by showing that either (1) the defendant did not actually believe the plaintiff was mentally ill, or (2) a

---

[46]The executive secretary was also joined as a defendant in this action, but in granting the rehearing, the appellate court did not rule upon his liability.

[47]*Pendleton v. Burkhalter*, 432 S.W.2d 724, 727 (Tex. Ct. App. 1968).

[48]Comment, *Malicious Prosecution as Basis of Recovery for Wrongful Instigation of Civil Commitment Proceedings*; 9 WAKE FOREST L. REV. 115, 119; Annotation, *supra* note 36, at 207.

[49]21 N.J. Misc. 1, 29 A.2d 395 (N.J. Cir. Ct. 1942).

[50]Annotation, *supra* note 38, at 204–205; 52 AM. JUR. 2d, *supra* note 35, at 216–217.

reasonable person possessed with knowledge of similar facts would not have suspected mental illness.[51] That is, the relevant question is not whether the plaintiff was in fact mentally ill but whether the certifying professional, acting as a reasonable, prudent person, actually believed the plaintiff was mentally ill.

A subissue of the probable cause element is *when* must the certifying professional have a probable cause belief of the plaintiff's mental illness such as to defeat a malicious prosecution action. Is it sufficient that at some distant time, prior to commitment, the physician had probable cause to believe the plaintiff was mentally deranged? Conversely, if the certifying professional initiates commencement proceedings without any belief that the plaintiff is mentally ill (for example, because the professional failed to examine the plaintiff), does a subsequent ruling that the plaintiff is mentally ill work retroactively to shield the professional from liability? Or, to constitute probable cause, must the clinician reasonably believe the plaintiff is mentally ill at a time contemporaneous with the initiation of commitment proceedings?

At least one court addressed the issue and determined that the certifying professional must have a probable cause belief of the plaintiff's insanity "at the time (or just before) the lunacy complaint was filed."[52]

Proceeding Terminates in Plaintiff's Favor. Before one can maintain an action for malicious prosecution, the allegedly malicious proceeding must terminate in favor of the plaintiff.[53] The most frequent issue raised in this context is "What is a favorable termination?"

To be "favorable," must the commitment proceedings terminate with an affirmative finding that the plaintiff is sane or competent? While such a finding would clearly be favorable to the plaintiff, a lesser standard will also satisfy the "favorable termination" requirement. For example, a finding that the plaintiff was not insane (as opposed to an affirmative finding of sanity) would also be a favorable termination.[54] Likewise, release of the plaintiff following examination has been held a favorable termination.[55] However, at least one court has held that a "favorable termination" does not result when the parties mutually agree to discontinue commitment proceedings.[56]

A minority of courts hold that the favorable termination requirement is not applicable when the plaintiff does not have an opportunity to defend herself or himself in the prior commitment proceeding.[57]

---

[51]Comment, *supra* note 48, at 123, *citing, Alexander v. Alexander*, 229 F.2d 111 (4th Cir. 1956); *Johnson v. Huhner*, 76 N.D. 13, 33 N.W.2d 268 (1948).

[52]*Pendleton*, 432 S.W.2d at 730.

[53]*See* Annotation, *supra* note 34, at § 4.

[54]Comment, *supra* note 48, at 125–126, *citing, Yelk v. Seefeldt*, 23 Wis. 2d 271, 151 N.W.2d 4 (1967).

[55]*Pellegrini*, 476 So. 2d at 1366.

[56]*James v. Brown*, 637 S.W.2d 914, 919 (Tex. 1982).

[57]See Annotation, *supra* note 34, at § 5, (*citing, Linder v. Foster*, 209 Minn. 43, 295 N.W. 299 (1940); *Hauser v. Bartow*, 273 N.Y. 370, 7 N.E.2d 268 (1937)).

Finally, at least one state supreme court (Florida) has ruled that a plaintiff suing for the malicious prosecution of insanity proceedings need not allege or prove that such proceedings terminated in his favor.[58] The result, therefore, is that liability can be assessed for malicious prosecution even though the plaintiff is found to be mentally ill.[59]

Plaintiff Damaged by the Proceedings.   The final element a plaintiff must plead and prove to be successful on a claim of malicious prosecution is that he or she suffered injury or damage as a result of the commitment proceedings. The injury, however, need not be physical. In fact, courts generally have been very lenient in determining what constitutes damages in this context because of the social stigma associated with lunacy proceedings. In other words, even if the proceedings terminate in the plaintiff's favor, a strong suspicion of insanity is likely to remain with that person. For example, a false accusation of insanity may lessen the chances of entering into a favorable marriage, may jeopardize the likelihood of procuring life insurance, and may preclude the opportunities for normal social intercourse.[60] Thus, in *Pendleton v. Burkhalter*[61] (the two doctors who tried to oust each other), the court held that the physician who was detained for only 3 hours while undergoing a mental examination sustained damages.[62]

The practical effect of such decisions is that if the other elements of the action are proved, some courts may hold that a per se presumption exists that the victim was damaged. That is, the mere fact that proceedings were wrongly commenced is evidence the plaintiff was damaged because of the attached social stigma.

Battery

A battery is committed when one intentionally touches another in a way harmful or offensive to the one touched.[63] Although this tort may be more frequently alleged in other contexts, such as when a therapist sexually exploits a client, the action is also infrequently alleged in the involuntary commitment context.

For example, in *Maben v. Rankin*,[64] Mr. Maben asked Dr. Rankin, a psychiatrist, to examine his wife's mental condition. When examined, Mrs. Maben told Dr. Rankin that she was not mentally ill but simply very upset because of her husband's offensive conduct, which included infidelity. When Mrs. Maben refused to be hospitalized, Dr. Rankin forcibly administered an injection. The next thing Mrs. Maben remembered was awakening in the mental hospital, where

---

[58]*Fischer v. Payne,* 113 So. 378 (Fla. 1927); *Hunter v. First Baptist Church,* 294 So. 2d 355 (Fla. Ct. App. 1974).
[59]*Fischer,* 113 So. at 381.
[60]*Timmey v. Bloom,* 14 Pa. D & C 288 (1929).
[61]432 S.W.2d 724 (Tex. 1968).
[62]*Id.* at 728.
[63]*See,* J. Smith, *supra* note 3, at 243; S. Halleck, *Law in the Practice of Psychiatry: A Handbook for Clinicians* 26 (1980).
[64]358 P.2d 681 (Cal. 1961).

she remained, against her will, for 15 days. During this period of commitment, Mrs. Maben received periodic electroshock treatments.

Evidence established that Mrs. Maben was not mentally ill, and she consequently obtained a $78,000 judgment against Dr. Rankin and the hospital. On appeal, the California Supreme Court declared: "The involuntary hospitalization of a person in a mental institution in violation of the statute constitutes false imprisonment. *Insofar as force is used to accomplish the unlawful detention, there is also liability for assault and battery.*"[65] Therefore, a battery will be found if physical force is intentionally used in an unlawful detention.

It is important to realize that the intent required in a battery situation need not necessarily involve the intent to cause harm—it is only the act itself that must have been intended. Therefore, a professional may have altruistic motives in committing an individual but still be liable for battery if physical force is used to accomplish the commitment.[66]

Unlawful Detention—Justified Commitment Converted to Unjustified Commitment

Clients who are lawfully committed to a mental institution have a right to be released when the reasons for their confinement cease to exist.[67] If not released, the client may have a cause of action against the hospital and staff for unlawful detention. Unlawful detention is similar to the tort of false imprisonment, with one distinct difference. A client who is *unlawfully* committed and detained has an action for false imprisonment, whereas a client who is *lawfully* committed but unlawfully detained has an action for unlawful detention.

An action for unlawful detention will generally arise in one of two contexts: (1) an involuntarily committed client is not released, even though the reasons that initially justified the commitment have since ceased to exist; or (2) a voluntarily committed client withdraws consent to be detained but is nonetheless still detained in the absence of commencing involuntary commitment proceedings.

An incredible example of the former context is the case of *Bartlett v. New York*.[68] Charles Bartlett was detained for 37 years in a state mental hospital, having been involuntarily committed under a diagnosis of "aimless wandering." In the 37 years of Charles' commitment, only 72 entries were made in his medical record; 47 of the entries reflected personal contact with physicians, and the remaining 25 entries consisted of administrative notes, such as transfers from one ward to another. During the first 25 years of his commitment, Charles was not permitted outside the locked hospital building except on supervised walking parties. For years, he received no treatment beyond an occasional interview with a hospital doctor.

---

[65]*Maben*, 358 P.2d at 683. The Supreme Court ultimately ordered a new trial in the case because the trial judge erroneously instructed the jury on points of law.

[66]J. Smith, *supra* note 3, at 244.

[67]*O'Connor v. Donaldson*, 422 U.S. 563, 576 (1975) (Burger, C.J., concurring).

[68]52 A.D.2d 318, 383 N.Y.S.2d 763 (N.Y. App. Div. 1976).

Charles' mother and sister visited him infrequently and were apparently "happy to have him retained at the hospital."[69] Although Charles consistently sought his family's help in securing his release, they gave him no assistance to that end.

A change in a state statute required the state to petition the court for authorization to retain Charles for another year. The court conducted a hearing but ordered Charles' release to outpatient care because the court found him not dangerous to himself or the community.

Charles subsequently brought an action against the state for both improper commitment and unlawful detention. The trial court dismissed both claims. On appeal, the court affirmed the dismissal of the improper commitment claim, holding that Charles' mental condition at the time of commitment justified his detention. As to the unlawful detention claim, however, expert testimony revealed that Charles should have been released to outpatient care very shortly after his commitment. The appellate court gave great weight to this expert testimony and accordingly ordered a new trial for the sole purpose of assessing damages.

There is no indication as to what amount Charles Bartlett was awarded by the trial court because there is no reported decision of the new trial.[70] However, 8 years earlier, a client who was unlawfully detained for 12 years received a $300,000 judgment.[71]

The second type of situation in which an unlawful detention action will generally arise is demonstrated in *Geddes v. Daughters of Charity of St. Vincent de Paul, Inc.*[72] The facts of this case were previously detailed,[73] but are briefly summarized here. The plaintiff, a 59-year-old woman, was taken by her brother to a hospital that she voluntarily entered, thinking she would receive treatment for her physical ailments. Upon learning that the hospital was not a general medical hospital but a sanitorium, the plaintiff requested her release. The hospital staff viewed these requests as customary, the usual type of complaint almost universal among psychiatric clients. Accordingly, the requests were ignored, and even though the plaintiff was considered a voluntary client, procedures to involuntarily detain her were not commenced. The court found the defendant liable and held: "[A]t some point subsequent to her entry in the hospital and during her stay therein, Miss Geddes withdrew her consent to detention in the hospital given on her original entry and that further detention at the hospital subsequent to such withdrawal of the consent constituted [an unlawful detention]."[74]

---

[69]*Id.* at 766.
[70]It is very possible that the case settled after the appellate court's decision and therefore never went to trial again.
[71]*Whitree v. New York*, 56 Misc. 2d 693, 290 N.Y.S.2d 486 (N.Y. Ct. Cl. 1968).
[72]348 F.2d 144 (5th Cir. 1965).
[73]*See* discussion *supra* at notes 33–35 and accompanying test.
[74]*Geddes*, 348 F.2d at 148. The court ultimately characterized the case as alleging a claim for false imprisonment. In doing so, the court held the plaintiff could not have technically entered the hospital voluntarily if she did not know it was a mental hospital or that she was to receive psychiatric treatments. Thus, because the plaintiff did not enter the hospital voluntarily and because she was not involuntarily committed, the court found she had been unlawfully committed. Therefore, the state was liable to her under a claim of false imprisonment.

Thus providers can be held liable for failing to release voluntarily committed clients if the client withdraws consent to be committed and the clinician does not initiate involuntary commitment.

Least Restrictive Alternative

Over the past 25 years, the social policy objective of "deinstitutionalization" has been increasingly advocated in an attempt to address the problems and abuses of the institutionalized mentally ill. Consequently, an important legal doctrine designed to accomplish this end has evolved—the "least restrictive alternative" doctrine. Strict application of the doctrine in the mental health context requires that treatment be no more harsh, hazardous, intrusive, or restrictive than necessary to achieve therapeutic aims and to protect the client and others from physical harm.[75]

The first application of the doctrine, in the involuntary commitment context, was in *Lake v. Cameron.*[76] *Lake* involved a 60-year-old woman who was involuntarily committed because she was diagnosed as senile. Despite this diagnosis, however, Ms. Lake was not considered a danger to herself or others. Consequently, Lake argued that she should be treated in a setting less restrictive than total confinement. The United States Court of Appeals for the District of Columbia agreed. The court held that "[d]eprivations of liberty solely because of dangers to the ill persons themselves should not go beyond what is necessary for their protection."[77] In other words, a client cannot be involuntarily committed and confined in a hospital if equally effective accommodations that constitute less of an infringement on the client's constitutional right to liberty exist. Since *Lake,* nearly every state has adopted the "least restrictive alternative" doctrine, either through legislation or judicial decision.[78]

The relevant question for present purposes is "What is the professional's liability for failing to provide care in the least restrictive environment?" The United States Supreme Court addressed this question in *Youngberg v. Romeo.*[79] The court held that when the physician makes a decision as to the least restrictive alternative for treatment, the decision is "presumptively valid."[80]

---

[75]I. Keilitz, D. Conn & A. Giampetro, *Least Restrictive Treatment of Involuntary Patients: Translating Concepts Into Practice,* 29 St. Louis U.L.J. 691, 692 (1985); J. Smith, *supra* note 3, at 489.

[76]364 F.2d 657 (D.C. Cir. 1966).

[77]*Id.* at 660 (footnotes omitted).

[78]*See* Keilitz, Conn & Giampetro, *supra* note 75, at 709–812.

[79]457 U.S. 307 (1982).

[80]*Id.* at 323. The Court emphasized the fact that the presumption existed only when the decision was made by a "professional." In a footnote, the court declared: "By professional decisionmaker, we mean a person competent, whether by education, training or experience to make the particular decision at issue. Long-term treatment decisions normally should be made by persons with degrees in medicine or nursing, or with appropriate training in areas such as psychology, physical therapy, or the care and training of the retarded. Of course, day-to-day decisions regarding care—including decisions that must be made without delay—necessarily will be made in many instances by employees without formal training but who are subject to the supervision of qualified persons." *Id.* at n.30.

The court reasoned that the professional should enjoy the favorable presumption because

> A single professional may have to make decisions with respect to a number of residents with widely varying needs and problems in the course of a normal day. The administrators, and particularly professional personnel, should not be required to make each decision in the shadow of an action for damages.[81]

Thus, because professional decisions are accorded this presumption, liability will be found only if the decision substantially departs from accepted professional standards such as to constitute malpractice.[82]

Note that the least restrictive alternative doctrine does not apply solely to the commit/do-not-commit decision; the doctrine is equally applicable to alternative treatment decisions *within* the mental hospital.[83] This is a reasonable expansion of the doctrine because "[i]t makes little sense to guard zealously against the possibility of unwarranted deprivations prior to hospitalization, only to abandon the watch once the client disappears behind hospital doors."[84] Thus professionals must be sensitive to the rights of clients even after the decision to commit has been made.

The least restrictive alternative doctrine has its critics. Some commentators[85] argue that the doctrine is medically ineffective because it has been viewed as the sole determinate in making placement decisions rather than being used as just one of many factors. The doctrine is often viewed as precluding consideration of some of the client's important and relevant needs.

To rectify this concern, the "most beneficial alternative" doctrine has been proposed,[86] emphasizing a balance between the client's civil rights and the client's treatment needs. That is, in balancing the client's interests, the client's family, the state, and the provider should consider a number of factors, including (1) relative risks and benefits of treatment alternatives; (2) family and community support available in the client's environment; (3) duration of the treatment; (4) likelihood that a client may pose a safety risk to the public; (5) availability, cost, and accessibility of alternative treatment; (6) likelihood the client will comply with the conditions of alternative treatment programs; and (7) mechanisms for monitoring and reviewing the client's compliance.[87] So far, the courts have *not* enthusiastically embraced the most beneficial doctrine.

---

[81]*Id.* at 324–325.

[82]*Id.* at 323.

[83]*Covington v. Harris*, 419 F.2d 617, 623 (D.C. Cir. 1969).

[84]*Id.* at 623–624.

[85]*See, e.g.*, Perr, *President's Message: The Most Beneficial Alternative: A Counterpoint to the Least Restrictive Alternative*, 6 BULL. AM. ACAD. PSYCHIATRY & LAW iv, v (1978). Irwin Perr is a past president of the American Academy of Psychiatry and Law.

[86]*Id.* at vi.

[87]Keilitz, Conn & Giampetro, *supra* note 75, at 696.

DUTY TO INITIATE INVOLUNTARY COMMITMENT

The previous section of this chapter revealed that a clinician is exposed to legal liability when she or he takes affirmative steps to civilly commit individuals who are not mentally ill. This section explores the circumstances under which a provider can be held liable for *not* taking those affirmative steps to civilly commit individuals who are mentally ill and who cause injury to themselves or others.

As a general rule, the law does not impose a duty on a person to initiate action for the protection of another, even if it is apparent that such action is necessary to protect the other person from injury.[88] This general rule has its source in the early common-law distinction between one who chooses to act but acts negligently ("misfeasance") and one who chooses not to act at all ("nonfeasance").[89] The reason for the rule may lie in the fact that by "misfeasance" the defendant creates a new risk of harm to the plaintiff, while by "nonfeasance" the defendant merely fails to benefit the plaintiff by interfering in the plaintiff's affairs and has, therefore, made the plaintiff's situation no worse.[90]

Exceptions to this general rule have developed, however, and are for the most part very recent developments in tort law. Two of these developments are the liability of providers for (1) failing to initiate an involuntary commitment and (2) failing to require the continued commitment of an indivdual who is being released.

The recent development of the duty to initiate an involuntary commitment is best demonstrated in the case of *Currie v. United States*.[91] On a hot August afternoon in North Carolina, Leonard Avery, a Vietnam vetcran, launched a one-man assault on the local offices of IBM. Dressed in army fatigues and carrying a .45 caliber semiautomatic rifle and homemade bombs, Avery shot and killed Ralph Glenn, Jr., and wounded several other individuals.

Avery, an employee of IBM, had been receiving treatment as an outpatient at the mental health clinic of the Durham VA hospital. He originally consulted the VA staff because he increasingly experienced "rage attacks." Consequently, Avery was given a psychological profile test and diagnosed as suffering from post-traumatic stress disorder. To treat the disorder, the VA doctors referred Avery to group therapy sessions and prescribed various types of antipsychotic medications.

Eventually, Avery began missing the weekly group sessions. After a period of continued absences, Avery was required to explain his absences. Avery angrily responded by threatening to blow up IBM's medical facility and personnel.

Because Avery was diagnosed as very mad, and not mentally ill, he was not involuntarily committed. The psychiatrists, however, notified IBM and several law enforcement agencies of Avery's threat. Despite these warnings, Avery launched his assault on the IBM building wherein Ralph Glenn, Jr., was killed.

[88]*See* RESTATEMENT (SECOND) OF TORTS § 314 (1965).
[89]*Id.* at comment C.
[90]W. Keeton, D. Dobbs, R. Keeton, & D. Owen, Prosser and Keeton on the Law of Torts 373 (5th ed. 1984).
[91]644 F. Supp. 1074 (M.D.N.C. 1986), *aff'd,* 836 F.2d 209 (4th Cir. 1987).

Glenn's widow (Ms. Currie) filed suit against the United States government, alleging that the negligence of the VA psychotherapists, in failing to commit Avery, was responsible for her husband's death. In essence, Currie advocated that the treating clinicians knew of Avery's violent propensities and therefore had a *Tarasoff*-type duty to protect her husband. The trial court agreed with Currie and held that therapists do have a duty to commit dangerous clients:

> The court believes that a psychotherapist, perhaps the only one with knowledge of the danger posed by his patient, may have a duty to protect society by taking the only practical action he can—which may include seeking the involuntary commitment of a patient whom he knows is dangerous. . . . Arguably, the client who will kill wildly . . . is the one *most* in need of confinement.[92]

Note that the duty to commit is just a different form of the traditional *Tarasoff* duty. Both the *Tarasoff* duty to protect and the duty to commit are based on the policy of protecting society from dangerous individuals. Under *Tarasoff,* however, the duty to protect focuses on potential *victims* and requires affirmative steps directed to them. A duty to commit, on the other hand, focuses on the *client* personally. Courts, recognizing a duty to commit, reason that by committing the client, the therapist is able to protect *all* possible victims and is therefore viewed as less intrusive than the *Tarasoff* duty to protect.[93]

On appeal, the Fourth Circuit Court was not convinced that the North Carolina Supreme Court would impose a duty to commit on psychotherapists when the intended victims had been warned. It is unclear, however, whether the Fourth Circuit Court would have so ruled had the intended victims not been warned of Avery's threat. *Currie* has perhaps the most dramatic facts of a duty to commit case, and even though the appellate court refused to find a duty to commit on the facts of that case, *Currie* is by no means the only case recognizing such a duty. Since the rapid advancement of *Tarasoff,* other jurisdictions have been willing to take the next step by recognizing a duty to commit. For example, the Wisconsin Supreme Court recently declared in *Schuster v. Altenberg:*[94]

> In the instant case, if it is ultimately proven that it would have been foreseeable to a psychiatrist, exercising due care, that by failing to take action to institute detention or commitment proceedings someone would be harmed, negligence will be established. . . . [W]e further find that a duty to institute proceedings may be triggered not only by the threat an individual client may pose to the public, but also by the threat an individual may pose to himself or herself.

---

[92]*Id.* at 1081, 1079, 1083. Even though the court recognized a duty to commit, the therapists and the VA hospital were found not liable in this case because the decision not to commit Avery was made in good faith.

Not only did Avery threaten IBM, he also threatened the therapists themselves. These threats were serious and direct. Therefore, the court reasoned that because the decision not to seek Avery's commitment involved serious personal risk to themselves, this fact evidenced the decision was "made in the utmost good faith" and that liability would not attach. *Id.* at 1085.

[93]*Currie,* 644 F. Supp. at 1079.

[94]144 Wis. 2d 223, 424 N.W.2d 159, 166, 170 (1988).

Similar positions have been taken by courts construing Pennsylvania[95] and Illinois[96] law.

Therefore, the growing trend is for courts to recognize a duty by therapists to commit clients who pose a threat of danger to themselves or others. The law, however, recognizes the difficulties in civil commitment decisions and will protect conscientious professional decisionmakers. However, the therapist who chooses not to pursue commitment of an individual who meets the statutory standards for commitment should carefully document the reasons for the decision and, when appropriate, obtain corroborating opinions from other professionals.[97]

Negligent Release

An action for negligent release differs from an action for failure to commit in that the latter can be characterized as failing to *initiate* a commitment, whereas negligent release is properly characterized as failing to *continue* a commitment. Perhaps no case better demonstrates the legal analysis involved with negligent release than *Perreira v. Colorado.*[98]

Seth Buckmaster had a long history of mental illness. He believed the police were controlling his thoughts and burning his feet with a radiation gun. These burns, however, were actually blisters that developed when Buckmaster's foot rubbed against his shoe.

In October 1979, Buckmaster was brought to Fort Logan Mental Health Center in Colorado, for the fourth time since 1975 and the third time in less than 6 months. It was learned that Buckmaster had been living on the streets for a considerable period of time and that he ate hardly any food. Consequently, Buckmaster was involuntarily committed on the basis that he was gravely disabled. That is, as a result of his mental illness, Buckmaster was unable to care for his basic personal needs.

Less than 2 months following his commitment, Dr. Anders (staff psychiatrist) released Buckmaster, despite his refusal to take any antipsychotic medication and the persistence of delusional symptoms. Evidence at trial established that Dr. Anders spent a total of 2 hours and 35 minutes with Buckmaster during the 2-month commitment. Furthermore, Dr. Anders and other members of the Fort Logan staff knew that Buckmaster, upon his release, intended to seek the return of a revolver the police had taken from him.

---

[95]*Greenberg v. Barbour,* 322 F. Supp. 745 (E.D. Pa. 1971) ("Dr. Hamann may also be guilty of negligence if he, having been fully warned of Hall's dangerous condition, did not act within a reasonable time to consummate Hall's admittance.")

[96]*Estate of Johnson v. Village of Libertyville,* 146 Ill. App.3d 834, 496 N.E.2d 1219, 1223 (Ill. App. Ct. 1986) ("It has been held that a mental hospital has a duty to control dangerous patients committed to its custody. The same considerations which require recognition of that duty constrain us to recognize a duty on the part of mental hospitals to control patients whom the hospital knows should be involuntarily committed.")

[97]Knapp & VandeCreek, *A Review of Tort Liability in Involuntary Civil Commitment,* 38 HOSP. AND COMMUNITY PSYCHIATRY 648, 651 (1987).

[98]768 P.2d 1198 (Colo. 1989).

In April 1980, approximately 4 months after his release from Fort Logan, Buckmaster was in Colorado Springs, where he created a disturbance at a convenience store. Buckmaster sat on the floor near the front door talking to himself and muttering profanities. The salesclerk told Buckmaster to leave, but he refused. The clerk accordingly called the Colorado Springs Police, who dispatched Officer Augustus Perreira. Upon arriving, Officer Perreira escorted Buckmaster out of the store to the parking lot, where a conversation ensued. Suddenly, Buckmaster pulled out a gun and fired several shots at Officer Perreira. Officer Perreira died instantly.

As a result of this incident, murder charges were filed against Buckmaster. Ultimately, however, Buckmaster was found not guilty by reason of insanity.

Officer Perreira's widow (Mrs. Perreira) then brought civil wrongful death action against Dr. Anders, Fort Logan Mental Health Center, and the state of Colorado. At the trial, Perreira presented expert testimony that Dr. Anders was negligent in releasing Buckmaster. The defendants countered this testimony with their own expert, who concluded Buckmaster was properly released from Fort Logan and that it was not reasonably foreseeable, at the time of his release, that Buckmaster would create a risk of harm to others. It was noted that despite all of Buckmaster's delusions, the only prior act of violence the defendants were aware of was an occasion when Buckmaster kicked his father in the shins. Even then, Buckmaster's aggression was provoked by his father, who threw an ashtray at him.

The jury, nevertheless, found that the defendants had negligently released Buckmaster and that they therefore were liable for the wrongful death of Officer Perreira. A judgment was entered in the amount of $150,000, the maximum statutory amount that could be recovered against the state for injury to any one person.

The case was ultimately appealed to the Colorado Supreme Court. There, the court acknowledged a cause of action for negligently releasing an involuntarily committed client could exist if the professional had a legal duty not to release the client. In other words, basic tort law provides that a claim based on negligence will succeed only if the claim is based on circumstances for which the law imposes a duty.[99] The legal duty that Mrs. Perreira alleged was a duty on Dr. Anders to protect her husband by *continuing* Buckmaster's commitment.

In determining whether or not Dr. Anders had a legal duty to protect Officer Perreira by continuing Buckmaster's commitment, the court considered several factors. One such factor was the foreseeability of harm that could result if protective action, for the benefit of others, was not initiated.[100] The *Perreira* court distinguished between the foreseeability of harm that could be caused by a mentally ill committed client and an outpatient. In the outpatient context, the therapist has limited opportunities to observe and determine the client's violent propensities. On the other hand, once a mentally ill person is involuntarily committed, the

---

[99]*Perreira,* 768 P.2d at 1208.

[100]*Id.* at 1208–1209. The court noted that other factors should also be considered: the existence of a special relationship, the social utility of the actor's conduct, the magnitude of the burden of guarding against the injury, the consequences of placing the burden on the actor, and other relevant factors based on the competing individual and social interests implicated by the facts of the case.

treating psychiatrist has adequate opportunity to learn of the client's condition, including any propensity to violence. Furthermore, the physician has a better opportunity to determine whether prolonging the client's confinement would further the best interests of the client and others.[101]

The *Perreira* court ultimately held that a therapist does have a duty of due care in releasing an involuntarily committed client to take whatever action is reasonable in view of the client's propensity for violence. For example, if the client has made specific threats against particular individuals during the term of commitment or has engaged in recent acts of violence during the commitment period,[102] such acts may require that the professional give "appropriate consideration to extending the term of the client's commitment or to placing appropriate conditions and restrictions on the client's release."[103]

The Colorado Supreme Court (*Perreira* court) is not the only court to recognize this cause of action. Courts in Delaware,[104] Kansas,[105] Nebraska,[106] North Carolina,[107] Ohio,[108] and Washington[109] have likewise recognized that a physician may have a duty to continue the commitment period.

Note, however, that the mere fact a recently released client injures someone does not mean liability will automatically be imposed on the releasing physician. The plaintiff must still show that the decision to release the client rose to the level of negligence, not just that it was clearly a wrong decision in retrospect. If the physician can show that he or she *considered* extending the commitment period but chose against that course of action, the courts will generally give great deference to that professional judgment.

In other words, if the professional conducts a thorough evaluation of the client's mental condition and diagnoses the client as not violent and accordingly releases the client, the professional will have discharged the legal duty, even if the diagnosis was in error.[110] Moreover, even if the clinician diagnoses the client as dangerous, the clinician will not be liable if the clinician rejects a decision to extend the commitment period in favor of a good faith decision to release the client under an acceptable treatment program.[111]

---

[101]*Id.* at 1212.

[102]The court also noted, however, "The absence of specific threats or overt violent behavior, however, is not necessarily conclusive on the issue of a patient's lack of propensity for violent conduct. The patient's history of behavioral disorders and present mental condition may be such that, notwithstanding the absence of specific threats and past or present violent behavior, a reasonably competent psychiatrist, utilizing accepted diagnostic criteria, would conclude that the patient's mental condition is such as to render the patient disposed to commit violent acts against others." *Perreira,* 768 P.2d at 1214.

[103]*Id.* at 1214.

[104]*Naidu v. Laird,* 539 A.2d 1064 (Del. 1988) (psychiatrist liable for actions of patient who was released nearly 6 months earlier).

[105]*Durflinger v. Artiles,* 234 Kan. 484, 673 P.2d 86 (1983).

[106]*Lipari v. Sears, Roebuck & Co.,* 497 F. Supp. 185 (D. Neb. 1980).

[107]*Pangburn v. Saad,* 326 S.E.2d 365 (N.C. Ct. App. 1985).

[108]*Littleton v. Good Samaritan Hosp. & Health Center,* 39 Ohio St.3d 86, 529 N.E.2d 449 (1988).

[109]*Petersen v. Washington,* 100 Wash. 2d 421, 671 P.2d 230 (1983).

[110]*Perreira,* 768 P.2d at 1218.

[111]*Id.*; *Littleton,* 39 Ohio St. 3d at 99, 529 N.E.2d at 460.

CONCLUSION

Any professional, regardless of specialty, may at some time be confronted by an emergency and asked to commit a client. And once a client is committed, a professional must ultimately face the decision of when to release the client. These are critical legal events because tort liability may be imposed if the provider is negligent in either initiating or terminating a civil commitment. The law, however, recognizes the difficulties in civil commitment decisions and protects conscientious professionals who follow the letter and spirit of the law.[112]

All clinicians, however, should be intimately familiar with the statutory civil commitment procedures *before* any emergency arises. If these statutory requirements are satisfied, the clinician will usually find that any significant possibility of liability has been avoided. Therefore, the practical application for protecting oneself from liability associated with the involuntary commitment process is *documentation*! In light of the difficulty involved in making commitment decisions, the court is not so concerned that the correct decision was made as it wants to be satisfied that a reasonable-under-the-circumstances decision was made. Documented evidence that consideration was given to commitment and implemented or rejected for some explained reason(s) will serve the therapist extremely well in defending these causes of action. Preferably, this evidence will include documentation of discussions with professional colleagues supporting the decision to commit or release the client.

---

[112]*See* A. Holder, *Erroneous Commitment,* 219 J.A.M.A. 1389 (1972); S. Knapp & L. VandeCreek, *supra* note 97, at 648.

10

Involuntary Civil Commitment: Clinical Duties

CLINICAL ISSUES IN INVOLUNTARY CIVIL COMMITMENT

The philosophical, ethical, and legal debates over civil commitment are both intellectual and emotional realities in clinical practice. The issues and conflicts surrounding commitment are of utmost importance in determining the way communities (and the clinician as an agent of society) treat individuals who are a threat to themselves or others. The clinician is faced with the practical realities of meeting the needs of the individual client, societal interests, and proper clinical practice. To that end, competent clinicians can proceed only in an atmosphere of ambiguity with good faith efforts to serve the client, the community, and themselves. The best efforts in this direction must be founded on a clear understanding of criteria for commitment and rigorous application of basic procedures that maximize positive outcomes for the client and the community while minimizing the liability hazards for the practitioner.

We now discuss criteria for commitment and procedures of commitment and the risks and recommendations associated with civil commitment. It is important to note that a provider is held to know the statutory requirements in his or her state *before* taking a civil commitment action (Smith, 1986). A first step toward avoiding a wrongful commitment suit is studying and discussing specific state statutory regulations. Our discussion, of necessity, deals with the topic in a more general way since it is too cumbersome to list every state law and there is considerable overlap from state to state.

Criteria for Commitment

Under most state laws, involuntary civil commitment is based on three to six criteria: (1) mental illnesss, (2) dangerousness (to self or others) or grave disability, (3) refusal to consent, (4) treatability, (5) lacks capacity to decide on treatment, (6) hospitalization is the least restrictive treatment. Each criteria is now discussed in relation to its clinical applications.

Mental Illness. Various state statutes widely diverge in their definition of what constitutes "mental illness." Some states leave the term undefined; others more or less precisely define it. The definition may be broad: a disorder that substantially disturbs a person's thinking, feeling or behavior, or impairs the person's ability to function. In some states, certain disorders may be specifically excluded (mental retardation, epilepsy, alcoholism, or drug addiction) or included (psychosis, organic brain syndrome). The practitioner must consult specific state statutes and then assess the extent to which the client meets the diagnostic criteria for an accepted disorder—usually a psychotic disorder or organic brain syndrome. Evidence that pertains to this judgment should be carefully documented. The clinician's judgment will not be expected to be infallible, but the procedures and processes of providing a diagnosis will be expected to conform to the standards of the profession.

Among the data that a provider should record are demographic factors (age, marital status, educational level, occupation, and ethnic identity); present difficulty (including signs and symptoms); a history of this problem (including past treatment, mental health status, emerging pattern, if any); history of drug and alcohol use (and their relation to present symptoms, if any); history of mental and behavioral problems; referral for physical examination and the relevant findings; collaborative interviews, including records of prior treatment; a mental status examination; other inventories and tests aimed at the same targets. To the extent that these data are missing and may arguably lead to a misdiagnosis, the provider is exposed to unnecessary claims of negligence. Unfortunately, the client may not be competent enough to provide such information or consent to the gathering of it from medical and mental health sources. Courts can be expected to be reasonable about lapses in the data if good faith efforts are demonstrated and verbatim responses are accurately recorded.

Dangerous to Self or Others, Gravely Disabled. In the 1975 case of *O'Connor v. Donalson,*[1] the Supreme Court declared, "A finding of 'mental illness' alone cannot justify a state's locking up a person against his will and keeping him indefinitely in custodial confinement." As a consequence of this finding, many states revised their commitment standards if they had been allowing the commitment of persons merely because they were in need of treatment. To be committed, a person needs to be determined to be dangerous as well as mentally ill. In addition to this ruling, some states enacted legislation to also allow commitment of persons who were mentally ill and "gravely disabled" (that is, so impaired that they were unable to meet their basic needs).

Despite the difficulties of predicting dangerousness (discussed in Chapters 3 and 4), the courts and state legislators still place responsibility for conclusions on this matter in the hands of practitioners (among others). In addition to "likely violence" (to individuals), some courts have also accepted nonviolent felonies and some forms of sexual deviation as acceptable evidence for commitment. The range of dangerousness is from "serious physical injury" to "substantial physical or emotional injury," or "substantial harm, whether physical or not" [see Alabama Code Section 229.1 (2), 1983]. Typically, danger to property alone is not considered

[1] *O'Connor v. Donalson* (1975), 422 U.S. 563.

sufficient evidence to warrant commitment, although a standard of "substantial property damage" has been enacted in some states. Ordinarily, the evidence for property damage must be substantial if it is to justify the deprivation of liberty involved in involuntary hospitalization.

As mentioned, issues concerning the imminence of harm, and the certainty with which dangerous acts can be predicted and managed, are central issues to the court. In hearings where these data are generally debated, much attention is focused on the client's history of overt acts. Such a history renders speculation about dangerousness less abstract, so several states require that a recent overt act, attempt, or serious threat of harm be in evidence for the conclusion of dangerousness to be reached (compare with Ohio Rev. Code Ann Section 5122.01, 1980). Although this is not generally true, to the extent that such evidence exists, such information should be carefully recorded and presented. In the absence of such evidence, dangerousness can be presented as a reasonable conclusion based on client dynamics. Whatever the clinical reality might be, involuntary commitment is unlikely if it is based solely on the presence of "destructive thoughts." And while at least one state statute (Arkansas, Section Rev. 59–408, 1980) permits commitments for dangerousness on the basis of "thoughts that create a grave and imminent risk," many courts would likely view this standard with skepticism.

Some states specify a time period for the commission of acts (including threats) that trigger commitment proceedings. In general, it is expected that the evidence for dangerousness be sufficiently recent to provide evidence of present danger, or that recent acts, coupled with a clear history, suggest the seriousness of the situation. Since we have already devoted considerable space to the criteria, risks, and procedures for assessment of dangerousness, further elaboration is not given here.

In those states where a standard of "gravely disabled" has been adopted, a majority of all commitments are made on the basis that the client is gravely disabled rather than dangerous. Gravely disabled is usually interpreted to mean that as a result of a mental disorder, the person is unable to provide for basic needs such as food, clothing, and shelter. Just what constitutes being gravely disabled is often a difficult thing to determine. It can be confused with an individual's preferred lifestyle or the fact that the person lives well below the usual standard, although the person is in fact meeting basic needs. Thus, one can only hope that providers will interpret statutes which allow commitments under this criterion on the same basis as the statute intends. The gravely disabled criterion is one that should go beyond the symptoms of mental illness and deal specifically with an individual's ability to meet basic physical needs without being so paternalistic that it allows every person who is in need of treatment to be involuntarily committed.

Refusal to Consent.   Although most states do not specifically require that a person refuse voluntary treatment, in practice, clients are involuntarily committed only if they refuse voluntary treatment or hospitalization. The provider would be well advised to pursue this issue with the client because in some cases clients are willing to accept voluntary hospitalization. In the instance that the client's final agreement to hospitalization appears only manipulative and the client is deemed to have no real motive to seek voluntary hospitalization, this fact should be documented and reported at the commitment hearing, along with other relevant information such as past admissions and withdrawal from treatment against medical advice. Since the need for involuntary commitment is often precipitated by the client's lack of insight into his or her illness, this fact is also relevant to an agreement to be voluntarily hospitalized.

Treatable. A number of states require evidence that a person has a treatable disorder as a condition of involuntary commitment. The provider needs to give some thought in these jurisdictions (and all jurisdictions for that matter) about the possibility for treatment and the availability of interventions the client needs. It must be made clear to the court that hospitalization is not a costly, useless endeavor but *could* have beneficial results.

Lacks Capacity to Decide on Treatment. Most state laws do *not* require a client to be incompetent to make specific treatment decisions before the client is involuntarily committed. The presence of this criterion in some states allows the hospital to insist that the client undergo certain treatment. The absence of this criterion in most state laws could result in a stalemate since the hospital may be limited in its ability to treat a hospitalized client who refuses treatment while simultaneously being required to keep the client. However, the absence of this criterion is perhaps a recognition that the client may not be competent to decide that hospitalization is needed, while on the other hand the client is competent enough to know that the risks of undergoing particular treatments such as electroconvulsive therapy outweigh the presumed benefits. When the capacity criterion is a part of the state laws, it is often thought of as a discrete impairment. Chapters 7 and 8 fully discussed the conflicts between the client's right to treatment and the client's right to refuse treatment. Readers may want to review this material.

Least Restrictive Alternative. Almost half the states have enacted into law the requirement that hospitalization is proper if it is the "least restrictive" of the client's freedom while still providing the necessary treatment. Nearly all states permit involuntary outpatient commitment, although this treatment option is rarely used. A core principle throughout all the states is avoidance of involuntary confinement if equal protection and treatment efficacy can be achieved by another means. Unfortunately, the "least" restrictive criterion is not easily defined. Some states, like Washington, have created screening agencies to determine proper placement of all clients, while other states, such as California, have provided a continuum of treatments so that clients may move sequentially along the lines of less restrictive alternatives.

Readers should now have a basic idea of the criteria necessary for involuntary commitment and some guidelines for minimizing risks of malpractice through failure to act, negligent diagnosis, and wrongful commitment. We now address the procedures and issues involved in voluntary commitment and ways of minimizing risks in the process.

Procedures of Commitment

Since procedures for civil commitment vary from state to state, providers must become familiar with state statutes' that will direct their specific activities. Despite some state differences, there are enough similarities to focus on general issues and guidelines.

Phase I: Initiation of Civil Commitment.   There are a number of situations in which a provider may function in relation to civil commitment. Perhaps the most common and perplexing situation is in the initial stage of commitment. States allow a variety of persons to initiate civil commitment: police; mental health providers; physicians; and in some states, family members or an interested person. Providers may find themselves in a variety of roles in this regard: initiating commitment on the basis of a direct relationship with the client, consulting with a client about a family member or friend, responding to a relative stranger who presents in an emergency situation, or consulting with a colleague who needs help making a decision.

In most states, the provider initiating the commitment must prepare a written petition stating that she or he believes the person meets the criteria for commitment or that the person needs emergency evaluation. Once access to the appropriate treatment facility is attained, personnel have a brief, prescribed time during which the client is evaluated, released, or required to attend a formal hearing. In the initial stage of commitment, a number of hazards effect clinical practice and can be handled in such a way as to minimize risk. The most general term to describe risk-reducing behavior of providers is *responsible,* which has particular meaning in reference to the initiation of civil commitment. More specific terms include independent, objective, or circumspect. We now clarify the operational definition of these various terms by describing some of the common pressures inherent in the initial stage of commitment.

Often a provider is asked to arrange hospitalization for a family member in an emergency situation. Family members may be justifiably concerned about possible harm the client may do or a potential suicide. However, at the same time they may misread the situation, overreact, or merely want to exercise control over the identified client's behavior. Family members may even try to manipulate the provider for genuine as well as devious reasons. Responsibility in these situations means making reasonable efforts to gather balanced information so that the decision arrived at reflects an independent, reasonably objective opinion based on an examination of the client. Finally, when the opinion favoring commitment is offered, the provider should be circumspect in regards to any statements made about the client. Statements should be limited to stating there is sufficient cause to conclude that the identified client is in need of emergency evaluation or that it is *likely* the client meets the standards for commitment. In this situation, the provider should not make a definitive judgment that commitment is warranted; this is the job of the treatment facility staff and the courts. Statements made in this context, or written on petitions for commitment, are for the purpose of raising reasonable questions for consideration rather than deciding answers to these questions. When rendering an opinion about the need for an emergency evaluation, the responsible provider should limit conclusions to those observed or verified by her or his examination of the client rather than repeating statements by concerned family members. Despite possible pressure from family members to "help" the identified client by making sure a commitment occurs, the provider needs to take an objective, independent position based on knowledge of the client and commitment criteria.

The provider's independence is exercised by finding evidence for mental illness (as defined by state statute) and in undertaking an assessment of dangerousness or suicide as elaborated in Chapters 4 and 6. Competent execution and recording of these tasks should be sufficient to minimize liability risks.

Another common situation in which a provider may initiate commitment procedures pertains to a client who has been undergoing treatment with the provider and thus is already known to the provider. To act responsibly in this context usually calls for more advocacy by the provider than when the client is a relative stranger. Helping the person gain access to the mental health system may be at the insistence of the provider. In this situation, it is more appropriate for the provider to give an opinion about the need for the client to be committed and treated. If the provider has considerable clinical information (likely in this context) that is relevant to the commitment, it should be disclosed on the petition for commitment. Also, it helps to remember that the provider is not in the position of final judge, only the initiator for the review. Keeping these facts in mind may alleviate conflicts within the clinician over the deprivation of liberty connected with commitment. Another important conflict- and anxiety-reducing procedure, especially if the situation is unclear, is to share the decision-making responsibility with a colleague, to not only reduce conflicts and anxiety but to protect both the client and the provider.

Phase II: The Emergency Evaluation.   Providers play a central role in assessments for commitment after a person has been confined for an emergency evaluation. Although many of the anxiety-arousing aspects of commitment decisions remain, the provider functions with less immediate stress under the restrictive but safe care of the hospital. In the hospital, the imminent likelihood of destructive behavior is greatly diminished. A number of professionals are available for consultation, many of whom will have access to the same observations, allowing clinicians to check their perceptions with one another. Although the time pressure is reduced, there is still limited time for assessment since the client has a right to a formal hearing within a reasonable period of time. The time period varies across jurisdictions, ranging from 2 or 3 days to weeks.

The treatment facility provider's role is to evaluate the client with regard to the specific commitment criteria and determine if the instigation is justified. During this evaluation, most states require clients to be informed of their rights and the time limits concerning emergency confinement. Since clients may lose their liberty, some courts have ruled that clients are entitled to be advised by counsel of their rights and can refuse participation on the basis of the Fifth Amendment. However, this is not general practice, and while it may protect the client's autonomy, it does not necessarily facilitate the client's health interests. If the provider is the instigator of the commitment proceedings, he or she should take care to offer relevant information while respecting the necessity and value of having the hospital staff render their own independent opinion on the need for commitment. It is now the emergency facility, or designated examiners, that have responsibility for formulating an independent decision.

Phase III: The Formal Hearing.   Some states hold preliminary hearings, which vary as to scope, formality, and purpose. Often the hearings are very informal, with only the proponent of the petition offering testimony. In some states, a preliminary hearing is dispensed with entirely—only a formal hearing is conducted. The formal hearing is intended to judge the relative interests of the individual and society. A hearing on civil commitment accords the client certain rights—to be present, to have advance notice, and to be represented by counsel. The rules of evidence vary across jurisdictions and differ from criminal proceedings in important ways. In most jurisdictions, the case is tried by a judge rather than by a jury. Narrative and hearsay testimony may be permitted if the judge feels capable of weighing and discounting less valuable testimony and because it is assumed that the proceedings are being conducted in the client's best interests rather than for the purpose of prosecuting the client.

Two rules of evidence are of special importance in these hearings. The first rule is that the therapist/client *privilege* is not recognized. Some courts have ruled that the therapist's privilege to refuse disclosure of the things learned and said in therapy will not be recognized in civil commitment hearings because it is the client's mental state that is at issue.

Obviously, the way in which therapist privilege is handled within civil commitment has important implications for the therapeutic relationship and the content of informed consent (see Chapter 8). The gravely disabled client may need to have information disclosed in the commitment hearing, whereas the dangerous client may be injured by information disclosed and opened to public scrutiny. The therapist needs to know before the hearing how privilege is to be handled in civil commitment and consider the implications of this procedure in their practice.

The second rule of evidence that differs from criminal proceedings is that the Fifth Amendment privilege is not honored in most jurisdictions. The client is expected to provide honest information and *may* have the right to disallow this testimony in later criminal proceedings if they subsequently or concurrently arise.

Thus the hearing can be a situation in which the client has minimal rights, and the therapist's participation in the process can have grave consequences.

At the commitment hearing, the petitioner usually presents evidence first and then is subject to cross examination. Subsequent witnesses can be called (obviously the provider could testify as either the petitioner or a witness). The client and counsel present a response that is followed by brief summaries by each side and a ruling by the judge or jury. A written transcript of the testimony and ruling is maintained.

Risk Reduction.   The risks of liability can be minimized to the extent a provider can avoid being the petitioner. Taking the role of the petitioner can have drastic, negative, and irreparable effects on a therapeutic relationship. In the case of dangerous/suicidal clients, it often means taking on a role that is perceived as adversarial, often as the betrayer of client trust. There are several ways of staying out of the role of petitioner. In some states, this role is designated to others during the emergency hospitalization period. Prior to hospitalization, the practitioner can encourage family or friends to initiate commitment through the police (in the case of a dangerous or self-destructive client) or by going directly to the local mental health authority. In these instances, the therapist can play a more peripheral role and avoid the position of instigator.

To a large extent, risk reduction must precede rather than follow decisions about commitment. In fact, the most promising risk-reducing activities are part of general practice decisions and include selecting clients at the initiation of treatment who fall well within one's field of competence and avoiding cases with a high risk of litigation (such as those people with a history of past suicide attempts or a history of dissatisfaction with past therapists). Further steps include case management practices that focus on becoming aware of problems and immediately addressing them, before they fester. It is especially important to be able to function effectively in the face of client anger and the anger of family members who may feel the therapy is having an adverse effect on them.

In the context of commitment, it is also important to be especially careful about dual relationships. At the point of a formal hearing, the presence of a dual relationship is likely to come to light. Depending on the situation, it could have negative effects on the commitment process and raise questions about the practitioner's bias or lack of objectivity. The possibility of dual relationships in the commitment situation frequently arises when the initiating petitioner is also a consultant or on staff at the institution in which the client may be committed, thus raising the possibility of a financial motive for an affirmative finding.

Release and Recommitment.   Most commitments are for time-limited periods (30 to 90 days), although the confining institution can release the client prior to the expiration of this period. If it is determined that the client needs further treatment, state laws usually allow the family or the treatment facility to re-petition before expiration of the initial commitment. This action requires further evaluation of the client in regard to current status. Recommitment can be ordered without evidence of a new dangerous act. Hospital clinicians need to provide accurate, objective testimony, and those who are put at risk (such as family members) may have the right to review records in order to offer their views on potential risks.

Commitment of Minors. In general, the procedures for committing minors differ from those governing adults. In some states, teenagers have the right to decline voluntary admission, but in most states a parent or legal guardian may at their discretion hospitalize a minor in a private hospital. In the most celebrated case on this topic, *J. R. v. Parham, 1979*,[2] the U.S. Supreme Court upheld such a procedure, ruling that due process was served if the parent consented and an independent judgment by the admitting professional concurred. In this situation, the provider is expected to offer an objective independent opinion, not just accept the parent's judgment of the situation. Given the lax standards for commitment and the lack of guidelines for decision making, commitment of minors is an area of professional practice ripe for litigation, especially if parents change their mind about the commitment and the hospital determines that the minor is in need of further treatment.

Many of these issues were addressed by the *J. R. v. Parham, 1979* opinion of the Supreme Court with differences of opinion in majority and minority views. These opinions differed in regards to the degree to which the absence of a formal hearing deprives minors of their constitutional rights. In particular, the minority opinion suggested that, if anything, children should be given greater, not lesser, consideration for due process because the effects of "erroneous commitment" would be even more tragic for children (who are confined longer), who may be more deeply scarred by the error, and who bear the scars of their formative years throughout the remainder of their life.

Important to our consideration here is that despite disagreements in their opinion, all justices agreed on the need for independent objective opinions from professionals. These opinions also reaffirm the suggestions made in this chapter for the importance of documenting historical and other information regarding the functioning and impairment of the identified client, regardless of age. Certainly, the rights of children, the rights of parents, the needs of society, the financial pressures on professionals, and professional standards are likely to conflict—providing an increasingly rich source of legal battles in the near future.

SUMMARY

Involuntary civil commitments raise a host of questions and issues regarding both the grounds for such commitments and the procedures that are to be followed. In balancing clients' health needs and their constitutional rights and society's safety needs, the provider is caught in a conundrum of conflicting needs, competing interests, and evolving doctrines. The ambiguities are plentiful. What

---

[2]*J. R. v. Parham,* 442 U.S. 584 (1979).

is dangerous? What is imminent? What is insane? In response to all these difficulties, it is essential that clinicians understand the statutory, civil commitment requirements and procedures in their jurisdiction, which will enable them to apply typical professional practices and their best judgment in making decisions.

Documented evidence of good faith efforts to consider the criteria, procedures, and client's best interests are of central importance in avoiding legal complications and negative and destructive relationships with clients.

REFERENCE

Smith, P. (1986). *Medical malpractice and psychiatric care* (p. 253). New York: McGraw-Hill.

Epilogue

Future Directions

Even though the practice of psychotherapy started as a highly private, inarticulate and, in some ways, informal undertaking with little public exposure, it has quickly evolved into an accepted treatment approach in the nation's health care system. Currently, the practice of psychotherapy, despite its relatively short history, has moved to a position where clear standards of practice are expected and where harm to the client is often attributed to failures by the therapist. Audiotape and videotape recordings and related research efforts have demystified and more clearly specified procedures and activities. Educational efforts have become more routine, systematic, and standardized with the corresponding development of well-accepted ethical guidelines. Licensing laws for the professions are now commonplace and based on the assumption that some control of practice is needed for the protection of the public.

The treatment of people with mental disorders no longer takes place in the cocoon of anonymity; it is now deeply embedded in the business of the health care industry. And practitioners are working not only for the client but for the state, especially in the case of high-risk clients. Here, the practitioner soon discovers that the provision of services carries with it a bundle of forms and obligations that will be examined in the light of day when things go wrong. And the examiners will not necessarily be psychological colleagues who share the same assumptive world and philosophical views of the mental health professions; they will be eager lawyers, angry clients, hurt relatives, and dispassionate judges whose views of personal responsibility, justice, equity, and due process may be both different and surprising to many mental health professionals. We are already starting to hear faint echoes of the old adage "Healer, heal thyself" as respected ethicists, lawyers, and some mental health professionals start to wonder aloud whether the client may not need more protection from the healer. This, ladies and gentlemen, is not a matter to be taken lightly.

But before things go wrong and end up in the judicial system, the wise practitioner will form the habit of following the highest standards of professional practice. As has been suggested, the lack of clear standards and the fluid nature of these standards, as well as the limitations of the legal system itself, ensure that interventions with high-risk clients will never be boring.

The future seems to hold numerous paradoxes and contradictions for the provider who is attuned to the complications of effective practice. While we cannot predict future trends with the precision and care we all hope for, some emerging trends that provide the basis for some interesting speculations about the future are obvious. One of the more dominant trends is that of the judicial system's growing intolerance of social wrongs that are not easily redressed. As a result, courts are accepting lower standards of precision in identifying the specific cause of social

219

harms before imposing liability. Individuals and organizations, with the means of ensuring against risk and spreading the cost of liability to the population at large, are becoming the targets of this trend. Social policy, or the principles believed to benefit society as a whole, is challenging individual culpability as the driving force behind legal liability. In light of this legal trend, the mental health profession's dramatic advances in the organized delivery of mental health services promise to continue in the relentless march toward closing the distance between the therapist's couch and the counsel's chair.

Index